The Commonw
International A

The Round Table journal (now subtitled *The Commonwealth Journal of International Affairs*) first appeared in 1910. The journal carried a number of articles recognised both by contemporaries and by historians as highly influential in the making of Commonwealth policy, including constitutional reform in India, the independence of southern Ireland, the League of Nations mandates system and the United Nations trusteeship system, British policy in East Asia, the building of the Anglo-American alliance, appeasement, decolonisation, and the transition to a new, multipolar Commonwealth.

This book brings together excerpts from some of the key articles published over the last one hundred years and features leading figures including;

- Lionel Curtis on Ireland, leading to the Anglo-Irish Treaty and the creation of the Irish Free State,
- T.E. Lawrence on the Middle East, a key influence on post-1919 state creation in the Arab Middle East,
- Philip Kerr on India, galvanizing attempts at constitutional reform in British India.

This selection provides a unique commentary on imperial/Commonwealth and international affairs and makes available to a new generation of scholars and students some of the articles now acknowledged as key influences in the evolution of British and Commonwealth policies.

This collection of essays is intended as a companion volume to *The Contemporary Commonwealth: An assessment 1965–2009*, edited by James Mayall, marking the centenary of *The Round Table*.

Alex May is Research Editor, *Oxford Dictionary of National Biography*, a project of the University of Oxford, and has been Honorary Secretary/Treasurer of the Round Table since 1997.

'Alex May, who is both the Secretary of *The Round Table* and its historian, is to be congratulated on assembling this selection of the best articles published in the journal over the past century. Both the anthology and his own incisive and informative Introduction provide a fascinating insight into the evolution of the Commonwealth idea, from its genesis in Milner's Kindergarten to current preoccupations with civil society, multiculturalism, multilateralism, and democratic governance'.

James Mayall *Emeritus Sir Patrick Sheehy Professor of International Relations, University of Cambridge*

'This fascinating selection from the work of one of the earliest think-tanks is not only a valuable historical document but contains much useful advice for today'.

Margaret MacMillan *Warden, St Antony's College, Oxford*

'For consistent, well-informed, high quality, and perceptive commentary on Commonwealth affairs and Britain's role in the world there is nothing to beat *The Round Table*. From its warnings of danger posed by German naval expansion prior to 1914 and the need to give the Dominions a say in policy-making if their military support was to be harnessed; through to under-standing the aspirations of Egyptian, Arab, Indian and African nationalists; appreciating the changing nature of Commonwealth relations as Dominion sovereignty was conceded, republican status accepted, and an inter-governmental Secretariat and other organs created, *The Round Table* has usually been ahead of popular opinion. This amazingly interesting collection of articles selected from a century's worth of lumpy bound volumes, with an introduc-tion by the current secretary of the editorial moot, catches both the flavour of the fast-changing Commonwealth and the quality of the journal'.

David McIntyre *Emeritus Professor, University of Canterbury, Christchurch, New Zealand*

'... a magnificent collection of great historic and contemporary significance...'

Don Markwell *Warden, Rhodes House, Oxford*

The Commonwealth and International Affairs

The Round Table Centennial Selection

Edited by
Alex May

Routledge
Taylor & Francis Group
LONDON AND NEW YORK

First published 2010
by Routledge
2 Park Square, Milton Park, Abingdon, Oxfordshire OX14 4RN

Simultaneously published in the USA and Canada
by Routledge
711 Third Avenue, New York, NY 10017

First issued in paperback 2014

Routledge is an imprint of the Taylor and Francis Group, an informa business

Typeset in Times New Roman by
Taylor & Francis Books

British Library Cataloguing in Publication Data
A catalogue record for this book is available
from the British Library

Library of Congress Cataloging in Publication Data
The Commonwealth and international affairs: the Round Table centennial selection/edited by Alex May.
p. cm.
Includes bibliographical references and index.
1. Commonwealth countries–Foreign relations. I. May, Alex (Alex Charles) II. Round table
DA18.C513 2010
327.09171'241–dc22
2009049004

ISBN 13: 978-1-138-88209-6 (pbk)
ISBN 13: 978-0-415-48523-4 (hbk)

Contents

Preface

The early years of the twentieth century saw the founding of leagues and societies devoted to promoting the unity of the British Empire. Among them were the Victoria League and the League of the Empire in 1901, the Empire Day Movement and the Tariff Reform League in 1903, the Royal Colonial Institute and the Empire Press Union in 1909, the Over-Seas Club in 1910, and the Empire Parliamentary Association in 1911. Apart from loyalty to the Empire, the most notable characteristic was the sense of anxiety underpinning their activities. The South African War of 1899–1902 came as a shock to the British psyche. Settler soldiers of Dutch descent had defied the might of the British Empire. The United States had already overtaken Britain in economic power; and Germany was now building a navy to match its industrial and military strength, threatening British supremacy on the high seas. Only by drawing on the resources of the whole British Empire, so ran the argument, could Britain retain both the Empire and a place in the first rank of nations.

The most interesting and enduring of the organizations created in the febrile atmosphere of Edwardian England was the Round Table, founded in 1909. Its eponymous journal began the next year. The Round Table had its origins in 'Milner's Kindergarten', the talented and impressionable young Oxford graduates recruited by Lord Milner and his successor Lord Selborne to help in the administration of the conquered territories in South Africa. Members of the Kindergarten were advocates of South African unification. They turned their attention also to the Empire. The Round Table was ostensibly a movement for the study of 'Imperial Britain'—the metropole, the Indian Empire, the Dominions, colonies, and other dependencies. In reality it was a pressure group for imperial federation, or the creation of a new imperial parliament and government representative of all the peoples in the empire, not just those in Britain. The first goal was to unify the Dominions of Canada, Australia, New Zealand, and now South Africa. From the beginning, to its critics at least, the Round Table movement aimed at something like a super-state.

Historians have debated whether imperial federation was doomed even in 1910. Most think it probably was. In any event it had little chance of success after the outbreak of the First World War, when imperial union gave way to internationalism (a gradual but distinct change recognized by all but the most obstinate of Round Tablers at least by 1917). Yet no one would deny that the Round Table played an important part in stimulating debate on the future of the British Empire, both before and after the war.

As Alex May's introduction to this volume makes clear, the *Round Table* journal was originally an offshoot of the Round Table movement and became its propaganda mouthpiece. Yet, under a succession of able editors, it soon took on a life of its own, and indeed became the primary focus of Round Table activities. Rapidly establishing itself as an authoritative source of news, commentary, and analysis on imperial and later Commonwealth affairs, it was regularly quoted in Parliament as well as newspapers and journals throughout the empire. Some of its articles had a direct impact on British policy as well as a more indirect influence through the shaping of debate. The *Round Table* reflected a distinct current of contemporary thought. Ironically, as Alex May again demonstrates, the journal's most important role was probably to help smooth the dissolution of the empire. It supported constitutional reform in India, and advocated independence for countries in the Middle East in the inter-war years. It stood for the virtual independence of southern Ireland and separate foreign and defence policies by the Dominions. The *Round Table* indeed popularized the very term 'Commonwealth' and its concept of an association of equal states cooperating freely, in contrast to the Anglocentric notion of empire. In more recent times, the journal has firmly urged a multipolar Commonwealth with an emphasis on democracy, human rights, good governance, sustainable development, and environmental responsibility, again in contrast to the intellectual climate in which it was conceived.

Some of the articles reproduced in this volume—such as those by Lionel Curtis on Ireland, Lord Milner on Egypt, and T.E. Lawrence on the Middle East—played an important role in helping to shape British public sentiment and the attitudes of British policy-makers. They are thus of historical significance. Others—such as those by Sir Frederick Whyte on the Balfour Report of 1926, Lord Hailey on colonial trusteeship, Elspeth Huxley on the dilemmas of colonial rule, or more recently Dawda Jawara on human rights or Sir Sonny Ramphal on the role of the modern Commonwealth—provide interesting and authoritative reflections on key issues of contemporary concern. Taken together, they provide a fascinating commentary on the transformation of the British Empire into the Commonwealth, a transformation in which the *Round Table* journal was both observer and participant.

The *Round Table* journal has of course changed substantially in the century since it was first published. Its articles are no longer anonymous. It is now largely written by scholars rather than journalists, politicians, or officials, and it reflects a broader range of opinion than it did in its early years. Yet its essentials remain the same. It is a highly-respected, wide-ranging, and influential source of commentary on all aspects of current Commonwealth concerns. If this collection of articles over the last hundred years—valuable as they are to historians—encourages more readers to read the current journal, it will have more than served its purpose.

Wm. Roger Louis

Introduction

The *Round Table* journal first appeared in November 1910, and, after a brief hiatus in 1982, is still published today. Initially sub-titled 'A Quarterly Review of the Politics of the British Empire', it reflected and indeed anticipated the evolution of the empire/Commonwealth, changing its sub-title to 'A Quarterly Review of the Politics of the British Commonwealth' in 1919, 'A Quarterly Review of British Commonwealth Affairs' in 1948, 'The Commonwealth Quarterly' in 1966, and finally 'The Commonwealth Journal of International Affairs' in 1983. Published quarterly until 2000, it is now published six times a year, with two or three of those 'special issues' focusing on a particular topic or theme. Its publisher's rubric states that it 'provides analysis and commentary on all aspects of international affairs', and 'is the major source for coverage of the policy issues concerning the contemporary Commonwealth and its role in international affairs'.

Published first at what may now be regarded as the high point of the empire (in confidence if not extent) – yet also a time when uncertainty of purpose and threats both external and internal were more than clouds on the horizon – the *Round Table* caught the imagination of political elites in Britain and throughout the empire. It rapidly carved out for itself an important role in the dissemination of information about and between different parts of the empire, analysis of the problems the empire faced, and attempts to find and garner political support for possible solutions. It was regularly quoted in parliament, and the South African prime minister Jan Smuts described it as 'the one thing of its kind which is read by nearly everyone who determines public policy or originates public opinion'.[1] For the last fifty years the journal has steadily become more oriented to academic than policy debate, but it still straddles the worlds of academia and policy-making in a way that is highly unusual amongst scholarly journals, a fact reflected in both authorship and readership. In 2009, the doyen of Commonwealth scholars, David McIntyre, asserted that it 'remained … the best means of keeping up with the Commonwealth into the 21st century'.[2]

Until 1966 all articles in the journal were anonymous – ostensibly to allow people in positions of authority to set forth their views without fear of embarrassment or adverse reaction. But anonymity also reflected the fact that, at least until the 1940s, most articles published in the journal were held to represent a collective and distinctive '*Round Table*' view. As one editor put it, in 1933, 'the Round Table expresses its own view in [the journal's articles], whoever writes them. It is this characteristic which gives us most of our influence'.[3] A few years earlier a prominent member of the editorial board had described the process of gestation: 'the line to be taken in the policy articles is thrashed out very earnestly, [and] the article is then drafted by the writer selected, circulated and thrashed out again'.[4] A later editor described himself, not unrealistically, as merely 'the scribe who puts on paper the collective views' of the editorial board.[5] The attempt to convey a distinctive and collective viewpoint was of course always only partially successful, and from the 1950s became much less so. By the time anonymity was abandoned it had served its purpose; but at least until the 1970s editorials in particular reflected a good deal of discussion and sometimes consensus amongst editorial board members, and the practice of relatively frequent editorial board meetings and discussion of contemporary Commonwealth issues continues to this day.

The role of the *Round Table*'s editorial board (or 'Moot', as it is known) has always been crucial in setting the tone of the journal, and changes in its composition, cohesiveness and political orientation have been reflected in changes in the journal. Initially, and for many years, it was small, extremely close-knit and centred around members of 'Milner's Kindergarten', a group of young Oxford graduates recruited to work in the administration and reconstruction of the southern African colonies following the war of 1899–1902, either under Lord Milner or under his successor, Lord Selborne. They included Lionel Curtis, the Round Table's moving spirit and an *éminence grise* of British imperial policy until the Second World War; Philip Kerr, later Lord Lothian, the journal's first editor, Liberal politician and British Ambassador in Washington during the early years of the Second World War; Robert Brand, later Lord Brand, a director of Lazard Bros and a powerful figure in the City; Geoffrey Robinson, later Dawson, long-time editor of *The Times*; Lionel Hichens, later chairman of Cammell Laird; and (Sir) Dougal Malcolm, later president of the British South Africa Company. Early recruits to the editorial board included the Conservative politicians Leo Amery and Edward Grigg (later Lord Altrincham), and the scholars Reginald Coupland and (Sir) Alfred Zimmern, whom Curtis persuaded to forsake the study of ancient history for the study of imperial history and international relations, respectively. From the 1930s Sir William Hailey, later Lord Hailey, perhaps the nearest to an imperial proconsul after Milner, was a powerful figure on the board, while Harry Hodson (later editor of the *Sunday Times*) began a 69-year association with the journal in 1930. Other recruits in the 1930s included John Maud, later Lord Redcliffe-Maud and one of the 'great and the good' of postwar Britain, and (Sir) Harold Butler, Director of the International Labour Organization, and later Warden of Nuffield College, Oxford. In the 1940s they were joined by the Conservative politician Henry Brooke, later Lord Brooke, the historian Nicholas Mansergh and the *Times* leader-writer

Dermot Morrah (who also served a 20-year stint as editor), but it was not until after the Second World War that the numerical preponderance of 'Kindergarten' members was broken, and not until 1963 that the last of the London-based 'Kindergarten' members died (Brand, active and indeed trenchant to the end; Richard Feetham, a 'Kindergarten' member who remained in South Africa, became a supreme court judge and remained in close contact with the Round Table, died in 1965). The tradition of frequent and long, sometimes weekend-long, editorial board meetings also lasted until the 1940s and 1950s, when they were replaced by more businesslike, shorter and eventually quarterly meetings – albeit supplemented by much correspondence and a panoply of sub-committees. The last weekend-long meeting devoted solely to the discussion of editorial matters was held (at Ditchley) in 1963. Since then, longer meetings have tended to take the form of seminars or conferences on current Commonwealth concerns.

The 1960s saw a wave of younger new recruits, including Leonard Beaton, sometime director of the Institute of Strategic Studies, and for five years Morrah's energetic successor as editor of the journal; (Sir) Michael Howard, later Regius professor of modern history at Oxford, and also briefly an editor of the journal; Douglas Hurd, later Lord Hurd of Westwell, diplomat and Conservative politician (including a stint as Foreign Secretary); (Sir) Jeremy Morse, later chairman of Lloyds Bank; and the diplomats (Sir) Humphrey Maud and (Sir) Robert Wade-Gery. From the 1980s the editorial board grew increasingly large (it now stands at around 35 members) and diverse (women, first admitted only in 1988, now account for around one-third of the membership), and although members in academic posts remain a minority they now constitute by some way the largest single group of members (diplomacy, non-governmental organizations and journalism also being well reflected). There is still a sense in which 'the Moot is not a committee, but rather a closely knit working group', as one member put it in 1951[6] – producing the journal being but the most important of the group's activities – but it is certainly no longer possible to speak of a collective '*Round Table*' view, and the balance of power between editor and editorial board has shifted irrevocably towards editorial independence. The journal now reflects this, with a wide range of viewpoints expressed in it, from a broad pool of contributors. Whereas in 1910–14 the editorial board or 'Moot' contributed some two-thirds of 'policy' articles (i.e. those not consisting of news round-ups, which the *Round Table* has always included, initially as 'chronicles' from different parts of the empire/Commonwealth, latterly in the form of a regular 'Commonwealth Update'), by the 1980s this had fallen to around one-sixth, where it remained into the 2000s. These, needless to say, now express the viewpoint solely of the author.

The *Round Table* was originally an offshoot of a Round Table 'movement', with branches around the UK and in each of the self-governing Dominions (Canada, Australia, New Zealand and South Africa). The purpose of the movement was ostensibly to discuss problems in imperial relations and the future of the empire, though there were always well-founded suspicions that, as one observer put it, 'the answers were already written out and reposing in Lionel Curtis's pocket'.[7] Having played an important role in the movement which eventually led to the unification of the four South African colonies in 1910 – by writing the so-called 'Selborne Memorandum' which gave official blessing to the process, organizing Closer Union societies within each of the colonies and working behind the scenes to bring leading South African politicians on board – Curtis and his colleagues hoped to play a similar role in relation to the empire, which many of them believed needed to be reconstructed on federal lines (with a federal government responsible to the electors in the Dominions as well as the UK) if it was not to disintegrate. As Curtis wrote to Milner, 'it becomes more and more apparent every day to my mind that the various countries included in the Empire must come to some definite business arrangement for the support and control of Imperial defence and foreign policy or the Empire must break up'.[8] There were various reasons for this conviction, the most important being the beliefs that the resources of the UK alone would prove insufficient to maintain the empire in face of internal challenges and external threats, that the Dominions would not remain content to allow their defence and foreign policies to be determined by a government responsible solely to the British electorate, and that the method of *ad hoc* co-operation which was increasingly characterizing the relationship between the UK and the Dominions would prove unworkable in the long term. While the populations of the Dominions were then small compared to that of the UK – with the consequences, first, that their contributions to the joint enterprise would be relatively small and, second, that Dominion electors would be greatly outnumbered by British electors – this was a time when it was widely believed that Australia and Canada in particular were potential giants, with the capacity even to rival the United States in terms of population and wealth.

With the support of Lord Milner and his political allies in Britain, and with financial backing from patrons including the Duke of Westminster, the Marquess of Anglesey, Sir Abe Bailey and most importantly the Rhodes Trust (which matched other donations on a '£ for £' basis until the end of 1915), Curtis embarked on a tour of the Dominions in 1909–10, setting up Round Table 'study groups' in each of the main cities. On his return, he set about producing a series of 'Round Table studies' which were distributed to the groups, interleaved with blank pages for comments; the comments were then collated and distributed, in order to provoke further discussion. Curtis's 'studies' made much of the external threats to the empire, particularly from Germany, and of the supposed unworkability of co-operation as a method of holding the empire together; they also dwelt at length on the Dominions' aspirations to full self-government, and on the inevitability of their wishing to take control of their own foreign policies as a result, for instance, of their wish to maintain racially discriminatory immigration policies, which Curtis contended would eventually lead to problems with China and especially Japan.

They were most notable, however, for popularizing the 'principle of the Commonwealth' (originally formulated by Alfred Zimmern in his work on Greek city-states), which Curtis defined as 'the principle of … entrusting sovereignty to all those whose sense of duty to their fellow citizens is strong enough to justify the trust'.[9] The British empire, Curtis contended, was not really an empire at all, in the commonly understood meaning of that word; rather, it was a 'commonwealth' which existed in order to promote self-government on a progressively wider basis.

Curtis's 'studies' came in for much criticism, and not just because of the sloppy scholarship underpinning his arguments. ('Their history is wicked', wrote the journalist Fabian Ware; 'how *dare* they do this sort of thing. It is really poisoning the wells'.[10]) Many members of the 'study groups' declared themselves unconvinced by Curtis's hostility to co-operation: most saw federation coming, if at all, as a result of a long process of evolution rather than a dramatic break, 'the final step', as the Australian F. W. Eggleston put it, not 'a first step'.[11] Others doubted whether Britain itself was ready to share responsibility for foreign policy and defence. There was much hostility to the idea of contributing to the costs of empire in India and the dependencies, many commentators suggesting that since Britain derived the greatest economic benefit from the empire it should continue to shoulder the burden of maintaining it. There was also much debate over the form, powers and financial arrangements of any new federation. These doubts were shared by many in the 'Moot' itself; 'I am an out and out imperialist and a great admirer of our friend L.C.', Milner wrote. 'But it is his work I admire not his philosophy. And I hate all kinds of flapdoodle more than words can say.'[12]

It was the outbreak of the First World War, however, which finally scuppered the Round Table 'movement'. Not only was there clear evidence that imperial co-operation did work – with troops from the Dominions and other parts of the empire fighting in every major theatre of the war – but also the Imperial Conference held in 1917 made clear that the premiers of Britain and the Dominions would reject federation outright while envisaging much closer and more continuous co-operation in the future. Curtis had been forced to publish his argument – as *The Problem of the Commonwealth* – under his own name in 1916; but the effect was more of a damp squib than the call to arms which he had initially envisaged. No one other than Curtis himself seemed to think that federation was then 'practical politics'. Most importantly, the allied victory ultimately removed the major external threat to the empire, and thereby undercut the single most compelling argument for constitutional reconstruction. While Curtis and a few others (notably Philip Kerr) retained a belief in federation as the only feasible solution to the 'imperial problem' in the long term, by the time the war clouds were again gathering, in the late 1930s, even Curtis recognized that a federation solely of Britain and the Dominions (and excluding the United States and western Europe) would make little difference to the balance of power.

Ironically, the First World War was also the point when members of the Round Table were closest to the centre of power in Britain. Milner was a member of the five-man War Cabinet; Kerr and Grigg served as Lloyd George's private secretaries, the former in particular credited with an influence out of all proportion to his official position; and various other members of the group were brought in to serve in different areas of the wartime administration. The Prime Minister himself described the Round Table at this time as 'a very powerful combination – in its way perhaps the most powerful in the country. … Behind the scenes they have much power and influence'.[13] As a result, members of the Round Table – and indeed articles in the journal, some of them reproduced in this volume – played important roles in a number of policy areas during the war and immediately after, including constitutional reform in India, the formulation of the League of Nations mandates system, and the fashioning of new British relationships with Ireland, Egypt and the Arab states. While individual members of the Round Table went on to hold other important positions of power and influence in later years, there was never again a sense of the Round Table as a group forming something approaching a cabal at the heart of British government.

While Curtis's hopes of imperial federation were never to be realized – and, indeed, according to most historians, were never likely to be, given the strength of Dominion nationalism – the Round Table editorial board, 'movement' and journal nevertheless played an important role in opening up discussion of imperial problems, including the long-term future of the empire, as even their fiercest critics acknowledged. Richard Jebb, who wrote *The Britannic Question* (1913) explicitly as an attack on the ideas of the group, thought that it 'has achieved a wonderful success … in organizing discussion of the whole [imperial] question … and the *Round Table* keeps up its level admirably'.[14]

Besides conveying information and opinion from different parts of the empire – itself an important task, given the lack of similar outlets at the time – the *Round Table* in its early years published a number of articles putting forward practical proposals for the improvement of Anglo-Dominion relations. Among these were suggestions that a Dominions Office should be created, separate from the Colonial Office (achieved in 1925), that the roles of Governor-General and British High Commissioner should be separated (achieved only in 1939 in the case of New Zealand), that other Dominions should follow the lead of Canada in creating departments of external affairs (achieved only in 1943, with New Zealand again the laggard) and that there should be an imperial secretariat separate from the British government (achieved, albeit with a different name and in very different circumstances, in 1965). Where the *Round Table* was less successful was in arguing for the creation of new machinery to co-ordinate the defence arrangements of the different parts of the empire, and in particular to bring the nascent Dominion navies into co-ordination with the Royal Navy: this was never achieved, except in wartime. On the main issue dividing the two main British political parties, 'imperial preference' or 'tariff reform', the *Round Table* consistently argued in favour of free trade, regarding imperial preference as retrogressive internationally, damaging to the trade and industries of the Dominions and *a fortiori* those of the dependent colonies, and of little benefit to the UK. This attitude continued (and indeed was confirmed) after the Ottawa agreements of 1932.

After the First World War, the *Round Table* welcomed the separate representation of the Dominions and India at the Versailles Conference and in the League of Nations, while calling for regular meetings between their and Britain's representatives. The *Round Table* also favoured annual imperial conferences, quasi-diplomatic communication between London and the Dominions by means of agents-general and high commissioners, and extending separate Dominion representation in foreign capitals. The journal welcomed the Balfour Declaration of 1926 (and its consequence, the Statute of Westminster of 1931), which recognized the legislative equality between Britain and the Dominions, though the journal was probably correct in its view that this merely regularized the existing situation. Privately, Curtis even went as far as to suggest that the Dominions should be encouraged to declare their independence from Britain: 'First let that position be accepted, and then let each Dominion set about to settle in conference with Great Britain and with the other Dominions what in future their legal and constitutional relations are to be, and let the conclusions arrived at be embodied in documentary form. ... Then, and not till then, shall we begin to know where we are'.[15] There is again some irony in the fact that an organization founded to promote the unity of the empire should in so many ways be encouraging its disintegration. But the irony is more apparent than real. In the Round Table view, a situation in which the Dominions played no part in the formulation of their own foreign policies and merely acquiesced in British policy while contributing little to it was one which benefited neither the Dominions nor Britain itself.

The *Round Table*'s use of the term 'Commonwealth' to describe the British empire – initially as a by-product of Curtis's 'Round Table studies', but more consistently during the First World War, when it was employed to evince an ideological dimension to the struggle between the 'British Commonwealth' and the 'German empire' – was an important factor in popularizing the term.[16] During the 1920s and 1930s it came into frequent, and from 1926 official, usage, though predominantly to characterize the self-governing parts of the empire; hence 'Commonwealth' referred to Britain and the Dominions, while 'empire' continued to be used to refer to India and the dependencies. This was not a distinction that the *Round Table* condoned: in the *Round Table* view, 'Commonwealth' was a better name for the whole of the British empire. Indeed, Curtis's 'principle of the Commonwealth' had been formulated primarily to suggest that India and the dependencies were all moving (albeit at different stages and at different speeds) towards self-government, and would eventually take their place on an equal footing with Britain and the Dominions. Curtis's elaboration of the 'principle' in his 'Round Table studies' had been attacked from all sides – by those (predominantly in Britain) who thought that India and the dependencies could never be self-governing, or at least could not be for generations or even centuries; by those (predominantly in the Dominions) who thought it a lot of eyewash designed if anything to strengthen British rule by yoking the Dominions to the imperial project; and by those (predominantly in India and the dependencies themselves) who thought it a typical piece of British hypocrisy. Nevertheless the 'principle' survived, and by the middle years of the First World War came to be the consistent, characteristic and frequently reiterated leitmotiv of *Round Table* thinking on the empire/Commonwealth.

Inevitably most of the *Round Table*'s interest in the non-self-governing empire focused, initially at least, on India – the 'jewel in the crown', the one country whose population outnumbered the rest of the British empire put together, but also the country with the most advanced and, after the First World War, most powerful national movement. (Indeed, the *Round Table* featured remarkably little coverage of the Caribbean, African, south-east Asian and Pacific colonies before the Second World War.) In 1912 the editorial board initiated an 'Indian Moot' of mostly relatively liberal members of the Indian Civil Service or India Office (notably including William Marris, later Sir William Marris, and Sir James Meston, later Lord Meston, both of whom had been seconded to work with the 'Kindergarten' in southern Africa). These officials argued that 'self-government' was 'one of the ideals at which our rule in India is to aim', and argued for an acceleration of the introduction of self-governing institutions and of the 'Indianization' of the Indian Civil Service, and for Indian representation in any federal reconstruction of the empire.[17] In 1916–18 Curtis travelled to India, where he talked both with officials and with Indian leaders including Gandhi, and wrote a series of papers advocating a system of 'dyarchy' – the creation of two parallel sets of institutions at provincial level, one run by the British-appointed (though increasingly Indianized) bureaucracy and the other by elected Indian representatives, with the expectation that gradually more powers would be transferred from one to the other.[18] Curtis's ideas had an important influence on the Secretary of State for India, Edwin Montagu, and on the 'Montagu–Chelmsford' reforms eventually embodied in the Government of India Act 1919. Curtis and his Round Table colleagues also played an important role in supporting the passage of the legislation, by lobbying in parliament and attempting to influence public opinion, both directly and via associations such as the Workers' Educational Association (WEA) and the YMCA.[19]

The Montagu–Chelmsford reforms of course failed to satisfy Indian national opinion, partly because of their inherent limitations and partly because their implementation coincided with a period of violent British repression, including the notorious Amritsar massacre. By the time of the scheduled ten-year review of the reforms (undertaken by the Simon Commission in 1927–30) it was clear that further reforms were necessary. The *Round*

Table supported the ideas coming out of the 'Round Table conferences' held in 1930–32 (which pointed towards advanced self-government at the provincial level and eventual Dominion status for an all-India federation which would include the princely states), and members of the editorial board again played an important role in the formulation of and especially in support for the Government of India Act 1935 – notably Philip Kerr (now Lord Lothian), who was Under-Secretary of State for India, chairman of the Franchise Committee which toured India in 1932 and a member of the Joint Select Committee which examined the Government of India Bill, and Geoffrey Dawson, who brought *The Times* firmly down on the side of the reforms and against the 'diehards' who opposed them.[20]

In the late 1930s there was a brief period of co-operation, when the Indian National Congress and other Indian parties formed provincial ministries under the Act, but the (British) Government of India's declaration of war without consulting Indian politicians in 1939 led to the ending of this brief experiment, and a further period of non-co-operation (in the form of the 'Quit India' movement) and repression. Leo Amery, wartime Secretary of State for India, sent Hodson and Coupland to India, the former as the Viceroy's Reforms Commissioner and the latter to conduct a study of the political situation (resulting in three wartime books, advocating an elaborate three-tiered federal system). Both were well placed to observe the ultimately unsuccessful Cripps Mission of 1942, which attempted to break the deadlock by offering full self-government after the war in return for support during it. On the crucial sticking point, the timing of further reforms, Coupland expressed the *Round Table* view when he said he could not see 'why … Winston and Amery worry overmuch' about Indian self-government during wartime: 'We are going to abdicate in a few years. … What does it matter if the Indian leaders are in virtual control of domestic government?'[21]

The *Round Table* has always covered international affairs more generally, as well as the politics and internal affairs of the empire/Commonwealth. The first substantial article in the first issue of the journal (excluding an 'introductory') was on 'Anglo-German Rivalry', which concluded that while much of the contemporary 'German scare' had been manufactured or exaggerated for journalistic purposes, there was a fundamental antagonism between British and German interests and ideas, and that war between the two countries was at the least very likely.[22] An article in the second issue, on the Anglo-Japanese alliance, pointed also to the threat (particularly to Australia and New Zealand) from Japan. Such articles tied in well with the organization's concern for greater imperial unity, at some points transparently so; similarly, the prewar journal was much concerned with the possibility of colonial neutrality during any major conflict (suggesting that this was an attempt 'to combine the advantages of membership of the British Empire, with avoidance of its risks and obligations').[23] That the Dominions rallied to the flag on the outbreak of war in 1914 was seen as a result of national self-interest as well as of imperial sentiment. Throughout the war, the *Round Table* continued to produce a series of articles portraying the conflict in ideological terms, as a clash between opposing principles; these articles were in many cases printed *en masse* for distribution in neutral countries as well as in Britain and especially the Dominions themselves.

For those associated with the *Round Table*, the most significant development of the First World War years, besides the eventual removal of the German threat, was the emergence of the United States as a major world power. From 1915 until the late 1960s, the *Round Table* included a regular quarterly survey of American politics, similar to those from various countries around the empire/Commonwealth. Moreover, throughout this period the journal was in the forefront of those urging 'Atlanticism', or a strong alliance between the empire/Commonwealth and the United States. (Curtis, in his 'Round Table studies', had described American independence as a 'schism' in the empire/Commonwealth, and there were many Americans who suspected the Round Table of seeking to re-incorporate the United States within the empire.) It would not be an exaggeration to suggest that after about 1915, the *Round Table* and those who wrote for it tended to see nearly all issues in international relations through the prism of Anglo-American relations. Initially unenthusiastic, the journal supported the idea of a League of Nations primarily as a means of preventing the United States from relapsing into isolationism, and Curtis was particularly keen for America to assume some of the 'burden' of administering as League of Nations mandates the territories wrested from Germany and Turkey.[24] The American Senate's rejection of membership of the League destroyed most of the value of the organization from the *Round Table* point of view, and throughout the 1920s and 1930s the journal tended to follow a consistent line, of downplaying the potential of the League to resolve conflicts, while urging that British policy should be framed with a view to rebuilding the wartime Anglo-American alliance. Hence the journal advocated ending the Anglo-Japanese alliance (which was disliked in Washington), opposed the Locarno pacts (which tied Britain into guaranteeing the borders between Germany, France and Belgium) and, in a curious inversion of its rhetoric towards the League of Nations, viewed the extremely nebulous ideas behind the Kellogg Pact (for the renunciation of war) as the most hopeful prospect for better international relations.

A desire to avoid European entanglements for the sake both of maintaining Commonwealth unity and of aligning British policy with that of the United States was a very important factor – along with 'guilt' about the terms imposed on Germany by the Treaty of Versailles, and annoyance at the intransigence of successive French governments – in leading some of those closely associated with the *Round Table* to urge what in the 1920s and early 1930s can be described as the conciliation of Germany, and what after the rise to power of Adolf Hitler has come to be known as 'appeasement'. Particularly prominent in advocating appeasement (and in ignoring the evidence of Hitler's unappeasability) were Lord Lothian and Geoffrey Dawson, both central figures in the so-called 'Cliveden Set' identified by Claud Cockburn,[25] but also in the Round Table group. The Round Table as a whole has consequently often been tarred with the brush of appeasement.[26] In fact, while the policy of distancing Britain from European commitments and of attempting to conciliate Germany was indeed common ground in the 1920s, such policies became much more contentious within the group as well as elsewhere in the 1930s. Leo Amery, Edward Grigg, Robert Brand and Harold Butler were amongst the most prominent 'anti-appeasers', and the journal as a whole tended to concentrate on advocating rearmament (which was supported by both appeasers and anti-appeasers) and opposing the restitution of Germany's former colonial territories (so-called 'colonial appeasement', which had been broached by Lloyd George as well as Neville Chamberlain). The *Anschluss* ended Lothian's support for appeasement, although Dawson continued to hold faith in it through and after the Munich agreement, primarily on the grounds that war would split the Commonwealth. Lothian's last article for the journal before his untimely death (while Ambassador to Washington, he died of a curable uraemic infection, having refused treatment because of his Christian Scientist beliefs) urged a 'Grand Alliance' of Western democracies, including the Dominions, to confront the Nazi menace,[27] a rallying-cry which set the tone for the *Round Table*'s wartime propaganda for the Allied cause.

The Second World War and its aftermath marked another and more decisive turning-point in the fortunes of the empire/Commonwealth, and consequently in the subjects covered and the views put forward in the *Round Table* journal. The fall of Singapore in 1942 seemed to many to symbolize the weakness of the empire and in particular its failure to gain the loyalty of its subject races; soon after, Patrick Duncan wrote from South Africa that even if the allies won the war, 'the British Empire will be gone beyond recovery'.[28] Thereafter the external context was characterized by Britain's decline from the world's largest creditor nation to its largest debtor; dependence on (rather than partnership with) the United States; eclipse as a major military power by Russia as well as the United States; and adjustment to the increasing rivalry between the latter, evident even in the final months of the war. Internally, the empire/Commonwealth was cast anew by a series of developments in the late 1940s: most notably, the disintegration of a common citizenship via the Canadian Citizenship Act of 1946, followed by the British Nationality Act of 1948; the independence of India and Pakistan in 1947; the triumph of *apartheid* in South Africa in 1948; the secession of Ireland and Burma the same year; and India's acceptance as a republican member of the Commonwealth in the London Declaration of 1949. While Curtis was still attracted by ideas of federation between Britain and the Dominions, even he could see that this would not work without the participation of other Western democracies, but more to the point he was now ploughing a lonely furrow. His colleagues in the Round Table accepted the altered circumstances with some regret but with realism. The empire/Commonwealth could no longer be conceived of in power-political terms, as a 'single unit' in international affairs; indeed, as the editor of the journal pointed out in 1950, 'no special apparatus for achieving a united Commonwealth policy either existed or was demanded by member Governments'.[29] Hopes of a more informal unity based on consultation and collaboration, and assumptions that Britain would still exercise a leadership role, survived a little longer, but were dealt a death-blow by the Suez crisis of 1956. Writing in the journal, H. V. Hodson attempted to counter the view that Britain's failure to consult its Commonwealth partners before acting 'outside previously declared policies, in a way that intimately concerned their interests, and might have provoked war' was a lamentable example of a Commonwealth member 'unwilling to fulfil the responsibilities of "belonging together"'.[30] Privately, though, another member, Denzil Marris, described Britain's actions as 'a negation of all that the Round Table [had] stood for'.[31]

The journal's main preoccupation in the 1950s and early 1960s was with the process of decolonization, and with the consequent rapid increase in the number of self-governing countries included within the Commonwealth. On the latter point, those who wrote for the journal were clear that every former colonial territory had the right to seek membership of the Commonwealth, and that there should be no attempt to create two or more categories of membership, or an inner and outer group – as advocated by the likes of Enoch Powell. They were also clear that applications for Commonwealth membership by newly independent states should be approved by all existing members, and not just by Britain. As regards decolonization, while it is increasingly difficult to speak in terms of a common '*Round Table*' viewpoint in this period, most articles in the journal supported the process, albeit frequently with reservations relating either to the speed of withdrawal (and the political and administrative unpreparedness of the newly independent nations) or to the wisdom of granting independence on the basis of existing colonial boundaries. Hence Lord Howick, a former Governor of Kenya, reflecting on the process in that country, asserted that the British government's aim should not be to gain 'a perhaps transitory popularity with the more impatient and vocal … Nationalists', but to give 'as good a chance as … possible … to a new and independent government to succeed'.[32] Elspeth Huxley highlighted the continuing existence of ethnic tensions in many countries, asserted that 'fitness for self-government presupposes a political unit which is, so to speak, self-governable', and implied (without stating explicitly) that the 'cartographer-countries' of Africa needed to be re-shaped in order for independence to be a success.[33]

Particular problems were identified in the Caribbean, where some form of federation or at least confederation was thought to be a necessary prelude to independence (and where the failure of the West Indian Federation was thought to preclude early independence for some of the smaller islands), and especially in central Africa. The presence of a sizeable settler population in the latter was believed to render the process of decolonization especially difficult. Articles in the journal initially supported the Central African Federation (bringing together Southern Rhodesia, Northern Rhodesia and Nyasaland), but soon advocated its dismemberment, on the grounds that it enabled the white minority in Southern Rhodesia to exercise excessive power over policy in the two other colonies. On Southern Rhodesia itself, the question of the future of white minority rule was highly divisive: some of the older members of the editorial board felt an instinctive sympathy with the settlers, whereas the younger members tended to see it as a test case for the Commonwealth's commitment to multi-racialism. Gradually the latter gained the upper hand – significantly, the liberal Southern Rhodesian Prime Minister from 1953 to 1958, Garfield Todd, was the journal's (anonymous) correspondent for much of this period – with the result that following the white regime's Unilateral Declaration of Independence in 1965, the journal advocated sanctions backed up by the threat of military intervention, and criticized the weakness of Harold Wilson's government's response. Nevertheless – and strikingly – the journal still did not come out in support of immediate majority rule, favouring instead as much as a generation of direct British rule during which African capacity for self-government could be built up.[34]

South Africa caused similar divisions within the editorial board, which included in the journal a range of opinions on the issues, from an article by the architect of *apartheid*, Hendrik Verwoerd, to an outspoken attack on white majority rule by Pat Duncan Jr (son of the 'Kindergarten' member Sir Patrick Duncan, and a member of the Pan Africanist Congress).[35] Increasingly the younger element prevailed. In 1951 Hodson, after extensive discussion, was authorized to state the *Round Table*'s view that there could only be one answer if Britain and other members of the Commonwealth were forced 'to choose between a uni-racial Commonwealth with South Africa as a member and a multi-racial Commonwealth without her'.[36] Nevertheless, South Africa's eventual departure from the Commonwealth in 1961 was regretted especially by the older members of the editorial board, and the *Round Table* carried a somewhat laconic editorial to mark the event.[37] Again it was several years before the journal came out uncompromisingly in favour of immediate majority rule.

The gradual evolution of the British empire into the Commonwealth has meant that no date can be singled out with certainty as the 'start date' for the modern Commonwealth. Indeed, historians, Commonwealth officials and other commentators have at various times argued for 1949 (the London Declaration, which allowed India to remain in the Commonwealth as a republic), 1931 (the Statute of Westminster), 1926 (the Balfour Declaration), 1920 (when Canada and the other self-governing nations entered the League of Nations as separate members), 1907 (when those self-governing nations had been recognized as 'Dominions') and even 1887 (the first meeting of colonial prime ministers). Undoubtedly the most significant date in the history of the modern Commonwealth, however, is 1965 – the date of the founding of the Commonwealth Secretariat. Until that point, the British Cabinet Office had organized all Commonwealth meetings and the Colonial Office and its successors (the Dominions Office from 1925, and the Commonwealth Relations Office after 1947) had acted as the hub for intra-Commonwealth communications; after it, the Commonwealth had its own organization and personnel, with the UK just one of a large and ever-increasing number of equal member-states (and indeed frequently in the minority on contentious issues).

The mid-1960s saw similarly extensive and significant changes in the *Round Table*. After a good deal of debate and soul-searching, the journal, with a few exceptions (notably the articles from Rhodesia in the late 1960s) dropped the practice of anonymity; the 'chronicle' articles from around the Commonwealth were discarded, and the Round Table groups which had provided them were allowed to wither; and a decisive step towards a more academic journal was taken with the recruitment of new, university-based editorial board members. The 'new' *Round Table* was launched to much fanfare in July 1966, and was initially successful in reversing the slow decline in subscriptions which had begun to threaten the viability of the journal. A combined financial and publishing crisis caused its closure in 1982, but this proved only a temporary setback, and in January 1983 the *Round Table* returned, with a new publisher, a highly regarded new editor (Peter Lyon, of the Institute of Commonwealth Studies, London, widely acknowledged as one of the leading academic experts on the Commonwealth) and an avowed mission to act as a 'think tank for the contemporary Commonwealth'.[38] In its new format as primarily a scholarly journal on the Commonwealth and international relations (with the bulk of its subscriptions coming from university libraries) it has flourished, moving to five issues a year in 2000 and six in 2007.

The creation of the Commonwealth Secretariat (and, the following year, its non-governmental counterpart, the Commonwealth Foundation) allowed the Commonwealth to develop a much sharper focus, albeit one which continued to reflect intergovernmental consensus rather than supranationalism. The *Round Table*'s coverage increasingly, and perhaps inevitably, followed the agenda set by the Commonwealth institutions, although at times, and in some areas, it anticipated and perhaps helped to shape that agenda. Reportage and analysis of the biennial Commonwealth Heads of Government Meetings (CHOGMs) and of the meetings of education, trade, finance and other ministers became a staple of the journal, as did commentary on the Commonwealth Secretariat's performance of its tasks. On the whole, the journal acted as a candid friend to successive Secretaries-General (the first four of whom published articles in it), with criticism of institutional or leadership failings tempered by acknowledgement of the difficulties each Secretary-General faced. On such matters as the financing of the Commonwealth Secretariat the journal consistently sided with the Secretariat against the more parsimonious member-states: 'the brutal fact is', Peter Lyon asserted in one of his last editorials, 'that in recent years CHOGMs have sought to load the ComSec with tasks while denying it adequate wherewithal in personnel and financial terms to perform such tasks'.[39]

Foremost on the agenda of the Commonwealth (and of the *Round Table*) in the late twentieth and early twenty-first centuries has been the promotion of democracy, human rights and good governance.[40] These values were of course particularly challenged by the white minority regimes in Rhodesia and South Africa, and it is much to the credit of those who ran and wrote for the *Round Table* that, after its earlier tergiversations, the journal was from the early 1970s (in contrast to the much more ambivalent attitude of British governments) unswerving in its hostility to those regimes. As regards the Commonwealth itself, the *Round Table* consistently supported and encouraged the move to a more rules-based organization, welcoming the Singapore Declaration of 1971 and the Harare Declaration of 1991, but calling for some means of policing the principles they committed Commonwealth member-states to, a number of years before the creation of the Commonwealth Ministerial Action Group (CMAG, a unique body amongst international organizations) at Auckland in 1995. The journal thereafter frequently warned against any dilution of CMAG's powers or any distraction from its efforts (as was thought to be the case when the issue of Zimbabwe's membership was handed over to a 'troika' of the leaders of South Africa, Nigeria and Australia in 2002). Commonwealth success stories included important roles in the ending of the military regime in Nigeria in 1999 and of one-party rule in the Maldives in 2008, but the repeated suspension of Fiji from the Commonwealth and the relative ineffectiveness of the Commonwealth in dealing with Robert Mugabe's regime in Zimbabwe highlighted the limited sanctions available to the Commonwealth. A number of *Round Table* articles also pointed to the weakness of the existing CMAG system when dealing with non-military undemocratic regimes, and its limited ability to stave off or engage with threats to democracy before they reached a critical point.

Other issues on the Commonwealth agenda which were also frequently aired in the *Round Table* from the 1980s onwards include conflict prevention and resolution (though here the journal repeatedly pointed to the almost total lack of Commonwealth involvement in some key disputes, such as that between India and Pakistan over Kashmir, or the civil war in Sri Lanka), sustainable development (especially in relation to Sonny Ramphal's promotion of a New International Economic Order, and the issues of debt and trade liberalization in the 1990s and 2000s), the environmental crisis, and the peculiar ecological and economic vulnerabilities of small states, which make up the majority of Commonwealth member-states. These latter can, indeed, be seen as something of a *Round Table* 'pet issue', particularly under the editorship of Peter Lyon, whose editorials and other publications helped to force the issue up the Commonwealth agenda.

The Commonwealth has frequently been derided, particularly in Britain, as a mere relic of the British empire, or a talking shop, with little relevance to the modern world. This view was early and perhaps most eloquently expressed by Enoch Powell (himself once an ardent imperialist, who had wanted to be Viceroy of India), writing as 'A Conservative' in *The Times* in 1964, where he described the Commonwealth as a 'gigantic farce'.[41] The *Round Table*, unsurprisingly, took issue with this view, denouncing 'the racists, the narrow regionalists and single-minded believers in national sovereignty' who propagated it.[42] During the 1970s and 1980s the journal frequently published articles setting out the case for the Commonwealth. By the 1990s the journal appears to have become either more relaxed or bored with such criticism, and articles defending the Commonwealth in general terms became less frequent. At the same time, the increasingly academic nature of the journal discouraged overtly normative approaches and diminished the extent to which it is possible to identify a common or '*Round Table*' view. Nevertheless there emerges from some articles, at least, in the 1990s and 2000s a strong sense, first, that its member governments have failed to make full use of the Commonwealth's potential, whether in conflict prevention and resolution, the promotion of good governance or trade negotiations; and, second, that the Commonwealth is an organization even more appropriate to the conditions of the early twenty-first century – with an emphasis on 'soft power', bridge-building and consensual decision-making – than the twentieth.

The Commonwealth of 2010 is of course a very different organization from the British empire of 1910, and in many respects its polar opposite, and the *Round Table* is a very different journal. Nevertheless, as the *Round Table* embarks on its second century, it is clear that, at the very least, the Commonwealth is still worth taking seriously.

Notes

1 L. Curtis to A. J. Glazebrook, 2 Sept 1921 [reporting conversation with Smuts], Round Table Papers, Bodleian Library, Oxford, c796, fols. 134–40.

2 W. D. McIntyre, *The Britannic Vision: Historians and the Making of the British Commonwealth of Nations, 1907–48* (London: Palgrave Macmillan, 2009), p. 89.

3 J. Dove to R. H. Brand, 23 June 1933, Lothian Papers, Scottish Record Office, Edinburgh, 276, fols 608–11.

4 L. Curtis to Sir A. Salter, 17 April 1930, Lothian Papers, 251, fols 596–99.

5 D. Morrah to L. Curtis, 16 January 1946, Curtis Papers, Bodleian Library, Oxford, 98, fol. 92.

6 V. Harlow to D. Morrah, 20 July 1951, Round Table Papers, Moot file.

7 Janitor [J. G. Lockhart], *The Feet of the Young Men* (London: Duckworth, 1928), p. 177.

8 L. Curtis to Milner, 31 October 1908, Milner Papers, Bodleian Library, Oxford, 195, fols. 155–58.

9 L. Curtis, *The Commonwealth of Nations* (London: Macmillan, 1916), p. 181.

10 J. E. Kendle, *The Round Table Movement and Imperial Union* (Toronto: University of Toronto Press, 1975), p. 175.

11 F. W. Eggleston to E. Grigg, 14 October 1913, Round Table Papers, c798, fols. 125–32.

12 Lord Milner to F. S. Oliver, 22 June 1914, Oliver Papers, National Library of Scotland, 86, fols. 40–41.

13 *Lord Riddell's Intimate Diary of the Peace Conference and After* (London: Victor Gollancz, 1933), p. 330.

14 R. Jebb to F. Ware, Jebb Papers, Institute of Commonwealth Studies, London, 2 June 1912.

15 Curtis to H. Wrong, 15 April 1926, Lothian Papers, 224, fols. 321–24.

16 See, e.g., S. R. Mehrotra, 'On the Use of the Term "Commonwealth"', *Journal of Commonwealth Political Studies*, 2/1 (1963), pp. 1–16.
17 Sir J. Meston, 'Memorandum on India and the Empire', December 1912, Round Table Papers, c826, fol. 87.
18 Curtis's Indian papers were collected and published together as *Dyarchy* (Oxford: Clarendon Press, 1920).
19 See D. Lavin, 'Lionel Curtis and Indian Dyarchy', in A. Bosco (ed.), *The Federal Idea, Volume 1* (London: Lothian Foundation Press, 1991).
20 See especially G. Douds, 'Lothian and the Indian Federation', in J. Turner (ed.), *The Larger Idea* (London: Historians' Press, 1988), pp. 62–76.
21 R. Coupland, Indian Diary, 10 April 1942 (p. 226), Coupland Papers, Rhodes House, Oxford, MSS Brit Emp s15.
22 See below, pp. 21–24.
23 [G. L. Craik,] 'Colonial Neutrality', *RT*, 1/4 (August 1911), pp. 435–42.
24 See below, pp. 37–39.
25 See N. Rose, *The Cliveden Set* (London: Jonathan Cape, 2000).
26 See, e.g., A. L. Rowse, *All Souls and Appeasement* (London: Macmillan, 1961); C. Quigley, *The Anglo-American Establishment from Rhodes to Cliveden* (New York: Books in Focus, 1981).
27 [Lord Lothian,] 'The Grand Alliance against Aggression', *RT*, 29/115 (June 1939), pp. 441–56.
28 P. Duncan to L. Curtis, 28 July 1942, Round Table Papers, c813, fol. 88.
29 [D. Morrah,] 'The United Nations in Action', *RT*, 40/160 (September 1950), pp. 299–303.
30 [H. V. Hodson,] 'The Commonwealth and the Crisis', *RT*, 47/186 (March 1957), pp. 114–20 (see below, pp. 102–05).
31 D. Marris to I. Macadam, 22 March 1958, Round Table Papers, Sydney Group file.
32 [Lord Howick,] 'Transition in Kenya', *RT*, 51/203 (June 1961), pp. 272–77.
33 [E. Huxley,] 'African Independence and After', *RT*, 46/181 (December 1955), pp. 17–26 (see below, pp. 95–99).
34 See below, pp. 120–23.
35 [E. Schuller and H. Verwoerd,] 'Apartheid in Practice', *RT*, 44/175 (June 1954), pp. 259–63; [P. Duncan,] 'Satyagraha in South Africa', *RT*, 43/170 (March 1953), pp. 130–37.
36 [H. V. Hodson,] 'Dr Malan and the Commonwealth', *RT*, 41/163 (June 1951), pp. 219–26.
37 [D. Morrah,] 'A Leaf Falls', *RT*, 51/203 (June 1961), pp. 219–23.
38 [P. Lyon,] 'The Round Table Revived and the Contemporary Commonwealth', *RT*, 72/285 (January 1983), p. 10.
39 [P. Lyon,] 'The Commonwealth in Crisis?', *RT*, 92/369 (April 2003), p. 188.
40 These and the other issues mentioned in the following paragraphs are dealt with much more fully in the companion volume to this, James Mayall (ed.), *The Contemporary Commonwealth: An Assessment, 1966–2009* (London: Routledge, 2009).
41 *The Times*, 2 April 1964.
42 [T. Raison,] 'The New Round Table', *RT*, 56/223 (July 1966), p. 214; see also [*idem*,] 'Is the Commonwealth a Farce?', *RT*, 54/215 (June 1964), pp. 215–21 (see below, pp. 114–17).

Part 1
The prewar empire (1910–14)

The Round Table

The first article in the first issue of the Round Table *set out the journal's stall. The editor's nonchalance about the sales of the journal was underpinned (though this was not widely known at the time) by extensive fund-raising and a '£ for £' arrangement with the Rhodes Trust (which lasted until 1915), but the journal's pitch for a select readership and its self-declared aim to dispel 'ignorance' were recurring themes. Many of the concerns raised in the editorial – the need to address popular 'misgivings' about the empire, the lack of imperial co-ordination, the threat from without – also featured prominently over the next few years.*

[Philip Kerr,] 'The Round Table', *RT* 1/1 (Nov 1910), pp. 1–6

It is a common complaint, both in Great Britain and in the Dominions, that it is well-nigh impossible to understand how things are going with the British Empire. People feel that they belong to an organism which is greater than the particular portion of the King's dominions where they happen to reside, which is one of the greatest of human fabrics, but which has no government, no Parliament, no press even, to explain to them where its interests lie, or what its policy should be.

Of speeches and writings about the Empire there is no end. But who has time to select what is worth reading from the multitude of newspapers and reviews? Most people have no access to the best among them, and such as have are haunted by the fear that what they read is coloured by some local party issue in which they have no concern. No one can travel through the Empire – without being profoundly impressed by the ignorance which prevails in every part, not only about the affairs of the other parts, but about the fortunes of the whole. This ignorance naturally leads to misgivings, and people are frequently involved in disputes and controversies about the Empire which in most cases would immediately be solved if the facts were known. The truth, of course, is that all who have grown up under the Union Jack are in their hearts devoted to it, for it stands to them for a great tradition in the past, a great inspiration in the present – as the writer in India shows[1] – and a still greater promise in the future. There is no British subject who has not subscribed in some way to the cost of keeping it flying in the heavens, and who does not cherish the memory of some friend or some hero of his own who has died for it. But many associate imperialism with the projects of jingoes and capitalists, and object to it, just because they admire the ideals of liberty, and justice, and personal responsibility upon which the Empire rests, and which such projects would destroy. Nothing is further from their minds than that the Empire itself should be allowed gently to dissolve so long as it is true to its traditions. For not they alone, but the world, would be poorer from its decay.

In order to dispel the ignorance on which misgivings rest, we need information of two kinds. On the one hand we ought to know the truth of what is going on in the several portions of the Empire. On the other hand we ought to be able to find out how the Empire is faring as a whole. But how is the truth to be found? No one who has other business on hand can follow affairs on the Indian frontier, the reciprocity negotiations between Canada and America, the proposals whereby the British Constitution is to be mended or destroyed in a federal reconstruction, the Asiatic menace in Australia, the complications which might follow in Africa from a revolution in Portugal, and steer his way to a clear judgement about each separately, or of the upshot of them all. That would be a task to be entrusted to a council of the wisest men to be found. […]

Failing, therefore, a body which can speak for every part, we must contrive a makeshift, and the makeshift is *The Round Table.* The aim of *The Round Table* is to present a regular account of what is going on throughout the King's dominions, written with first-hand knowledge and entirely free from the bias of local political issues, and to provide a means by which the common problems which confront the Empire as a whole can be discussed also with knowledge and without bias. For that, in the opinion of the promoters, who reside in all parts of the Empire, is what is most needed at the present day.

In order that *The Round Table* may achieve its first aim and may truly represent the opinion of all parts it has been arranged that each part of the Empire should provide its own correspondent, whose business it will be to present the views of that part frankly, with local knowledge, and local ignorance perhaps, about its own concerns and the interests which it shares with the rest. The greater part of the Review will thus consist of articles actually written in the different Dominions and Dependencies. There will be no censorship of opinion. But it is an essential condition laid upon every writer that he should neither misrepresent facts nor persons nor subserve the interest of any party in the locality where he resides. Personal bias cannot be entirely excluded. But the reader will at least know that what he reads is straightforward opinion, and not a careful paraphrase of the facts put forth by a cunning partisan.

If this part of the programme is fulfilled, *The Round Table* will present as true a reflection of the present state of affairs as it is reasonable to expect. It will reveal the wide divergence of opinion on common concerns. It will give readers the structural ideas in current controversies, and explain the broad movement of events. It will help them to understand the meagre cablegrams which flash fitfully across the wires, and to correct the glaring errors in fact and quotation which every citizen abroad notes in the news from his own home.

But this is not enough. The founders of *The Round Table* have an uneasy sense that times are changing, and that the methods of yesterday will not serve in the competition of tomorrow. They feel that if the various communities of the Empire have common interests they are singularly badly equipped to pursue them. If there is a conflict between the political systems of the British Empire and of Germany, as the writer on foreign affairs thinks,[2] and if, as Captain Mahan says, 'the balance of forces influences continually and decisively the solutions of diplomacy,' it is an anomaly that there should be no means of marshalling the whole strength and resources of the Empire effectively behind its will, when its mind is made up. If its weight in the counsels of the world depends in the long run on man power and the type of human being that becomes a British subject, it is strange that its people should be left to drift to foreign lands, and that there should be no joint authority to assist the migration of British citizens from one portion of the Empire, where they are superfluous, to another where they are urgently required. If there is a common problem such as Asiatic immigration, there should be some other means than the circulation of formal official despatches, or a meeting of Premiers only once in four years, whereby it can be publicly discussed, and a decision quickly reached. […]

The Round Table will thus be concerned solely with Imperial affairs. Nothing else, indeed, would justify its production, for there is already a plethora of admirable journals which at times discuss the problems of the Empire. But these journals have a common quality, which diminishes their value for our purpose. They are all written for a particular public and from the point of view of a particular locality. As is but natural the Editors have to consider the wishes of their readers, who are more anxious to learn about budgets which lighten their breakfast tables, or land laws which reach into their purses, than to follow misty proceedings at a distance, which may affect their careers not today or tomorrow, but in the far future. The ordinary journal, therefore, cannot help representing local prepossessions and being influenced by the local atmosphere, and if it is to sell at all it must concern itself with much besides the Empire.

It is a main object of *The Round Table* to escape this quality, for its value would disappear if it could be accused of local bias. It will do so, it is true, at the expense of being, perhaps, somewhat unsaleable. But this prospect does not dismay the promoters, who do not seek a large circulation or publicity but hope to create a review which will be of interest to all parts and will gradually accumulate the material on which a sound judgement of the Imperial problem can be based. […]

Much that relates to the several portions of the Empire may appear obvious and commonplace to dwellers in these parts. But they should remember that such articles are produced not for those who know the facts, but for people at a distance who are ignorant of them. *The Round Table* does not aim at propounding new theories or giving voice to ingenious speculations. It will serve its purpose if it contributes to the better understanding of the problems of the Empire and to their solution, and if no one ever raises the charge against it that it has distorted the truth for its own ends.

The German menace

The threat to the British empire from Germany was a frequent theme of articles published in the journal between 1910 and 1914 – not surprisingly, since it was also the main reason put forward by those who wanted a greater degree of imperial unity (and Dominion contributions to the common defence). Kerr's characterization of the antagonism as reflecting a clash of ideologies drew on long traditions of British self-satisfaction (perhaps even self-delusion), but it also had important implications for British imperial policy, as regards the 'ends' of British rule.

[Philip Kerr,] 'Foreign Affairs: Anglo-German Rivalry', *RT* 1/1 (November 1910), pp. 7–40

The central fact in the international situation to-day is the antagonism between England and Germany. It is the universal element which every foreign minister has to take into account in appraising his country's fortunes, and it is the topic which dominates all others in the columns of the world's press which are devoted to the discussion of foreign affairs. Much that is absurd, it is true, has been said in England about Germany's reputed plan, prepared in every detail, for a sudden and unprovoked attack on the heart of the Empire, on a date which is almost due. There is, too, ground for suspecting that minor candidates in the heat of an election conflict have employed this tale for party advantage. Even wilder stories have been circulated in Germany about England's supposed design of destroying Germany's fleet before it is full grown and then marching an army on Berlin! That tale, also, has been exploited for party purpose in the Fatherland. But underlying these exaggerations there is a solid substratum of truth. It is an old and a true saying that there is no smoke without fire. Anglo-German rivalry does not exist solely in the minds of panic-mongers and Chauvinists, nor can it be dispelled by the amicable disclaimers of pacificists and 'cordiality leagues'. It is an all-pervading reality.

If this be so, the solution of this rivalry between the great military power of Europe, and the great sea-power of the world is the most difficult problem which the Empire has to face. […]

Modern civilization is a compound of ideas contributed by a number of peoples. To the Jews it owes the idealism of its religious belief, to the Greeks the conception of liberty, to the Romans the sanctity of law, to the Teutonic peoples its respect for personal rights.

It is within the British Empire that the spirit of individualism has grown to its full maturity. For of all the Teutonic peoples the Anglo-Saxons alone have been free from the cramping necessity of subordinating their development to the exigencies of war. Scarcely ever have they heard the drums of war in their homes, for nature has provided in the Channel a better defence than walls of steel.

The unconscious working of this intense spirit of individualism runs through the whole history of the Empire. It is the keynote of the long struggle of the people first with the feudal barons and later with the crown, and when, after two revolutions, the victory was won, the constitution which enshrined the liberties of the British people was transplanted to America, Africa and Australia. Once an attempt was made to force some reluctant colonists in America to contribute to the common defence, and the issue has moved England to protect her dominions ever since at her own expense. Moreover, in conceding self-government to the young communities overseas, she handed over to them the vast wealth of the lands they dwelt in without reservation, and without even attaching to them the burden of debt she had incurred in acquiring them. To this day the tradition has run on, for, to the wonderment of the world, she gave self-government to the Transvaal four short years after the termination of a long and costly war, again without casting upon it any share of the cost or making conditions about its contributing to the common defence. Under no political system but the imperial system could the French Canadian or the Boer retain his language, his customs and his racial individuality. Even in America, where personal freedom has been carried to the point of weakening the rule of law, the new-comer has to submit to a far straiter discipline than the immigrant to any of the British domains. With the backward races it is the same. For the first time in history conquered peoples, incapable of maintaining order among themselves, were governed not mainly in the victors' interests, but in their own. Slavery, though the tradition of all the ages, was obviously inconsistent with personal freedom, and was abolished throughout the Empire a century ago.

Let us look at the other side of the picture. The peoples of the Continent were not so fortunate as the Anglo-Saxons. Nature afforded them no better protection from foreign attack than a narrow stream or a mountain pass. Europe has been torn by the ambitions of kings and the brutal savageries of war. The struggle for personal rights has been impeded by the constant necessity of submitting to a rigid and uniform discipline. Personal freedom has had to be sacrificed to national liberty. The continental spirit, therefore, is very different from the British spirit. It is the spirit which accepts authority readily, and subordinates the individual to the will of the community. It is a spirit which produces an intense corporate life and a splendid eagerness in the individual to sacrifice his personal desires for his country. But it is also the spirit which is prone to follow the allurements of ambition, and to exalt the claims of a nation above the rights of mankind.

The continental spirit finds its most characteristic embodiment in modern Germany. The Germans give free play to individualism in many respects.

They are not false to the dominant characteristic of the Teutonic peoples. But their history has taught them the bitter lesson that the citizen can only be free when the State to which he belongs is strong enough to guarantee his freedom. Individualism, paramount in other matters, stops at the entry to the political field. They have never known the political liberty of the British subject or the American citizen. To their minds it conflicts with national interests. Just in so far as the interests of the individual are allowed to prevail the effective power of the state is diminished. The political organization of the British Empire is designed to promote the development of the individual, the political organization of Germany to promote the efficiency of the state. It is only by realizing that to the German the interests of the Fatherland far transcend all other claims that one can understand the German character, and so the German policy. […]

The aims and interests of Germany alike point to a policy of expansion. Time is on the side of her rivals, Russia, America and the British Empire, who are rich in vacant land, and unless she can grow in wealth and population as they grow, she is bound in the long run to fall back in the race for world supremacy which it is her fixed determination to win. Of all things she fears the effective union of the British Empire for defence. In the long run it is mathematically just as certain that she will defeat England alone in a contest of wealth and numbers, as it is that she will be beaten by the combined peoples of the Empire. That is why she thus feverishly augments her armaments, and plans to master Europe, for it is only by making herself invulnerable at home that she can hope to use her strength effectively on expansion abroad. […] Nobody has ever described the inevitable result of the policy to which Germany has committed herself better than the great Treitscke,[3] the national historian of Germany.

'If', he said, 'our empire has the courage to follow an independent colonial policy with determination, a collision of our interests and those of England is unavoidable. It was natural and logical that the new great power of central Europe had to settle affairs with all great powers. We have settled our accounts with Austria-Hungary, with France, with Russia. The last settlement, the settlement with England, will probably be the lengthiest and the most difficult'.

Unfortunately, Treitscke's doctrine is the belief of the mass of the German people. The essential fact is that an overwhelming majority of Germans regard war with England as inevitable. Germanism, they say, must and will prevail, for it is the most vital and the most self-sacrificing of the forces of the day. England, the colossus with the feet of clay, the plutocrat who can neither fill nor effectively defend the vast lands she owns, lies across her path. The prospect of gaining a new colonial dominion, or of winning the first place in the world, may be remote, but it is hopeless so long as the British bar the way. Once that obstacle is torn away, at least there is a chance, and the blind instinct of expansion makes every German resolve that he will not abandon the struggle till the question of British supremacy has at least been put to the test. […]

What is England to do? She has no desire to thwart German ambitions so long as they do not involve injury to her own citizens or destruction to the free institutions of the Empire. The idea that she is jealous of German progress is absurd. During the years of her supremacy has she lifted a finger against the United States, which have now a population twice her own and resources immeasurably greater? No, for the ideals of the United States, like her own, are essentially unaggressive and threaten their neighbours no harm. But Germanism, in its want of liberalism, its pride, its aggressive nationalism, is dangerous, and she feels instinctively that if it is allowed to become all powerful it will destroy her freedom, and with it the foundation of liberty on which the Empire rests. […]

Imperial defence

Written to coincide with the Imperial Conference held in London in May and June 1911, Kerr's editorial was the nearest the Round Table *came to endorsing Lionel Curtis's thesis that there were only two possible long-term outcomes for the relationship between Britain and the self-governing Dominions: federation and independence. In other passages Kerr dwelt on the anomaly in the status of the Dominion navies, the disparity between British and Dominion defence expenditure, and the impossibility of a Dominion remaining neutral in a war involving Britain without declaring its independence.*

[Philip Kerr,] 'The New Problem of Imperial Defence',
RT 1/3 (May 1911), pp. 231–62

[…] During the last fifty years the Empire has faced and solved the problem of its own internal government. The principle of complete autonomy in local affairs has now been established as the basis of the internal government of the Empire – a solution which no one is ever likely to question again. But scarcely has the old problem disappeared than a new problem has begun to arise in its place. Hitherto the external relations of the Empire have been regarded, by the Dominions as well as by Great Britain, as the proper concern of the British Government. During the last few years, however, the Dominions have realized that they can no longer ignore foreign affairs. In numberless ways they are finding themselves affected by what goes on beyond their borders. And as they are affected they are considering by what means they are to safeguard their national interests. How are they to do so without obtaining a real influence over the Foreign Policy and the defensive arrangements of the Imperial Government? It is obvious that foreign policy and defence cannot continue to be the sole and exclusive concern of the United Kingdom. Indeed, they have already ceased to be so, and it is the instinctive apprehension of this fact and of its far-reaching consequences which is the cause of the present general feeling of unrest about the future of the Empire. […]

It is quite clear that Great Britain alone cannot indefinitely guarantee the Empire from disruption by external attack. The further one looks ahead the more obvious does this become. A nation of 45,000,000 souls, occupying a small territory and losing much of the natural increase in its population by emigration, cannot hope to compete in the long run even against single powers of the first magnitude – with Russia for instance with its 150,000,000 inhabitants, with America with its 90,000,000, with Germany with its 65,000,000, increasing by nearly a million a year, to say nothing of China with its 430,000,000 souls. Far less can it hope to maintain the dominant position it has hitherto occupied in the world, with a dozen new powers entering upon the scene. Each of these powers, of small account by itself, is already an important factor in the scale which measures the balance of power. And as they are steadily increasing in wealth and population, it is only a question of time before some of them will become first-class powers in their turn. What will be the position of the Empire then, if it has to depend upon the navy of England alone? Obviously the day must come when, if the Empire is to continue, it must be defended by the joint efforts of all its self-governing peoples.

It is not, however, on this ground that a reconsideration of the relations between Great Britain and the Dominions about foreign affairs and defence is becoming urgent. Great Britain can probably defend the Empire, at any rate if the international situation is favourable, for some, perhaps for many, years to come. The other half of the difficulty is far more pressing and far more dangerous. It is simply impossible for the Dominions to set up independent foreign policies and independent defensive systems of their own without destroying the Empire, even if foreign powers refrain from attack. Suppose the present tendency [is] carried to its logical conclusion. Instead of there being one government responsible for the safety of the Empire there will be five. Each of these governments will be free to pursue any policy it likes and each will have military or naval strength with which to back its policy. Each of them, therefore, may involve itself in war. And if the policy of one government, or the use it makes of its navy, does lead to war, what is to be the position? Are the other governments to be involved? The Dominions, not unreasonably, do not admit their responsibility for the policy of Great Britain, because they have no share in framing it. Is Great Britain to be responsible for the policy of the Dominions? Australia, for instance, is committed to the policy of Asiatic exclusion – a policy which may lead to international complications of the gravest kind. Are Great Britain and the other Dominions committed to support this policy and are they responsible for making the naval and military preparations necessary to guarantee its being carried into effect? On the other hand Great Britain is responsible for maintaining intact the Imperial system as a whole. Is her government not to know what resources in men, ships and money can be depended upon, in making her dispositions for defence? And are the Dominions to be left to frame policies which may render it impossible for England to make the international agreements by which alone the safety of the Empire can be maintained? […]

Obviously, the principle of complete local autonomy, admirably as it works for the internal politics of the Empire, cannot be applied to foreign affairs. The Empire will infallibly disappear if any one of five governments can involve it in war. Even if in its weakness and confusion it is spared by foreign powers, it will break up of its own accord, for every one of the five nations of which it is composed will declare its independence, rather than remain a part of a system in which it may find itself at war by the deliberate policy or imprudent folly of any one of four other governments, over none of which it has any sort of control. The conclusion is inexorable. Either the nations of the Empire must agree to co-operate for foreign policy and defence, or they must agree to dissolve the Empire and each assume the responsibility for its own policy and its own defence. There is no half-way house between the two positions. […]

Yet it will not be easy to find a satisfactory method of Imperial co-operation for foreign policy and defence. There are many difficulties in the way, and many prejudices and traditions to overcome. There are difficulties, too, both on the side of Great Britain and on the side of the Dominions.

In the case of Great Britain the difficulty will come over the control of policy. […] She will, naturally, be reluctant to part with any share of the control, especially to young nations inexperienced in international affairs. But she must recognize that the old system cannot continue. The Dominions are no longer colonies. They are nations. Even if they were anxious to remain hermit states they could not do so. In the modern world, with its rapid system of intercommunication and the delicate equipoise of international credit, they are bound to be vitally affected by what goes on beyond their borders. Any war between first-class powers must ruin many thousands of people in each of the Dominions. Markets where they have been accustomed to sell their goods will be closed. Shareholders will lose their dividends and perhaps their capital. Labour will find no employment. The price of money will rise. Business will stagnate, enterprise will be checked, and the whole process of their national life will be unhinged. And if England is involved the position will be still worse. […] What would be the effect on the Dominions of a war between England and a first-class modern power, even if they tried to avoid being involved? Dominion merchandize, worth hundreds of millions of pounds, and on whose safe delivery the living of their populations depended, would be liable to instant capture at sea.

Moreover, Great Britain must realize that the Dominions have vital interests of their own entirely distinct from hers, and of which she has little understanding. They are committed to policies – such as Asiatic exclusion – which vitally affect foreign powers. They cannot allow their foreign policy to be decided for them by a government which does not represent them. Nor will their growing self-respect permit them to shelter behind a navy which will retain command of the sea only if Great Britain diverts to a barren expenditure on armaments revenues which are urgently needed for social reform. It is obvious that if Great Britain were ten times as rich and populous as she is and could guarantee indefinitely the safety of the Empire from foreign attack, the day has gone by when she can control the foreign relations of the Dominions, or act in her own discretion on their behalf. Unless the Dominions have a real share in the control of the Imperial policy they will be driven to adopt policies of their own – policies which must be framed in the light of purely local interests and which may therefore conflict with it. Great Britain must recognize also that co-operation in foreign affairs and defence does not mean that her government will listen to the views of the Dominions and then, on the ground that her population is three times as large as that of the Dominions combined, declare that she must be left to decide knotty problems as she thinks fit. […] If the Dominions and Great Britain are to co-operate over foreign policy, the policy must be a true Imperial policy based on the needs of every part.

In the case of the Dominions the difficulty will arise over the responsibility for the defence of the Empire beyond their own territory. The Dominions admit their responsibility for defending themselves. But they do not admit that they have any obligation to keep peace and order in India, to protect Egypt or the African dependencies from external invasion, or even to support Great Britain if she were involved in a European war, though there is little doubt that in practice they would come to her assistance as best they could. But this state of affairs, which exists because they have never yet had to provide entirely even for their own defence, cannot continue. […]

The changing raj

Written by two relatively liberal members of the Indian Civil Service (ICS) and India Office, this article sought to extrapolate from the experience of the Ripon and Morley–Minto reforms the guiding principle of British policy in India. The authors suggested the need for Indianization of the ICS parallel with political reforms, and made clear that they ultimately envisaged a self-governing dominion within the British empire (two decades before this became official government policy). Nevertheless their assumptions about Indian fitness for self-government and their disparaging (and misjudged) views on the Indian National Congress were very much of their time.

[William Marris and M. C. Seton,] 'India: Old Ways and New',
RT 3/9 (December 1912), pp. 52–80

[…] The time is quickly approaching when no longer can the English in India be content to do their work empirically; to go on trusting for guidance to their own sense of right and justice and expediency, avoiding a philosophy or a creed whenever they can, and, when they cannot, professing one only of the vaguest, and not troubling seriously about any apparent divorce between their principles and their practice. For we have been challenged to recognize, and we have recognized, that in our management of India the people of India must henceforward take an increasing share. It is time that we defined our ideas; that we knew more clearly what it is that India wants, and how far and by what stages we are going to assist her to get it. […]

Government being the art of management on the largest scale, it seems axiomatic that self-government in minor affairs should precede self-government in greater. Lord Ripon's institution of town councils and district boards was designed as an introduction of the Indian public to the task of administration.[4] Both town and country boards are, in the main, elective; their members are chosen by electors enrolled either on a property or educational qualification or for good repute; they discuss all questions of concern to their town or county; they vote resolutions, and a majority decides. To all appearance the foundation stone of self-government has been well and truly laid. But, in fact, the best friends of the system must acknowledge that after many years of patient trial it still affords an uncertain basis for the future political structure of the country. District boards exist chiefly on resources beyond their control, because there is no such community of interest or opinion among a scattered agricultural people as would lead them, left to themselves, to endure the common sacrifice of self-taxation. They are still artificial creations. The district officer is chairman, he arranges the budget, and the board is little more than a consultative body, useful chiefly for purposes of information, and valued by its members, and by them alone, for the opportunities it gives of intercourse with the authorities. Its mainspring is official, and its estimation is that of a minor honorific distinction. […]

Until quite recently criticism of government has centred in the Indian National Congress, a self-elected body which meets once a year and makes speeches and passes resolutions, often in the same set terms year after year, attacking the government policy. India's future historians may treat with respect this first amateur attempt to create an indigenous organ of politics. But looking only to actual facts, one is constrained to say that it has not been a success. Hampered from the first by its lack of a mandate, the Congress has suffered also from dissensions as to leadership and methods, and from the aloofness of the Mohammedans; but it has been even more discredited by the ignorance it has shown of practical politics, and the empty wordiness of its harangues. There has been little reasoned criticism, and the debates have not affected its prearranged and stereotyped resolutions. Hitherto it has not had, nor has deserved to have, much effect in influencing the actions of Government.

But it seems likely that activities hitherto manifested in the Congress will now be mainly diverted to the legislative councils, the character of which has been entirely altered by the changes made by Lord Morley.[5] In the past, a minority of Indian members had attended the Council meetings with small hope of even influencing a division. Convinced by the unrest which marked the beginning of Lord Minto's rule, that the moment had come for giving the Indian representatives a larger voice, Lord Morley greatly increased the number of Indian elected members, and gave them power of asking questions, discussing financial policy, and moving resolutions on all matters except a few specially reserved affairs. In the provincial councils he even disdained to keep an official majority, so that the non-official members, if united, can now actually defeat the Government over a provincial legislative measure, or carry through Council a Bill to which Government is opposed. […]

So far the reformed councils can point to no great achievement. Interpellations are still verbose and inordinately numerous. Resolutions are the plaything of the eccentric member, though it is conceivable that in the future they may be a powerful weapon of attack. But budget discussions have been more illuminating and useful than in the past. And private members' Bills dealing with particular points of Indian personal law – as, for example, the law relating to marriage, or the law of Mohammedan money-trusts – will certainly be important, not merely for their educative value, but as serious contributions to the Statute Book. Mr. Gokhale's Bill providing tentatively for free education[6] was important as the first constructive attempt of a non-official member to direct public policy into an entirely new route. It failed, because the Government were able, without difficulty, to show that it was practically unworkable. But it is only the forerunner of many other legislative proposals of a far-reaching character. Already a Bill to stop the dedication of girls in Hindu temples has been put forward by a private member. Undoubtedly the increased number of Indian members will arm the councils with new power to deal with such difficult and delicate questions; and we may be quite sure that both by resolutions and by legislation the Indian members of the council will succeed more and more in directly influencing the course of policy. […]

Meanwhile it is something gained that the Secretary of State has been induced to define the intentions of His Majesty's Ministers. He is reported by the *Pioneer* as follows: They wished first to devolve on the provincial governments as many functions of government as could be safely entrusted to them; secondly, to employ as many Indians in the public service as could reasonably be employed; and thirdly, to arrange for the supremacy of British rule in India as the best method of securing the happiness of the people of India. […] It is, of course, in reconciling the second and the third of Lord Crewe's objects that the real difficulty of the whole Indian problem lies. The increased admission of Indians to the service, which is the Government, means no other thing than the decreased admission of Englishmen to it. How is this compatible with the maintenance *in perpetuum* of British supremacy? Lord Crewe spoke guardedly of the immediate or the perceptible future; and rightly so. But if no one supposes that in five years England will have ceased to be administering India, can we feel equal confidence as to the outcome, fifty or a hundred years hence? Is there any imaginable position of stable equilibrium under the action of the two varying forces, which we may look to, not indeed as the sure and inevitably final goal, but with sufficient confidence to give us a creed and to steady our steps upon a strange, new road?

The public service of India is also the government of India. To realize this we must drop all preconceptions of a parliamentary legislature controlling a ministerial executive, distinct from and directing the whole public service of the country. In India, service and executive are one and indivisible; and it would be truer to say that they control the legislature than vice versa. To the highest grades of the service the Indian is as yet admitted only by competing with Englishmen at the Civil Service examination in London. Below those grades he has generous opportunity, and no changes which may be found desirable in the secondary service have any bearing on our present question. But the government of the country, the heads of the great departments, the secretaries, the heads of provinces, the executive councils are practically drawn from the same privileged, superior service. The legislative councils in which, under Lord Morley's scheme, non-official Indians bulk so largely, and in which are centred the nationalists' hopes, are still something of an excrescence upon the system of administration. They legislate, and legislation is an important function of government. But the whole course of legislation in India could be arrested without necessarily bringing the machine to a standstill. The councils do not control supplies, and they do not make and unmake governments. They can debate, ask questions and move resolutions which may be entitled to respect, but are not binding on the Executive. They are a legislature but not a parliament. […]

The process of nationalizing the administration may proceed in more ways than one. You may indeed enlarge the powers of the legislative councils until they become the government; but you may also take Indians freely into the public service, until a due proportion find their way into the executive; or you may combine the administrative with the constitutional change. […]

There is no more important and difficult duty before the Indian administration at the present moment than gradually and steadily to introduce a well-tested element of Indian material into the structure of the Government. Not merely to satisfy Indian ambitions – that is a secondary aim – but as the directest step towards the ultimate solutions of the political problem of the country. […]

Australia and the Japanese menace

In the face of Britain's diminishing naval supremacy, there was much debate about the future role of the Dominions in imperial defence – and whether they should seek to build up their own forces or contribute to those controlled by Britain. Following the Imperial Defence Conference of 1909, Australia began to increase dramatically its expenditure on its own navy, New Zealand contributed a battlecruiser to the Royal Navy and Canada prevaricated between the two policies. F. W. Eggleston, presenting 'the Australian view' in a composite article (with the British view being given by Edward Grigg), highlighted in particular the supposed threat from Japan to the 'White Australia' policy as a reason for not being able to rely fully on British protection, and for proceeding with a separate scheme.

[F. W. Eggleston,] 'Naval Policy and the Pacific Question',
RT 4/15 (June 1914), pp. 391–462

[…] The main factors which enter into the question of the security of British interests in the Pacific are fairly simple. We have on the one hand the unquestionable preponderance of Japanese power. The first question is, how far is that power limited by countervailing factors and tendencies. The overwhelming preponderance of Japan in the Pacific is not questioned, and need not be closely examined. It is Japan first and everyone else nowhere. Japan is in a position, so far as her naval and military offices are concerned, to work her will. Her fleet is a growing one. Ministerial programmes contemplate increases, and though public feeling protests against the taxation, it has not shown any disinclination to maintain the present policy. It is, of course, true that the efficacy of any warlike armaments is strictly limited. Questions of distance affect very much the power of a great nation to work its will. But the distance of Australia from Japan is counterbalanced by the extraordinary difficulty which Australia would have in defending her coast line and preventing a lodgment in unoccupied parts where agricultural settlements would grow up impossible of displacement.

The instability of conditions in the East will have one of two issues, either of which is big with menace for other countries in the Pacific. Either Japan will obtain a dominant interest in China, or she will be disappointed. In the one case, backed by the immense resources of China, she might be inspired to extend her sphere of power; in the other, deterred from her immediate object she might turn towards an object to be gained with more certainty. It would be dangerous to rely upon the supposed internal difficulties of Japan. […] It is indeed dangerous to calculate too closely the conditions which seem to limit the efficacy of the overwhelming armaments of Japan. We know that the fleet is there, and that we have nothing to match it. We have no idea how it may be used by the statesmen of Japan in two, ten, or twenty years time. Thus for all practical purposes it must be assumed that the Japanese Fleet stands at its face value and that it is the dominant force in the Pacific.

It is next to be considered whether the Anglo-Japanese treaty is a sufficient guarantee of British interests in the Pacific. It must be remembered that a treaty is merely a contractual obligation. It is secured by no independent guarantee, but only by the mutual self-interest of the contracting parties. Are the respective interests of Great Britain and Japan in the maintenance of the treaty of sufficient strength to secure its observance?

The interest of England in the observance of the treaty is obvious. The treaty enables Great Britain to do without a fleet in the Pacific. Great Britain has enormous interests in the Pacific which can under these circumstances only be protected by Japan. Japan indeed is the only nation that can protect them, and therefore it is essential to Great Britain to secure her alliance. But what *quid pro quo* does Great Britain give for this service? Great Britain has no fleet in the Pacific, and, therefore, can do no service to Japan there. Japan has no interests in the Atlantic, and therefore Great Britain cannot render any services to Japan there. Under these circumstances the treaty cannot be regarded as a safeguard. It is dangerous in that it leads to the diminution of English power in the Pacific. If questions arose between the Empire and Japan in the Pacific, the Empire would be helpless. In order to retain the virtue of the treaty so far as was possible, Great Britain might have to sacrifice her interests on the question raised. Such a sacrifice would probably be at the expense of the outer Dominions.

Are the interests of any part of the Empire likely to come into conflict with those of Japan in such a way as to make war a possibility? It should be pointed out at once that the character of the respective interests of the Dominions concerned in the Pacific varies considerably both in kind and intensity. It is important to emphasize this because at present it is a strong but unacknowledged factor in the discussion of all Pacific questions. A nation which is only concerned in protecting commercial interests is in quite a different position from a nation which believes that the lives, the happiness and the personal well-being of its subjects may be in question – particularly if the danger be held to arise from a race whose civilization is alien, and whose victory would mean deprivation of privileges and traditions which have grown into the life of a people. It cannot be denied that this difference of interests affects the attitude of Great Britain and the Dominions towards Pacific questions. The interests of Great Britain are primarily commercial, the interests of the Dominions are personal. Great Britain has protected her Empire by a world wide naval supremacy. This supremacy is becoming increasingly difficult to maintain; if it is not kept up to the full, and so long as the British Government has the sole disposal of the forces of the Empire, it is likely to concentrate where English interests are personal and not where they are merely commercial. An alliance may be a very good protection for merely commercial interests. It is quite another thing to rely on a treaty where personal interests are involved. It is true that a more intense feeling of national sympathy between all parts of the Empire would give the British peoples that personal interest in extra-European problems which is necessary, but that sympathy needs development and a full understanding of those problems which does not at present exist. […]

What policy should be adopted towards meeting the dangers which seem to threaten the Pacific communities? Up to the last few years the policy of what is known as the Blue Water School of naval strategists has been dominant. This school held the view that the true policy was concentration of the naval forces of Great Britain where the danger was likely to arise. In case of difficulty the command of the sea should be obtained at the earliest possible moment by attacking and defeating the enemy at its strongest point, and then all else would be easy. Isolated raids in outer seas were contemplated, but it was felt that they could be punished at leisure when the principal enemy was defeated, and that, this being the case, such raids would not often be attempted. An admiral of this school would (quite rightly) consider the bombardment of Sydney with equanimity. It would use up the enemy's powder and could be compensated afterwards. According to this theory, the fleets of the Empire should be concentrated (as they have been) in European water to meet a possible attack by Germany. The wisdom of this policy is not questioned. Germany is a potential enemy of the whole Empire.

It is questionable, however, whether the policy is applicable at all to the present circumstances where a potential enemy of great power exists in the

East; and is not controllable by European forces. An attack by Japan might not involve any European complication at all. It could not justify England's attacking Germany and securing the command of the sea. She could not send her fleet away without forfeiting her potential command of the sea to Germany, an invitation which might easily be accepted. She could not get any guarantee from Germany without giving substantial compensation. If such a state of affairs could arise, the theory of the Blue Water School is not applicable at all. That theory only applies to a simple situation, and not to the 'two ocean' dilemma which now confronts the Empire. […]

Another factor is the question of control. Assuming that a fleet could be detached from the Atlantic, would it come at any time when it was called for by a Dominion? If a Dominion were attacked, no matter on what provocation by her, the British fleet would no doubt be available to get her out of the scrape, but the action of armaments is not merely *ex post facto*. They are used in peace to give support to policy. A fleet in the Atlantic is of little weight in assisting the settlement of grave issues in the Pacific. This is especially the case where the interests of the Pacific Dominions are not directly shared by the British people. Such a divergence of interests between Great Britain and the Dominions should not be slurred over in the supposed interests of unity. It must be faced. It is useless to believe that statesmen or populace in England understand the point of view or realize the dangers of the Dominions. Under democratic conditions the only defence is self-defence. The dangers which face Australia are unique. They affect no nation in the world to anything like the same degree as they do Australia. It is not conceivable that British Ministers, as things stand to-day, could secure greatly increased sacrifices from the British electorate.

These facts show conclusively that some effort has to be made in the Pacific Ocean to-day by the people who border on that ocean to defend themselves, and that those peoples should determine the policy upon which their defence is to be conducted. […]

Notes

1 [William Marris,] 'India and the English', *RT* 1/1 (Nov 1910), pp. 41–57.
2 Kerr himself: 'Foreign Affairs: Anglo-German Rivalry', *RT* 1/1 (Nov 1910), pp. 7–40 (see following extract, pp. 21–24).
3 Treitschke is intended (Heinrich von Treitschke).
4 In 1882 the Viceroy, Lord Ripon, had introduced reforms which included the election of members of town councils and district boards, albeit on a restricted franchise, and alongside nominated members.
5 The Indian Councils Act of 1909, generally known as the 'Morley–Minto reforms' (after the Secretary of State for India, John Morley, and the Viceroy, Lord Minto), introduced elected members of provincial legislatures and the (all-India) Imperial Legislative Council, although again on a restricted franchise, and with the majority of members still nominated.
6 In 1911 G. K. Gokhale introduced an Elementary Education Bill in the Imperial Legislative Council, which was voted down by the official majority.

Part 2

The First World War and its aftermath (1914–21)

War aims

Throughout the period 1910–14 the Round Table *had warned of the danger of war with Germany. When war eventually came, the journal portrayed it as the outcome of a conflict between the principles of 'autocracy' and 'Commonwealth'. (The fact that Russia was on the side of the Allies was an inconvenient fact seldom referred to.) The espousal of the 'Commonwealth' ideal clearly had important implications for the future of the empire, especially in India and the dependencies. It also led those who wrote for the journal to align themselves with those calling for a reshaping of the international order, though only relatively late in the war with those calling for a new international organization to police that order.*

[Philip Kerr,] 'The Principle of Peace', *RT* 6/23 (June 1916), pp. 391–429

This war is a war for principle, and those who are in doubt about its justice or its necessity are chiefly those who are unable to discern the principle which underlies it, and in consequence naturally regard it as a dogfight between nations, the outcome of no higher impulses than envy or ambition, or 'because something angers them in each other's smell'. The principle which is at stake is […] whether Europe is to develop along the lines of the free commonwealth or under the lowering domination of an overweening militarist State. […]

A Commonwealth is a society of human beings living in one territory united by a common obedience to laws the purpose of which is the enlargement of liberty. It is not an abstract personality, like the Prussian State, claiming unquestioning obedience from its citizens. Nor is it a voluntary association of people temporarily united by bonds of interest or contract. It is a community the members of which are individually dedicated to promote one another's liberty and welfare, in obedience to the principles of justice and truth which they embody in their laws.

It is, indeed, a misnomer to speak of the commonwealth at all. It is nearer the truth to speak of the people or the nations of the commonwealth, for it is the people who are the commonwealth, and what unites them is not loyalty to a government, but loyalty to one another and to the principles which inspire their constitution and their laws. The constitution of the commonwealth is based upon love for and trust in the individual; for the excellence of the community is taken to consist in the prosperity, happiness and good conduct of its members, and in nothing else. Accordingly the qualities which it seeks to develop in the citizen are not docility or obedience, but character – that is self-reliance, self-respect, a high sense of duty towards others, grasp of and fidelity to principle and right. Its institutions do this in two ways: first, by ensuring that liberty and opportunity without which the individual cannot freely follow truth and justice, and do the best work for others; and, secondly, by throwing upon all those citizens who are sufficiently educated and sufficiently civilized to be able to subordinate their own interests and desires to the general welfare the responsibility for the laws by which they are governed. Liberty, indeed, is the life blood of the commonwealth, because only in freedom can a man serve his neighbour as he should. But liberty is inseparably yoked with responsibility. Hence democracy, in the sense that public policy and the law which governs social relations should be determined by the free votes of all qualified citizens, who thereby become solely responsible for the conditions under which they live, is an invariable characteristic of the true commonwealth. […]

In their external relations the people of a commonwealth are necessarily peaceful and humane. Because their institutions and their laws are primarily concerned with the welfare and the liberty of the individual, and with securing the best and fullest conditions of life for all, they set up no barrier between themselves and their fellow-men. While they have a prior and special obligation to their own members, and are primarily concerned with the development of their own institutions and civilisation, they recognise that, in essence, mankind is one community and that all the lesser communities into which it is at present subdivided, ought to co-operate in making the world a better place for all to live in. While, however, they have no desire to interfere with others, to impose upon them their own customs or ideas, or to rule over them, they cannot be totally indifferent to conditions outside. They cannot divest themselves altogether, in the spirit of Cain, of all responsibility for the welfare of the rest of mankind. Their external policy, therefore, tends to fall into two natural halves. First, to co-operate with other civilised peoples in defining the law which should govern the relations of States towards one another and prescribe their mutual rights and duties. Second, to uphold the treaties and declarations which secure the reign of law in the international sphere against those backward or selfish peoples who would upset them in their own interest. And this may mean the assumption, as trustees for civilisation, of the task of education and government among those races who have proved unable to resist for themselves the corrupting influences of civilisation, in order to restore those conditions of liberty and opportunity for the individual in which the people can learn to govern themselves. Thus the attitude of the people of a commonwealth to external affairs is a responsible solicitude that others should enjoy the same benefits of freedom and the rule of law as they themselves enjoy, and a resolute determination to protect and, if possible, improve the safeguards for liberty and justice which exist throughout the world. […]

As against these ideals, Prussia has set up another set of values. The root principle of Prussianism is worship of the 'State-idea'. The State is not the citizens. It is something above and beyond them. It is not even a paternal institution watching over the welfare of its people. It is rather the creator of the nation, for it is only in being organised into his proper niche in the vast mechanism of the State that the individual acquires his highest character and development. The State is thus an abstract personality possessed of 'divine right', whose authority it is impious to question. And the primary function of the citizen is to serve the State to which he belongs, and to obey its commands, with absolute and unquestioning obedience, whatever they may be. […]

In its external policy the Prussian State is necessarily militarist and ruthless. The State is an end in itself. It is utterly self-centred. It is above morality. Its interests are supreme, and to them not only must its own subjects sacrifice themselves, but its neighbours must be sacrificed also. This conception sets up a barrier between the members of one State and another. Their common humanity is hidden in the fact that they are seeking to promote the ends of institutions which, by their nature, are rivals. The world, therefore, instead of being conceived as a single family of human beings, all of the same blood and nature, but grouped into communities, united in friendly co-operation under the reign of law, is regarded as a number of States, whose interests are always competitive, and at times inevitably in violent conflict. […]

It is no use to expect too much at the end of this war. But there is the whole difference in the world between aiming at the creation of an international system based upon the principle of law – law which is recognised to limit the sovereign independence of all States – and acquiescing in a return to an international system which is based upon the balance of forces. The one leads on to an ever closer association between the great nations, and the ever increasing application of justice to human affairs. The other leads back inexorably to Armageddon. […]

The creation, therefore, of a treaty system guaranteed by all the chief civilised Powers, and establishing that 'international system which will secure the principle of equal rights for all civilised States' of which Mr. Asquith spoke a few weeks ago, is the second and the greater half of the settlement at which we must aim at the end of the war. It is an end in itself. It is also the best security against any new attempt by Germany, or any other Power, to upset the settlement or to attack the liberties of their neighbours. Prussian militarism in the full sense of the word can only be destroyed by the people themselves. It rests upon the worship of the State and of racial ascendancy, and the docility and failure of character, which makes the vast majority of Germans so 'organisable', so invariably compliant with the commands of authority whatever they may be. These characteristics cannot be changed by the sword. They must follow a change of mind and of heart, and the birth of moral courage in the people, which will hearten them to overthrow the absolutism of their rulers and take charge of the conduct of their own affairs. But the foundations on which they rest will be destroyed when all hope of achieving their purpose has disappeared. With the promises of Kultur and of the ruling caste wholly unfulfilled, with only some millions of killed and maimed, a mountainous debt, and the execration of the civilised world, to show for their attempt at world dominion, with no chance of repeating the attempt, because the peoples they have repressed and used are free, yet with their own national liberty not only untouched by the victors but guaranteed under international law, it is inevitable that the German people should have their eyes opened to the iniquity of the doctrines by which they have been betrayed, and begin to build up a democratic commonwealth for themselves. […]

America and global responsibility

The Round Table *had taken little notice of the United States before 1914, but from 1915 it regularly included contributions from there, and the promoters of the journal became early advocates for Atlanticism. Much emphasis was put on the need to prevent the US relapsing into isolationism. Curtis (who was meanwhile working behind the scenes to influence the League of Nations mandate system) gave this position an added spin, advocating American responsibility for the bulk of the territories taken from Germany and Turkey. The scheme of course came to naught, but throughout the interwar period the journal continued to emphasize the need for an Anglo-American alliance and for a US share in the 'burdens' of empire.*

[Lionel Curtis,] 'Windows of Freedom', *RT* 9/33 (December 1918), pp. 1–47

The future position of America in the world, not that of Germany, Austria, or Turkey, is the great issue which now hangs on the Peace Conference. […] From the moment of her independence the American Republic endeavoured to treat the American continents as a world apart, as though she were unconcerned in the rise or fall of states in Europe. The present war was needed to show that the Atlantic is now narrower than the Straits of Dover before the days of steam, and that while despots rear their heads in Europe, freedom has no sanctuaries. America, as well as England, now sees that the world is one. Their isolation, which was never splendid, is now impossible. […]

That the balance of power has outlived its time by a century, and that the world has remained a prey to wars, was due to the unnatural alienation of the British and American Commonwealths. So far the position has been that Britain stood somewhat aloof from the struggles of Europe, knowing in her heart that she must at need stand ready to intervene, in order to redress the balance of power when threatened. Her power, as well as her will to step in, were somewhat in question. Doubts upon either point encouraged Germany to believe that she might, by cajolery or force, avert British intervention in her schemes of conquest until it would be useless.

As to America, it was not even a question of doubts. If five years ago a responsible American had foretold the present position, his friends would have summoned a mental specialist. Not Theodore Roosevelt himself would have thought that to-day, with two millions of men in Europe, an American President would be taking the lead in dethroning Emperors, in erecting Republics, and redrawing the map of the world. The incredible has happened, and now it seems so obvious, that people are apt to assume that it could not have happened otherwise. America no longer stands, contrary to her old habit, clean outside the world-old struggle of freedom with despotism. The British and American Commonwealths are now together in that struggle, and will stand together by the law of their being, once for all. Their union with France, Italy and the smaller races of Europe struggling for liberty, deprives the balance of power of its meaning. […]

But what is the effect of this victory to be on Asia, Africa, and the scattered remnants of primitive society who inhabit a hundred Pacific isles? In the end the effect must be that they too will achieve the arts of governing themselves. But the question, how soon that end can be reached, depends upon a right understanding by the free nations who now control the world of the delicate and complex nature of the problem. Failure to grasp it will not only delay the achievement of the end, but may yet set the civilised world by the ears. […]

The crux of the problem lies in the fact that none of the territories outside Europe detached by this war from the German and Turkish Empires can in the near future provide peace, order, and good government for themselves. How to provide government for these territories is the most difficult of the questions which the Conference has to face. From a hundred lips and pens the answer will come that the solution lies in international control. The League of Nations will solve the problem. […]

The Inter-State Conference of the world, of which the Peace Conference will constitute the first meeting, will be a scaffolding, and invaluable as such. But it will not constitute a world government; if the burden of a world government is placed upon it, it will fall with a crash, and the whole world will be involved in the disaster. Before it can become the government which the world needs, and be really capable of discharging the functions of government, it must consist of representatives sent to it, not by the governments of nations, but by their peoples. And those representatives must be able to impose and collect taxes by Acts which need no ratification by the governments and legislatures of existing nations. If and when those conditions are realised, the League of Nations will have developed the structure of a world government. Until it has done so, it remains a scaffolding, indispensable so long as it is treated merely as a series of platforms from which its artificers can raise walls of stone, which have their foundations in the bed-rock from which the stories are hewn. But plastered with phrases, and made to look like stone, that scaffolding is the greatest danger which can threaten mankind. To bring the fable to its application, if ever a League of Nations, clothed with the appearance, but not with the attributes, of a government is used to administer vast territories which cannot as yet govern themselves, it will collapse. Those territories will be involved in its ruin, which will shatter the fabric of civilised society. […]

Let us recognise at once that the burden borne by the British Commonwealth is now overwhelming. It is answerable for the government of 373,000,000, or nearly one-third of the races who cannot as yet govern themselves. A fraction of this burden rests on South Africa, the merest atoms on Canada, Australia and New Zealand. The rest lies with crushing weight on the 45,000,000 of the British Isles. That it is not shared by the 100,000,000 who inhabit the United States is the tragic result of the schism of 1775. Had the British Commonwealth not been disrupted, the vast administrative resources of the most vigorous people in the world would have been used in the discharge of this, the greatest of all human functions. As it is, the brain-power and energy by which these vast multitudes are controlled has all to be drained from the British Isles, to the great detriment of its own internal efficiency. And these Islands have now lost at least a million of their most promising youth. It is not in her own interest, at any rate, for England to assume, as a result of this war, additional burdens which any other Power is equally capable of discharging. In its own interest, if not in the world's, the British Commonwealth should restrict its claims to territories, control of which is essential to the safety of others for which it is already responsible. […]

The time has come for America to consider this whole matter on grounds wider than those created by her citizens in founding Liberia. The lesson of facts is nowhere more clearly written than in the experiment which she has made there. In tropical Africa, as in the Pacific, the only hope of these races who cannot as yet govern themselves of ever learning to do so is in tutelage by some great democratic civilised nation. Once for all the League of Nations will render obsolete the old pernicious idea of empire, rightly abhorrent to American tradition. The duty of external government can now once for all be placed on its right footing of trusteeship to society at large, if at this juncture the greatest and wealthiest of all democratic nations will not shrink from assuming her share. Is it too much to ask that in this crisis of human destiny America shall forget to think of herself, and think rather of those infinitely wider interests, to vindicate which she has sent two million Americans to Europe, and in doing so has saved freedom for mankind? Having put her hand to the plough, can she look back? Can she now shrink from the dignity of her calling? […]

Disengagement in Egypt

Milner had begun his overseas career as an official in Lord Cromer's administration in Egypt, and had followed this with a popular book, England in Egypt

(1892), extolling the virtues of British rule. Nevertheless the revolt of 1919 convinced him that it was necessary to disengage from Egypt by acceding to the bulk of the nationalists' demands. His article for the Round Table *followed a visit to Egypt from December 1919 to March 1920 as head of a commission of enquiry but appeared at a time when the British government was reluctant to accept his conclusions. Eventually Britain issued a unilateral declaration of Egyptian independence in February 1922 (while holding back on four 'reserved points').*

[Lord Milner,] 'The Situation in Egypt', *RT* 10/39 (June 1920), pp. 520–35

[…] That Great Britain can keep her present hold on Egypt by force, is not open to question. The Nationalist leaders themselves are the first to admit it. She could do so, even if a majority of the people were disposed to rebellion, and as a matter of fact rebellion against the existing regime is as alien to the temper of the fellaheen as it would certainly be fatal to their interests. The outbreak of the spring of 1919 was due, in the main, to temporary causes incidental to the war, and even so it was confined to the riff-raff of the countryside, and found little support among the genuine peasantry. But, on the other hand, there is a violent spirit of revolt against British control among the leaders of native public opinion. The native Press, the native Courts, the officers of the native Army, the native officials in the public service are all, in greater or less degree, affected by it. Unless something can be done to stem the tide of disaffection, it will be increasingly difficult to find natives of standing to fill the high offices of State, and we may be forced to take the administration of the country entirely into British hands. That is a prospect so formidable, so complete a reversal of the policy we have hitherto pursued, that it is impossible to contemplate it without extreme aversion.

Is there no way of avoiding such a disaster? Or, to put the question in a more definite form, is there no way of reconciling the aims of British policy in Egypt with what is sane and reasonable in Egyptian Nationalism? Fundamentally this should not be impossible. It would not be in the interests of England, nor has it ever been her desire, to convert Egypt into a Crown Colony. The Egyptians who keep on fulminating against our supposed policy of 'Colonialism' are simply beating the air. Great Britain has certain vital interests in Egypt, and those interests are of a permanent kind. They are more important than ever to-day, having regard, in the political sphere, to our increased responsibilities in the Near East, and, in the economic sphere, to our growing dependence on Egyptian cotton. But these are not interests, the defence of which necessarily involves our taking charge of the whole government of Egypt. A peaceful and progressive Egypt in friendly alliance with Great Britain, and screened by that alliance from international interference, would completely serve our purpose. There is nothing in this incompatible with the ideal of Egyptian independence, reasonably interpreted. And, on the other hand, there are many Nationalists whose hostility would be completely disarmed, if they were convinced of the sincerity of our repeatedly expressed intention to help their country to stand on its own legs. Too much must not be made of their reluctance to come into the open to curb the extravagance of the present agitation. It is not easy for them to do so, as long as the controversy is confined to catchwords. What self-respecting Egyptian can be expected to say that, *in principle*, he is not in favour of the 'complete independence' of his country? But once let the discussion turn upon the practical steps which must be taken, if that independence is to be real and lasting, and many even among advanced Nationalists will be ready to admit, that Egypt is still far from fit to dispense with British assistance, and that in certain respects she must always stand in a closer relation to Great Britain than to any other foreign country. Despite the differences between us, and the bitterness which those differences have recently engendered, there is in the minds of thoughtful Nationalists a strong underlying sense of the comparative unselfishness of British policy; and, in so far as their country remains under foreign influence at all, they would prefer that influence to be British.

It must be admitted that we have done little of recent years to encourage these moderate elements of Egyptian Nationalism. It is not sufficient for them that we should go on repeating that the ultimate aim of our policy is to enable Egypt to govern herself, that we are only her guides and teachers, and that this tutelary relationship is essentially transient. The answer is obvious: 'You have been here for nearly forty years, and how much nearer are we to the goal to which you profess to be directing us?' To that we may reply that Egypt really is nearer the goal, that the progress she has made in forty years is not only material, but intellectual and moral, that the number of native Egyptians capable of taking part in the work of government, and indeed actually engaged in it, is constantly on the increase. It is really absurd to contend that the Egyptian people are not much freer to-day, not much nearer to anything that can be truly called independence, than they were in the time of Ismail. And we may reply further that it is quite untrue to say that we have ever taken all power into our own hands, or that Egyptian Officials, Egyptian Ministers and Egyptian Khedives have been mere puppets, and not partners with us in the work of government. The system of dualism which has in fact existed may have had many defects, but it has been not a sham but a reality. And in so far as our authority has at any time prevailed, it has always been exercised not for our own advantage but in the interests of the great mass of the Egyptian people.

But when all this has been urged, can we honestly go on to say that the progress of Egypt towards an independent national life has been as rapid, or that our efforts in that direction have been as consistent and as wholehearted, as they might have been? To build up an independent Egypt was, indeed, always the policy of Cromer, but in his later years the goal towards which he strove seemed in his own eyes to be receding further and further into the distance. And since Cromer's day British policy has swayed backwards and forwards, and measures have sometimes been adopted which it is difficult to reconcile with any policy at all. The time has certainly come to review the whole position, and to consider, if possible in concert with moderate native opinion, what practical steps can now be taken to accelerate the pace of Egypt's political progress. […]

The problem is not insoluble, if only it is approached in the right spirit. This is not a matter for bargaining. The settlement of it ought not to be a haggle, one party trying to grab as much as it can, the other to yield no more than it is obliged to. Rather should British and Egyptians alike regard themselves as associates in a difficult enterprise – the elaboration of the best practical system of government for Egypt. There is one test only – the good of Egypt – by which every point of difference regarding the distribution of political power should be tried. That Egyptians should want to be masters in their own house is most natural, and we have no desire to prevent them, provided that the house is kept in reasonable order. The genuine independence of Egypt, within the British ring fence, is an object at which we too should aim.

But if Egyptians are to believe that we are really sincere in these views, something more must be done on our side. The vague expression of good intentions is no longer enough. A definite scheme needs to be put forward, showing how far we are prepared to go at once, and under what conditions we may go further hereafter. For then moderate Nationalists will have something to work for. They will be able to come over to the side of Government without exposing themselves to the charge of want of patriotism, and may even succeed in persuading some of those who are now wasting their time in barren polemics, that it is only by co-operating with the British and not by seeking to thwart them that Egyptian Nationalism can ever hope to attain its legitimate ends.

Nationalism in Asia and the Middle East

T. E. Lawrence, better known as 'Lawrence of Arabia', was a close friend of many on the Round Table*'s editorial board, and it was Curtis who secured for him the fellowship at All Souls College which enabled him to complete* Seven Pillars of Wisdom. *In this article, Lawrence stated boldly his view that the peoples of Asia and of the Middle East in particular were 'catching up' with the West in terms of political evolution. Lawrence's views were one factor which helped persuade British policy-makers not to try to impose colonial-style regimes when awarded the League of Nations mandates for those territories.*

[T. E. Lawrence,] 'The Changing East', *RT* 10/40 (September 1920), pp. 756–72

A picture-writer once coined a phrase, 'The Unchanging East', and Time has turned round and taken revenge upon him. The East is today the place of change – of changes so great and swift that in comparison with it our Europe is standing still. We have been much engaged lately, making wars and peaces, looking at our own hurts, and trying to restore the balance of the times, and so we have not always been able to spare attention to what Asia is doing or thinking. We have tried to deal with her on the old traditional lines, and to our dismay she has not reacted properly. There have been outbreaks, unrest, protestations, and we, lacking the knowledge of movements there, have missed the sequence and find ourselves reduced to force, as our last remedy and restoration.

Yet there is urgent need for comprehension, of a careful study of our possessions in Asia, in order that we may regain touch with their opinion. We are all agreed as to the need of this stock-taking, though few of us will agree later on the lessons of it. We sent out a commission to India, which considered reform in India; we sent out a commission to Egypt, to consider reform in Egypt. We heard talk the other day in the House of Lords of a commission for Mesopotamia. Even Malta has had one. These all have been piecemeal affairs, conducted by statesmen in blinkers, forbidden to see anything except the political conditions of the province to which they were addressed. None of them gave us a general survey of the new Asia: none of them described the disease as well as the remedy. This disease is physical, material, moral, mental, all you will. It is the civilisation-disease, the inevitable effect of too close contact with the West. The aborigines of Australia got it when they met us, and they died of it. There were biological reasons why their frames were too weak to stand contact with a body social so different from their own. Asia is tougher, older, more numerous, and will not die of us – but indubitably we have made her very ill. Europe is not a thing easily digested.

We see the strain we have put on Asia soonest in the domain of matter. We evolved our own machinery in long centuries of struggle and invention, years in which the face of Europe gradually changed, without any too violent misery, to suit the new ideas: we had pack-horses, solid wheels, springless waggons, coaches, railways, motor cars, aeroplanes: we found the progress indecently fast at times, and put men with red flags to walk before the machines while we breathed – but what of Asia, which has stepped in a lifetime of thirty years from saddle-donkeys to Rolls-Royce cars, from blood-mares to aeroplanes? We grew by slow stages of muskets from bows to automatic guns: it took us five hundred years. The marauder of the desert laid away his spear just before the war, and to-day goes out on his raids with a Maxim. We invented the printing press four hundred years ago, and served a long apprenticeship by way of wooden types, screw and lever presses, steam presses, electric presses, to the cheap speed of the modern newspaper. The East has side by side the old-fashioned scribe, making each year a poorer living, and the linotype. The vernacular press came to them full-born. These are the material sides. Asia has in thirty years leaped across a stage which took us hundreds. She has not done it very well, perhaps, no better than parts of Russia, parts of the Balkans, parts of South America: the important part is that she has done it, and the Asia of Kinglake and Lamartine is wholly gone. Our eyes show us this, and some of us, the mediævalists, lament it. However, that is just a pose. The clock has never been put back: but the simplest thing in the world is to push its hands a little forward, and there are so many people pushing Asia that it is rather difficult to realise what the unassisted speed of its own ticking is. We will hardly learn this till they stop tinkering at it: yet it is important for us to learn it, since the earth is just a track along which countries and continents race with one another, and for all we know Asia may be gaining on us mentally.

This mental and moral growth is so hard to measure. The material changes prepare our heads to note great change in other ways, but their apprehension stays uncertain. There has been a change in ideas: we hear the people of Asia talking about representative government and parliaments. In our fathers' days they were governed by theocrats and autocrats. We think how long it took England to conceive and bring forth a House of Commons, and we begin to be astonished at this headlong Asia. There are labour troubles in Cairo and Bombay, a general strike in Mecca, trades union congresses in Constantinople. This disease they have caught quickly. Self-determination – yes, they have adopted that: League of Nations – they care more for it than we do. Things must be moving. Before the war we saw their politics changing, as the old springs of action became exhausted, and new motives came into play. In our fathers' days the East, and especially the Middle East, this side of Afghanistan, was logical, similar and simple. These countries, Persia, Turkey, Egypt and the rest, were old-established governments, of sultans and princes ruling by right, often by divine right, basing their regulations on the dictates of the state religion. The men were Moslems first, or Christians, or infidels of some sort. Later on, if there was any reason for it, they might be Turks or Arabs, but about this they were not too certain: the important thing was the faith. We cannot sneer at them. Only too recently, in the manuscript and crossbow days, we were like them. About 1870, though, we began to see stirrings of a new idea, the sense of nationality, which had been invented in Western Europe, and had moved slowly south and east, causing turmoil and wars in the separate countries as it passed. Nationality is a turbulent principle, and has cost probably as many lives as religion, in its much briefer reign. […]

This new condition, of a conscious and logical political nationalism, now the dominant factor of every indigenous movement in Western Asia, is too universal to be extinguished, too widespread to be temporary. We must prepare ourselves for its continuance, and for a continuance of the unrest produced by it in every contested district, until such time as it has succeeded and passed into a more advanced phase. It is so radical a change in the former complexion of Western Asia as to demand from us a revision of the principles of our policy in the Middle East, and an effort to adjust ourselves, that the advantage of its constructive elements may be on our side.

This new Imperialism is not just withdrawal and neglect on our part. It involves an active side of imposing responsibility on the local peoples. It is what they clamour for, but an unpopular gift when given. We have to demand from them provision for their own defence. This is the first stage towards self-respect in peoples. They must find their own troops to replace our armies of occupation which we are going to withdraw. For this they must be armed, and must learn by having arms not to misuse them. We can only teach them how by forcing them to try, while we stand by and give advice. This is not for us less honourable than administration: indeed, it is more exacting, for it is simple to give orders, but difficult to persuade another to take advice, and it is the more difficult which is most pleasant doing. We have to be prepared to see them doing things by methods quite unlike our own, and less well: but on principle it is better that they half-do it than that we do it perfectly for them. In pursuing such courses we will find our best helpers not in our former most obedient subjects, but among those now most active in agitating against us, for it will be the intellectual leaders of the people who will serve the purpose, and these are not the philosophers nor the rich, but the demagogues and the politicians. It seems a curious class to which to entrust the carefully begun edifices of our colonial governments – but in essence it will not be dissimilar to the members of our own House of Commons, whom we entrust with our own liberties. They will not wish to take charge, but we can force their hand by preparing to go. We do not risk losing them to another power – for the Englishman is liked by everyone who has not too much to do with him, and the British Empire is so much the largest concern in the world that it offers unrivalled inducements to small peoples to join it. Egypt, Persia and Mesopotamia, if assured of eventual dominion status, and present internal autonomy, would be delighted to affiliate with us, and would then cost us no more in men and money than Canada or Australia. The alternative is to hold on to them with ever-lessening force, till the anarchy is too expensive, and we let go.

The Anglo-Irish Treaty

Another striking example of the Round Table *facilitating the process of imperial retreat came in the form of Curtis's article for the journal on the situation in Ireland, written after he had travelled there incognito to assess the situation. He condemned British methods of violence and advocated offering full Dominion status to the South (while insisting on separate institutions for the North). His article was brought to Lloyd George's attention by Edward Grigg, and was a factor in the decisive shift in British policy which ensued. Curtis was subsequently secretary to the British delegation for the Anglo-Irish Treaty and then for two years Colonial Office adviser on Irish affairs, reassuring the Irish Free State government on the scope of Dominion self-government.*

[Lionel Curtis,] 'Ireland', *RT* 11/43 (June 1921), pp. 465–534

This is no agrarian disturbance of the old recognised type, but a highly organised rebellion. The fact has never been squarely faced, and the consequences are apparent in the methods adopted. Martial law was proclaimed in patches, and seems to be imposed on the Continental idea that it is of the nature of a punishment. In South Africa martial law existed merely to ensure the conduct of operations on lines which were both efficient and civilised. It meant that one man was solely responsible for all operations, with absolute authority to enforce discipline. Martial law, properly so called, simply means that the will of the Commander-in-Chief is law. He enjoins all authorities to carry on in accordance with ordinary law, except in so far as he may vary it for military reasons. Accordingly he adapts his system to local conditions. In peaceful areas he leaves things very much as they are under normal conditions. In disturbed areas the system is adjusted to local requirements. We do not hesitate to say that all operations should be placed under one commander-in-chief, and martial law extended to the whole of Ireland. The commander-in-chief should stand in the same relation to the Viceroy as Lord Roberts stood to Lord Milner. Both should be made to realise that we are not fighting a foreign force, but our own kith and kin, inhabiting a country which must always live in some kind of political communion with Great Britain. And whatever is done must be done by the Government itself in the light of day and with full responsibility. There must be no winking at unjustifiable excesses on the part of policemen because for the moment they seem to be serving a purpose, or because there is a risk of destroying the zeal of their servants. Whatever measures are taken should be ordered and directed by people who are not themselves under the influence of passion.

The methods adopted in the last year have restored the control of the Government to this extent, that the courts have been able to function and the police to leave their barracks and take the initiative. Eye-witnesses who attest to the undisciplined conduct of the Black and Tans often go on to say that things would be worse but for their activities. On the other hand, they have driven moderate and respectable elements of the population into tacit or open sympathy with rebellion. We are bound to say that the temptation to fight Sinn Fein with its own weapons has not been resisted. The destruction of life and property is a crime, except in so far as it is done by orders given from above in pursuit of a policy publicly avowed and approved by Parliament. Crime cannot be met by crime, or murder by murder. […]

Surely it is dangerous to burke the fact that if the Act[1] leads, as it is intended to lead, to the establishment of a parliament for all Ireland, that parliament will be nearly as well situated as those in the self-governing colonies to demand and obtain additional powers. We say nearly, because Great Britain, so long as the British Commonwealth exists, can always maintain its naval control unimpaired. But were a United Ireland once vested with a parliament of its own resolved to assume control of its own taxation and customs, it is difficult, in the light of history, to argue that Great Britain could or would continue to resist that demand. Our conclusion is that, if the present Act were to achieve its avowed purpose, Ireland would presently attain full control of her customs and all her sources of revenue. And in doing so she would also acquire the power to withhold any contribution to Imperial expenses. In this measure Great Britain was, in fact, committed more deeply than was realised or intended.

How comes it, then, that the South of Ireland continues to resist this measure? The answer to this question brings us to the root of the whole problem. Gifted and intelligent as the Irish unquestionably are, they lack the qualities which a people can only gain from the conscious control of their own affairs. This long-standing defect, for which Ireland is not mainly responsible, has been aggravated to a fever of unreason by the war and the violence which preceded and has followed the war. The whole question might easily have been met by a federal solution applied in time. Delay has produced a temper in Ireland which objects more fiercely to such a solution even than to remaining as she is. For that very reason the present Act is not supported by more than a few dozen voices in the South of Ireland. Want of experience in handling facts has left the Irish mind out of touch with actualities. No cure will now reach the root of this malady which does not give Ireland the strongest dose of responsibility which she herself is able to take. And this is exactly what she would get if the present Act succeeded in its purpose. There could only be one end to the controversy. If a Government of Conservative complexion refused the demand, a Liberal or Labour Government would grant it when the turn of the tide came. But, even so, the final steps would only be achieved after friction and controversy with Great Britain, more acute, perhaps, than attended similar struggles in the case of the Dominions. Such friction will greatly delay the creation of better relations between the two islands. If the fullest measure of autonomy is the only cure, and if under the present Act that full measure will result, it is surely wise to eliminate this period of friction, and grant forthwith everything which it lies within the power of any future Government, however extreme, to concede. This course would have an element of finality which the Act as it stands has not. […]

The danger lies in the fact that the leaders of this movement are asking for terms which if any British Government accepted on paper they could not deliver in fact. When one asks a spokesman of Sinn Fein whether the demand for Irish independence includes the whole Island, the answer is: 'Absolutely so.' Now, even assuming that four-fifths of the Irish people are anxious to renounce their status as British citizens, which they certainly are not, it is certain that at least one-fifth are immovably resolved to retain that status. Men whose whole lives are inspired by one idea find it difficult to realise the idealism latent in the minds of ordinary commonplace people. We have met Sinn Feiners who seemed genuinely startled to hear that if the establishment either of self-government in the Transvaal or of the Union of South Africa had meant that British citizens were to renounce their citizenship, civil war would have been the result. It surprised them to be told that had General Hertzog won the recent election and declared a republic, shopkeeping Britishers in that country would have sprung to arms. These men, who are ready, nay eager, to die for an idea, have little recognised the strength of an ideal opposed to their own, for which a substantial proportion of their own fellow-countrymen are also prepared to die. Nor do they realise that their demand, if conceded, would place them in the very position which they now execrate. In the first month of their existence the forces of a Republican Government in Dublin would, in Northern Ireland, be engaged on the same fell work that the forces of the Crown are now doing in Kerry and Cork. They would be copying the methods of the British Government in coping with tactics perfected by themselves. […]

The feelings which separate North and South have been terribly deepened by the character which the present struggle has assumed. Southern Ireland must be free to choose its rulers, and Ulster must have time to see how she uses that freedom before a new prospect of unity for Ireland can dawn. The apostles of a violence unrestrained by civilised conventions scarcely realise the obstacles they create to their own ends, to whichever party they belong.

To say that the hands of the Crown forces are as red as those of Sinn Fein is no answer. The Government is one thing, and the people of Ulster another. The Imperial Parliament is as powerless by its mandates to effect a genuine organic union between North and South, as it was to unite Upper and Lower Canada. It tried and failed. The plan which succeeded was the work of Canadians and based on agreement between the electorates of Ontario and Quebec.

More instructive still is the case of South Africa. So long as there were three parties to the dispute, Great Britain as well as the Dutch and British in South Africa, a settlement was hopeless. The only final solution lay in Union, but Union was impossible so long as the question was at issue, whether South Africans were to retain or lose their status as British citizens. The pact of Vereeniging settled that question, and within eight years the British and Dutch were united by a settlement made by themselves in their own country which the British Government were able to accept without the alteration of a single word. The secret lay in first eliminating questions at issue between South Africa and the British Commonwealth. The principle of this precedent has, we suggest, a real application to Ireland. If matters can be finally placed on a footing which leaves no further bargain to be struck between Great Britain and Ireland, and which still makes North and South feel that each can meet the other free from fear of compulsion from outside, the unity of Ireland, however distant, will at last be in sight. […]

Notes

1 The Government of Ireland act 1920, which provided for separate parliaments in Northern and Southern Ireland, with powers somewhat short of Dominion status.

Part 3

The interwar empire/ Commonwealth (1921–39)

The Commonwealth and the League

> *At the time of the League of Nations' inception, the* Round Table *had seen it primarily as a means to securing the active participation of the United States in international affairs; America's refusal to join the League was interpreted as largely destroying the organization's value. Yet the great mass of public opinion in Britain and the Dominions remained supportive of the League, viewed it as providing the mechanisms to solve most international problems, and saw it as to a large extent removing the need for imperial or 'Commonwealth' co-operation. Throughout the interwar period the* Round Table *therefore invested much effort in exposing the limitations of the League, and the dangers of allowing the empire to disintegrate.*
>
> [Philip Kerr,] 'The New Imperial Problem', *RT* 13/51 (June 1923), pp. 459–93

[…] If we take a broad survey of the world to-day, what are the fundamental facts, not the disputes and problems of the hour, with which we have to deal?

The first fact is that Europe has been Balkanised. Before the war Europe consisted of two great political combinations, the Triple Alliance and the Triple Entente, with a number of minor neutral states. To-day it consists of 25 almost unrelated states, each with an army, each with an exclusive tariff, each in financial tribulation, with the League of Nations trying to exercise a feeble unifying influence over Europe and the whole world. But not only is Europe Balkanised, but the war is not yet over. The passions it let loose in the breasts of the two primary combatants, France and Germany, have resulted in another war in a new form in the Ruhr, partly a dispute over reparations and security, partly an explosion of unsatisfied hatred and fear. No progress towards the real pacification and economic reconstruction of Europe can take place until exhaustion or wisdom has brought the combatants in this war to a more reasonable temper. […]

The second fact is that Russia has ceased to be part of Western civilisation, and has become a law unto itself. There is no doubt that the full communist experiment has failed. But the future of this great aggregation of 130,000,000 people is quite uncertain. As the unity and authority of the Communist party declines, as private enterprise extends its scope, especially as the great figures of the Revolution, like Lenin, disappear, Russia may enter upon a new period of anarchy, or it may fall a prey to a new military despotism. It hardly seems likely to join the ranks of the Western democracies for some time. Yet its future affects not only the question of peace, but of the economic restoration of the world, for Russia is one of the great markets for the manufactured goods of other countries, and one of the great exporters of the food and raw products also produced by the Dominions.

Thirdly, there is the United States. Is she coming back into the world? If so, it is the biggest fact of all. Her entry into the war was decisive. Her whole-hearted participation in the task of making the world not only safe for democracy, but ordered so that every nation shall be free to work out its own salvation for itself, would be not less decisive. It would at once bear down the scales, now trembling in doubt, against anarchy and reaction, and in favour of freedom, order and peace. For the moment the issue is uncertain. For a number of reasons, mostly domestic, the United States reacted into isolation after the war was won. She is clearly not going to undertake any such responsibility for the internal affairs of Europe as was imposed upon her under the Treaty of Versailles. Europe she now regards as a glorified Balkan peninsula, and she thinks it ought to settle its internal problems for itself. […]

The primary concern of the British Commonwealth in Europe is not only that it should return to political and economic sanity as soon as possible, but that in doing so it should not revert to that system of armaments, alliances and the balance of power which has always ended, in the past, and which must in the nature of things end in the future, in world wars. How is that to be done? Is the Treaty of Versailles, apart from reparations, with its basing of Europe on nationality, its disarmament of Germany, and the League of Nations, a good beginning? If so, what is needed to make it more effective? If not, what is the alternative? [. …]

This review is a loyal supporter of the League of Nations. Obviously the ideal which underlies it is sound and the great hope of the future. Unless the nations of the world are willing to meet regularly round a table, air their grievances and prejudices, and discuss publicly and in Parliamentary form the problems of the world, there can be no hope of lasting peace. A permanent return to the policy of national isolation and the religion of national selfishness must lead to competitive armaments and another world war. The League of Nations, or some modification of it, is absolutely essential to progress towards the abolition of war, security for national freedom, and the evolution of some more intelligent system of adjusting international disputes than armaments and trial by battle.

The Round Table further supports the existing system of representation within the League.[1] In gatherings the main purpose of which is the free discussion of world problems every national governmental entity should be represented, and the more voices that can be raised by the democratic and progressive peoples the better. It is clearly undesirable, as it is politically impossible, that in such a gathering as the Assembly of the League the British Commonwealth, with its peoples scattered all over the face of the globe, should have but a single voice. The more vigorous the activity of every part of the British Commonwealth in the League, after consultation with one another, the better.

On the other hand, it is neither common sense nor in accord with the facts to believe that the League of Nations is now, or can be, for many years to come, an effective alternative to the existing system of maintaining the security and freedom of nations. A considerable change both of heart and of mind among the peoples of the earth must come about before the nations can abandon defensive armaments or do without the machinery and methods of diplomacy. The only alternative to every nation being prepared to defend itself and its rights is the formulation and enforcement of laws governing all nations, and while the League of Nations is the means of gradually bringing this about, it is obviously a long way from having succeeded yet. Under the existing Covenant the League of Nations has no executive authority, no money, and no force, save what its members voluntarily give it from day to day. It is in its very nature an organisation for consultation, with a permanent machinery for dealing with relatively non-controversial matters. Its ability and power either to execute its own decisions or to defend its members depends entirely upon the willingness of the leading nations composing it to act on its behalf.

Therefore, for much time to come, the practical conduct of the world's affairs will run on very much the same grooves as during the nineteenth century, with the League of Nations exercising a progressively more potent influence on the attitude of all nations. Anybody who stops to consider the ambitions and policy of nations like Russia, or Japan, or Poland, or tries to estimate what Germany or Italy will stand for a few years hence, or speculates on whether the war-fever has passed from the Mohammedan countries, or on what may happen in China, or on the difficulties which the colour question will introduce into international relations as Asia and Africa stir into life, must realise that we have not yet passed out of the era of force in human affairs, and that it is still as impracticable to rely upon nothing but sweet reasonableness in international affairs as it is to abolish the machinery of law and order, with its policemen and prisons, inside the civilised state.

For these reasons *The Round Table*, while supporting the League of Nations to the full, remains an enthusiastic and unrepentant believer in the British Commonwealth of Nations. The time may come when the League of Nations may be able to induce world opinion to create an organic system which will end war by creating the machinery necessary to adjust international problems by constitutional and legal means. When that time comes we can cheerfully merge the British in a world Commonwealth. In the meanwhile the British Commonwealth not only gives freedom and security to its members, but … so far from impeding progress towards that ideal, helps enormously towards it. […]

What the world needs now is not more self-determination, more Balkanisation, but some measure of unity. The greatest cause of war to-day is that self-centred nationalism that refuses all association or comradeship or partnership with other nations. There is only one instance of peoples rising above this devastating and unchristian passion, and that is the British Commonwealth. Yet that unity is based, not upon coercion or authority, but upon the exercise of a free choice. If the nations of the British Commonwealth cannot resist the Balkanising tendency and maintain their unity, what hope is there of the League of Nations giving unity to nations divided by race, language and colour? For if the League is to be effective, it will not be merely because 70 suspicious and selfish nations agree to sit round a table, but because it develops a spirit of brotherhood and self-sacrifice among its members, a sense of living for something greater than themselves, which will lift them to the level of subordinating their separate ambitions to the common good, and of shouldering their share of the responsibility of maintaining world peace. Where does that spirit exist to-day, except among the nations of the Commonwealth which sprang to arms directly the Prussian challenge was thrown down, and brought men by the hundred thousand from the ends of the earth in defence of human freedom?

From every point of view, therefore, whether from that of freedom and self-defence, or of exerting influence for peace and sanity in the conduct of the world's affairs, or of helping forward the League of Nations in its drive for world unity and world peace, it seems to *The Round Table* that the unity of the Commonwealth ought to be preserved. […]

Atlanticism

Philip Kerr's editorials in the Round Table *made it one of the most consistent (indeed persistent) advocates of Atlanticism in interwar Britain. In this article he surveyed the problems in the Anglo-American relationship (especially over inter-allied debts) and acknowledged the depth of American isolationism (including the unlikelihood that America would join the League, at least for a number of years), but claimed to detect signs of a new and pro-British internationalism in such matters as the recent Washington treaties on naval armaments.*

[Philip Kerr,] 'Anglo-American Relations', *RT* 17/65 (December 1926), pp. 1–17

Ever since the Treaty of Paris in 1783 it has been an axiom of British statesmanship to keep on friendly relations with the United States of America. The motives for this policy have varied from time to time. In the earlier days the reasons were partly sentimental and partly the fact that, in the event of war, Canada would be extremely vulnerable. Later there was added the reason that the United States had herself become an international Power of the most formidable kind. The policy of friendship was put to a severe strain during the Napoleonic era, when it broke down for a time in 1812, and again during the American Civil War. It has by no means always been a popular policy in

Great Britain, for often the so-called ruling classes have had but little sympathy with either the international manners or the domestic methods of the eldest daughter of their own civilisation and stock. None the less, with a singular persistence, uncommon in the foreign policy of any nation, Great Britain has remained faithful to the tradition that war with the United States must be ruled out of the category of contemplated possibilities, and that her own policy must be regulated accordingly.

Never was the policy of friendship pursued more faithfully than by Sir Edward Grey during the difficult blockade controversies which preceded the entry of the United States into the great war, and by Mr. Lloyd George during the Peace Conference at Paris and the negotiations which later led to the Washington Conference and to the treaties concluded there for the limitation of naval armaments and for the regulation of the Pacific. The case for such a policy had been immensely strengthened by all that had happened in those eventful years. On the one hand, a war between Great Britain and the United States would not only put the British Commonwealth to such internal and external strain that its existence might be seriously impaired, but it would probably draw half the nations of the world into the struggle and destroy Western civilisation itself. On the other hand, co-operation between the English-speaking nations of the world in supporting the League of Nations or some similar organisation for the settlement of international disputes by sensible means would bring a political experience and an amount of financial and naval power to the support of world law and world peace which would probably ensure that mankind would never again have to suffer from so protracted a disaster as the world war of 1914–18. […]

The simple truth is that it is very difficult for Great Britain and the United States to understand one another. Great Britain has long been well educated in international politics. One of her main characteristics is a high sense of public duty both in domestic and international affairs. Her instinctive judgment that the peace and political progress of the world depend upon an intelligent co-operation by the English-speaking nations with the rest of the world in a league of all nations is indestructibly sound. The United States, on the other hand, has for 150 years been educated in exactly the contrary idea, that it is her duty to keep the rest of the world at a distance – under the Monroe doctrine – so that she can work out her own contribution to the political and social life of the world free from interference. The whole notion that she has a duty to co-operate actively with the hardened sinners of Europe in securing world peace still seems to her traditionalists to be contrary to the Monroe doctrine, and it will clearly take time for a nation of 120,000,000 people to realise the new responsibilities which power and modern invention have thrust upon them – they are really the logical outcome of the Monroe doctrine – and to make up their minds how they are to discharge them.

These differences make understanding difficult. For instance, to the American, who is dedicated to the idea that it is the primary duty of man to govern himself and support himself economically, and who knows nothing about the conditions of Asia or Africa, Great Britain appears to be incurably imperialistic, as proved by the vast amount of territory and peoples she has brought under her control all over the world. To the Briton, who is dedicated to the idea that the performance of public duties must come before the attainment of personal success, America appears incurably selfish as a nation and wedded to the sordid pursuit of the almighty dollar. Yet to the first charge the Briton replies that he does not seek empire for the sake of bossing his neighbours, but because the substitution of political order for chaos is the first and necessary step towards liberty and self-government, as well as towards better trade. And to the second charge the American replies that he is far more interested in developing an economic system which will abolish the slums and poverty which still disfigure Britain, and will create order out of economic chaos, than in accumulating dollars for himself. The truth is that there are mixed motives on both sides, that Great Britain is mainly busy about politics while America is mainly concerned with economics, and that the solution both of the political and the economic problem is essential to the peace and prosperity of mankind.

None the less it is becoming more and more obvious every day that it is only a question of time for the United States to play her full part in the international world. That she is slow in making up her mind to act may be annoying to the rest of the world. But it is not reasonable to expect a nation of 120,000,000 people, utterly inexperienced in international affairs and with a century and a half of tradition in favour of isolation, to plunge into almost unlimited international responsibilities at President Wilson's command. No doubt, too, when she does emerge once more from her isolation, as she emerged in 1917, her policy will differ in emphasis and detail from Great Britain's, just as President Wilson's definition of war aims differed from Mr. Asquith's. But there is not an atom of evidence to show that in fundamental moral or political purpose the policies of the two peoples will not run just as much on parallel and sympathetic lines as they did during the great war and the Peace Conference. Great Britain will, for instance, always be actively interested in Europe. The United States, on the other hand, like the Dominions, will probably insist that her active co-operation must be confined to problems which are real world problems and that Europe must manage her own internal problems for herself. Again, the American approach to international problems will be mainly economic, while the British approach is mainly political.

But these are matters of detail. The fundamental thing is that the hope of world peace depends upon the English-speaking nations co-operating actively with the other nations in establishing order, justice and reason where international chaos now largely reigns, and that public opinion in the United States is steadily moving in that direction. […]

The Balfour Report and Commonwealth co-operation

In 1925 the Dominions reacted angrily when the UK government merely informed them of its intentions regarding the Locarno treaties (whereby Britain guaranteed the borders between Germany, Belgium and France); this seemed to undermine the process of Commonwealth co-operation to which the UK government had committed itself. Partly in response to this crisis, the 1926 Imperial Conference saw the issuing of the Balfour Report, explicitly avowing the equality of status of the Dominions. The independence of the former Dominions is most frequently dated to the Statute of Westminster 1931, which embodied in legal form the Balfour Report. In this commissioned article, Whyte rejoined the problems of constitutional status and Commonwealth co-operation.

[Sir Frederick Whyte,] 'The Imperial Conference', *RT* 17/66 (March 1927), pp. 225–41

The ninth Imperial Conference has come and gone. It was heralded in the Press of two hemispheres in every tone of hope, scepticism and apprehension; and its accomplished work has since been described in widely divergent estimates. The apprehension arose from a too ready acceptance of certain demands at their face value and from the consequent doubt whether any formula – even the most innocuous – could possibly secure the assent, let us say, of General Hertzog and Mr. Coates. The subsequent divergence of estimate was mainly a question of attitude. Those who consider only realities have accepted the estimate of *The Times*, that the Imperial Conference 'has provided an agreed and authoritative picture of the Empire as it is'. And, on the other hand, those who, with a relish for 'imponderables', find greater significance in a 'state of mind', will not quarrel with the description of Lord Balfour's Report as the Magna Charta of Commonwealth Liberties. *The Round Table*, true to its function and its name, accepts both the objective and the subjective estimates as indispensable facets of one and the same truth.

'L'Angleterre', says M. Henry de Jouvenel, 'a reconquis ses Dominions en les émancipant', or, to put it in the more controversial words of another commentator, 'till there is full freedom to separate there can be no spontaneous will to remain united'. These imperfect epigrams state a psychological truth which has a great political significance. They are not equally true of all parts of the Commonwealth, for each part has its own 'state of mind'; but they are true, in different measure, for all, because they reveal the immanent principle – now authoritatively proclaimed – on which the whole Commonwealth rests. Equality of status has been sought and found in Dominion autonomy; and the strength of our unique constitutional structure lies in the fact that it combines the benefits of union with those of independence. The Imperial Conference of 1926 has dissolved the Downing Street 'complex', and the Commonwealth is now, in very truth, a Round Table.

Now, in acknowledging gratefully that Lord Balfour and his colleagues have done good Imperial service, let us take stock of the new position, if indeed it be new. To be sure, none of the principles are new: the novelty lies in the explicit recognition of the conclusions to which they logically lead. What, then, are the essential features of this 'authoritative picture of the Empire as it is'?

The British Empire is unique; it defies classification: and it bears no resemblance to any known political organisation. Its principal figures – Great Britain and the Dominions – 'are autonomous Communities within the British Empire, equal in status, in no way subordinate one to another in any aspect of their domestic or external affairs, though united by a common allegiance to the Crown, and freely associated as members of the British Commonwealth of Nations'. Equality of status is thus the root principle, 'but the principles of equality and similarity, appropriate to status, do not universally extend to function. Here we require something more than immutable dogmas'. In other words, we must recognise facts. And the recognition of facts, in one vital region, at all events, follows at a later stage in the Report, where the Conference unanimously recognises 'that in this sphere [i.e. foreign affairs generally],[2] as in the sphere of defence, the *major share* of responsibility rests, and must for some time continue to rest, with His Majesty's Government in Great Britain'.

These two passages, read together with the paragraph on 'Negotiation', and with the references to the Policy of Locarno, are as important as anything in the whole record of the Conference. These passages make no reference to any general and mutual obligation which might follow action under the negotiation clause, but they appear to warrant the conclusion that, though the *active* share in war rests in the unfettered discretion of each Government, the inevitable status of belligerency at times when Great Britain or any other part of the Empire is at war was, by inference at least, assumed in the Conference. Let us note that the initiative leading to war is entrusted to each and every self-governing partner in the Commonwealth as an essential function of equality of status in domestic and external affairs. It follows that, in the discharge of this virtually sovereign function, each partner in proposing to act in its own interest, ought so to act as to conserve the interests of the whole. This obligation underlies the whole accepted procedure for the negotiation of foreign treaties.

Here is unity in belligerency, accepted so to speak *in embryo*. But, since war is only the pursuit of policy by special means, the pursuit of policy *ab initio* must imply a general unity of purpose capable of definition for particular major issues. We believe that there is a real though undefined unity of purpose, and that the forces animating it are so powerful that no Dominion Government can ignore them. It is true that recent history still leaves a good deal of evidence of disunity too prominently in the foreground, but time will correct this perspective by revealing to all concerned the true character of our Imperial relations. And it is because the Imperial Conference has described these relations in a lucid and authoritative statement that its achievement, both practically and psychologically, stands high.

Now, our unity of purpose can be stated in terms which easily command universal assent so long as they express the general philosophy of the Commonwealth. It is the descent from the general to the particular that is our difficulty. Let us consider the matter once more in the light of its most recent test. Diplomatic unity, which is only unity of purpose canalised towards an immediate aim, implies consultation and agreement as the preparation for action. The theory of our diplomatic unity held good for a while after the war, but suffered a serious reverse at Locarno. The preparation for Locarno actually entailed nothing but the supply of information to the Dominions of what Great Britain proposed to do. There was no effective consultation and no agreement. From that General Smuts drew the conclusion that, if the Locarno method became a precedent, 'more and more the foreign policy of the British Government would become simply that of Great Britain.' […]

The Commonwealth must be something more than a picture of the British nations enjoying free institutions: it must show a positive purpose.

There can be no more positive aim in the modern world than the establishment of peace on new international foundations. It has often been said that peace is the greatest of British interests, and never was that truism truer than it is to-day. Only in the last resort of war can any real peril now assail the British Empire; and, therefore, both as an insurance for our interests, and as an expression of the inner spirit of our own family relations, the League of Nations is an instrument peculiarly appropriate to our peaceful purpose. Without it, the world would be condemned to a precarious reliance on safeguards which provide no safety.

The League is a world-wide organisation, and the absence of Russia and the United States only serves to throw into bolder relief its well-nigh all-embracing character. None the less, it is not a vessel of unlimited capacity; and to use it as a vat in which to blend all the discordant elements of the world, is to court disappointment. If it has great possibilities, it has also its limitations; and those who recognise both aspects of its character do it no disservice. The British Commonwealth is committed, irrevocably and sincerely, to its underlying principle; but in contemplating the magnitude and the multiplicity of the problems which are gradually being placed within its jurisdiction, we cannot fail to see that it will soon be beyond the power of any Member-State to bear a responsibility, proportionate to its power, in all the obligations which may arise. Every State will have its own geographical sense of proportion; and if Great Britain loses hers by becoming a predominantly European State, she may lose her overseas perspective and strain her relations with the Dominions. She cannot help being a great World-State and must play a part in the League commensurate with her responsibilities and with her history. But the nature of her responsibilities and the lesson of her history alike warn her that no regional obligation should be permitted to overshadow her general mission. Her influence in Europe will be the more decisive if she confines her commitments to issues of first-rate importance which, by their very nature, are something more than a purely European concern.

A policy based on these principles should secure the willing assent of the Dominions. If properly executed it will express the spirit of Locarno, but not the method; but before it can be executed it must be conceived as the offspring of the Commonwealth as a whole, and not merely the child of Great Britain. To-day it is no more than a project, unembodied and without form; and it can only find its true embodiment through the process of organised consultation upon which the British Commonwealth ought to embark forthwith.

Dominion status for India

While far from endorsing the Indian National Congress demand for full and immediate self-government for India, Lord Lothian (the recently ennobled Philip Kerr) and the Round Table played an important role in the early 1930s, by advocating an advanced form of self-government for India, and arguing against those diehards such as Winston Churchill who pressed for the retention of the status quo. Lothian served as Under-Secretary of State for India and chairman of the Indian Franchise Committee, which helped pave the way for the Government of India Act 1935. Subsequently The Times *(under the editorship of Geoffrey Dawson) and the* Round Table *argued strongly for the reforms, which combined provincial self-government with the promise of an all-India federation (and which indeed led Congress to participate in elections and in provincial administration for a few years before the Second World War).*

[Lord Lothian,] 'India: Constitution or Chaos', *RT* 21/82 (March 1931), pp. 239–73

The Indian Round Table Conference has opened a new epoch in the history both of India herself and of the relations between India and Great Britain. […] For the first time a delegation of some eighty Indians, representing all races and religions and classes in India (though not the Congress party) sat round a table with a delegation representing all parties and both Houses of the British Parliament to discuss, on a basis of complete equality and with nothing excluded from the purview of the Conference, what the future of Indian government should be. For the first time Indian Princes and their Diwans sat round a table with the representatives of all classes in British India, also on terms of complete equality, and agreed together that the basis of the new constitution should be the inclusion of all-India within a single federal constitution under which responsibility both for central and local government should rest, subject to certain limitations, in Indian hands. For the first time the representatives of Great Britain declared that the time has come for the primary responsibility for Indian government to pass from British to Indian shoulders, provided that a constitution can be drawn up and accepted which would do justice to the minorities in India and which could reasonably be expected to give stable government to a united India, and, subject to certain safeguards and reserved powers for which Great Britain will remain responsible, in the interests no less of India than of Great Britain, during the period of transition. […]

There is little doubt that the completeness with which the Round Table Conference and afterwards the mass of British public opinion accepted the principle that Indians should in future, subject to safeguards, be responsible for their own government both in the centre and the provinces came with a shock of surprise and dismay to those who have been familiar with the India of the past, in which the whole effective responsibility for Indian government has rested in British hands. It seemed so reckless and gigantic a move forward in a continent containing as many people as Europe without Russia, and divided within itself as Europe is divided. It seemed all the more dangerous in face of the recommendation of the Simon Commission that strong government should be maintained at the centre while full responsibility was being introduced in the provinces, and even of the more 'advanced' proposal of the Government of India that in the next period there should be a kind of irresponsible executive 'dualism' at the centre.

But there is no doubt that, except in certain relatively narrow circles, the discussions of the Conference convinced, not only the British members, but public opinion outside, that the time had come when, in India, as in Canada, South Africa, Ireland and elsewhere, a definite and irrevocable breach must be made with the old type of empire, that India must follow in the footsteps of the other Dominions and be free to work out her future by constitutional means in her own way. People came to this conclusion, not only because it was right in itself and the only course consistent with the new British Commonwealth, but because it was the only way of avoiding, both for India and Great Britain, the disasters of the American revolutionary era. Some have believed that the transition to responsibility could come gradually, piecemeal and almost imperceptibly. There is no evidence in history to justify this belief. The transfer of governmental power from one set of hands to another is a tremendous event, and it takes place, not imperceptibly, but either by war and violent revolution or by definite constitutional action. The most important decision of the Round Table Conference was that the time for a constitutional revolution had arrived. […]

The old India has gone, or is rapidly going, and with it the old British raj is inevitably going also. Indian life and society are seething with the same forces, the same hopes and aspirations, the same discontents as Europe and Asia and America since the war. The old form of government through a bureaucracy, efficient but detached from the new life stirring among the people, is as inadequate for modern India as it has proved to be for Great Britain, Europe and America. The Civil Service – already in course of rapid Indianisation – can be preserved, but the ultimate decision in determining the policy to which it is to give effect must now rest with a body amenable, in constitutional ways, to Indian opinion. Not only is such a step right in itself and the logical result of the Pronouncement of 1917, and of British institutions themselves, it is the only way of avoiding in India government by repression, which, when it is continued by an alien Power against the consent of the governed, never has lasted and never can last in the modern world.

The alternatives which lie before India to-day are chaos or constitutionalism. Despite Mr. Winston Churchill and his friends, the third policy, of trying to maintain the old British raj through the resolute determination of a British Government to govern India, whatever the cost, is an alternative no longer. The consent of all classes in India – Princes no less than British Indians – to such a solution has clearly been withdrawn, and British public opinion, in the light of the history of the rest of the Empire since the beginning of the century, and of the ideals for which it fought during the war, would simply refuse to be a party to the continued repression and bloodshed by which the old British raj could alone now be maintained. The Round Table Conference was certainly right in thinking that the one hope for the future was to place the responsibility for Indian government, subject to safeguards and reserves in the transition period, as far as was practicable, on Indian shoulders under a sane and well-balanced constitution.

It is perfectly true that, without faith and co-operation on both sides, the attempt to create a self-governing constitutional India may fail. The task is the most gigantic to which two peoples have ever consciously set their hands. There are forces of violence, of communalism or parochialism, of race, of suspicion and ignorance and distrust, both in India and in England, which will certainly work, not to build, but to disintegrate and destroy. The overthrow of the democratic regime in Russia by the Bolsheviks and the destruction of parliamentarianism in China by militarists and party discord, may still be repeated in India. It is said that the responsible politicians will be swept aside by the extremists and that minorities like the Moslems and the Sikhs, States like Afghanistan or Nepal, communist and terrorising groups, will sweep the inefficient executives and legislatures aside. It is certainly possible that the attempt to create a workmanlike federal constitution may break down and that India may break up, first into a Moslem and a Hindu India, and later into a number of national States, as Europe did after the Renaissance and the Reformation. None the less, to proceed along the line of constitutional self-government is the only possible or hopeful way forward to-day. Moreover, the forces which are making for success are far more powerful than is always realised. For a century India has been accustomed to constitutional and legal procedure: the habit of order is strong, as are the Civil Service and the Police; the doctrine of non-violence makes a widespread appeal; and behind all, during the period of transition, stand the army and authority of Great Britain, which, even if she is now ready to transfer responsibility for government to Indian hands, is certainly not yet ready to see the hopes of peaceful constitutional self-government destroyed by an organised military violence which she is still perfectly able to control. […]

The problem of India to-day is not dissimilar in fundamentals from that of Europe in the last few centuries. India is moving towards democracy, and as the unifying power of the British raj disappears, the racial, linguistic, religious and other differences which have lain dormant begin to show themselves in the struggle for political power. The revival of communalism in India since the 1920 reforms is an example of this process. These same communal forces in Europe gradually destroyed the unity once given to it by Rome, the Holy Roman Empire and the Roman Catholic Church, and eventually broke it up into twenty-six national States, each so intensely and nationally self-conscious that losing all sense of their common European nationalism they armed themselves in fear and hatred of their neighbours, and from time to time plunged into fratricidal war. The problem in India is to find the right balance between communalism and nationalism, so that minorities may feel security and have an opportunity of reasonable self-expression, and yet remain loyal, co-operating members of one Indian nation embracing them all. To press either minority rights or national uniformity too far would be to smash the structure of Indian constitutional unity before it has had time to come into being. […]

We shall not attempt to anticipate the criticisms of the proposals of the Round Table Conference which will come from India. The primary difficulty in India will probably be to secure the abandonment of the campaign for immediate independence by non-violent civil disobedience – a method which seems to promise the millennium if only its adherents are heroic and self-sacrificing enough – and the co-operation of all elements in the far more difficult, laborious and less exciting task of agreeing upon a constitution which will actually enable Indians to become responsible for their own government. Yet, that is the real test of Swaraj. Whatever the precise status of India, the primary necessity is to draw up a practical federal constitution and to obtain the assent of the main elements of Indian opinion to it. Can India, like Ireland, develop the statesmanship which will recognise this: can she agree to accept a constitution and work it successfully? On the answer by Indians themselves to that question will depend whether India is to be a self-governing constitutional unit or not. […]

In a difficult and dangerous situation, the road of responsibility, with safeguards, is the only road which may lead India past the Scylla of chaos and dismemberment on the one side, and the Charybdis of military and party despotism on the other side to constitutional self-government. And it is the only road by which it is now possible to win over India to contentment as a Dominion – an equal partner within the charmed circle of the British Commonwealth of Nations.

Trade and tariffs

Despite the urgings of Leo Amery and others, the Round Table *had always maintained a sceptical attitude towards 'tariff reform' or 'imperial preference', as advocated by Joe Chamberlain and his followers. The depression of the 1930s inclined many imperialists to seek refuge in empire protectionism – a policy given concrete form in the Ottawa agreements of 1932. The* Round Table *was never convinced by the arguments for protectionism, and urged (unsuccessfully) that the empire should continue to work towards global free trade. The journal's promoters were particularly worried by any idea of including India and the dependencies in protectionist schemes.*

[H. V. Hodson,] 'Imperial Preference', *RT* 22/86 (March 1932), pp. 246–65

[…] We have thought too long of a system of imperial preference as implying fresh restrictions upon trade, and thus fresh dangers to our economic welfare. The Ottawa Conference will fail if it does not approach the problem from precisely the opposite standpoint. The purpose of an imperial economic system is to cause trade to flow not less but more freely. We want to exchange more of our products for more of the products of our fellow members of the Commonwealth. No member has, in the long run, any interest in cramping the trade of the world, and negatively we do not wish an imperial preferential system to diminish world trade just as, positively, we wish it to enlarge empire trade. An imperial economic policy, therefore, which was only a super-nationalism in the field of trade and tariffs, imposed upon the unrestricted nationalism of the parts, would be a disaster to the Empire and to the world; it would strangle the trade by which everyone of us must live, and, what is more, would contain the germs of its own defeat. An Empire still divided by high tariff walls, and ringed about by an almost unscaleable barrier against the rest of the world, would be an Empire doomed to decay if not to disruption; yet it is the inevitable conclusion of economic policies urged upon us by some who most emphatically profess and call themselves imperialists.

We shall therefore not make much progress at Ottawa if we have not at the back of our minds the conception of trade as a mutually advantageous interchange of goods and services. Within the limits set by considerations of defence, social policy or monetary difficulties, the more trade the better for everybody. Tariffs, in this light, far from being in themselves a national asset, are an unfortunate necessity imposed by the action of others or by fundamental national policy. If a tariff is valuable in itself, a reduction of the tariff on British imports is as harmful as a reduction of the tariff on imports from foreign countries, and the 'sacrifice' must only be made for an equivalent return, which itself takes the name and appearance of a sacrifice by the other party to the reluctant bargain. Let there be no more talk of 'mutual sacrifices' or 'concessions' to be made at Ottawa. The basis of the new imperial economic system must be mutual advantage or it will be an unsubstantial, jerry-built makeshift doomed to early collapse. Buying and selling are reciprocal functions and the wealth that goes into a country by purchase should be regarded with no greater suspicion than the wealth that goes out by sale. If the world has not yet learnt that lesson then we had better shrug our shoulders and wait until the complete breakdown of international exchange drives us to a system of barter which would teach us the lesson painfully in words of one syllable. […]

The general attitude of Great Britain is perfectly clear. We are a great trading nation, absolutely dependent for livelihood on the maintenance of world trade. Roughly 60 per cent of our exports go to foreign countries. Nearly one half of our vast overseas investments have been made outside the British Empire. It may be that if we had placed more of our capital in the Empire, and particularly if we had invested more in commercial enterprise there and less in foreign government loans, our export trade would have been less precarious and less dependent on the policies and prejudices of foreign countries. Certainly we would be glad if the percentages were more favourable to the imperial link, and perhaps the Ottawa Conference may help to bring about such a change, but in the meantime our existing position cannot be left out of account. Nearly £200 millions of our normal annual receipts, as a country, come from invisible items, other than long-term interest, directly or indirectly dependent on the commercial prosperity of the world at large, an amount which we cannot afford to see further diminished. Our position as manufacturers and bankers for the world, on which our livelihood depends, has been based on cheap food, cheap raw materials and the stimulus of free competition. […]

In hazarding the established benefits of our former policy, we are motivated partly by the need to defend ourselves against the effect of tariffs elsewhere on our own balance of trade, partly by the desire to arrange a common economic policy with the rest of the British Commonwealth. If we, for that purpose, are prepared to forsake free trade it is more than reasonable to expect the Dominions at the same time to modify their policy of high protection. Of imperial preference Great Britain must demand that it should expand rather than diminish the aggregate of international trade, that it should enlarge her exports and not merely injure her competitors in one market so as to intensify their aggression in others. That is not an impossible demand. It is false economics to contrast our imperial and our foreign trade and to assume that a rise in the one must necessarily be accompanied by a fall in the other. […]

But if our aggregate of trade is to be enlarged our imperial policy must be flexible enough to allow us to take advantage of any special opportunities that may arise outside the Empire. It would be foolish to shut out the rest of the world for ever from advantages which the members of the Commonwealth accord to each other, and to make those advantages wholly dependent on such exclusion. Since the British market is as important to the foreigner as the foreign market is to Great Britain, we should fear tariff retaliation not so much for its direct injury as for the harm it would do to world trade as a whole, but the repercussions upon our own position would be serious enough. Moreover, our imperial ties would be no more than fetters if, while suffering all the disadvantages of protection, we were to be prevented from reaping its benefits in securing special concessions from foreign countries on the strength of the bargaining power that it would afford. […] The point is not by any means of purely British interest. South Africa has already, for what seemed to her good and sufficient reasons, concluded a commercial treaty with Germany by which that country receives all the subsequent preferential advantages extended to Great Britain, and there is no saying when opportunities may not arise for making other special arrangements, say between Canada and the United States, or Australia and Japan. […]

At all costs the Ottawa Conference must bring about a net lowering of tariff barriers, so that each of the participating countries may receive a balance of advantage through the profitable expansion of trade. We believe that the best way of achieving that purpose is for Great Britain to be prepared, if necessary, to enter into separate gentleman's agreements with groups or individual Dominions, as a preliminary to a general accord which might mature only after years of experience, and in any case fitted mentally into a scheme of what intra-imperial trade really ought to be in relation to world trade as a whole. Such a plan would avoid some of the pitfalls that lie in the path of imperial preference when it turns towards the other parts of the Empire. India, for instance, as her representatives have frequently pointed out, is not in a position either politically or economically to grant any substantial increase of imperial preference; were she then to share fully in the advantages which the Dominions had secured in exchange for enlargements of their own preferences to British products they might legitimately complain. Should the colonies participate in those advantages or not? Only those most ignorant of the structure of the Commonwealth could imagine that a simple Act of the Imperial Parliament can establish in the colonial empire a system of reciprocal preferences, or 'Empire Free Trade', or for that matter any other alteration of fiscal policies. Ceylon, the West Indian Islands, the African territories and other colonies have in these affairs a large measure of self-government with which we would attempt to interfere only at grave peril to the amity that exists between them and ourselves. In West Africa by the Treaty of St. Germain-en-Laye, in the mandated territories by the terms on which we hold the mandates, we are bound not to establish preferences against foreigners. And over the whole of the non-self-governing Empire trade policy must be guided by the consideration that any attempt to build barriers against the rest of the world and make the colonies just such a private preserve as they were in the eighteenth century would arouse the dangerous resentment not merely of the colonies themselves but of the whole of the foreign world. […]

Any system of imperial trade regulation, including preference, which is to be of lasting value […] must take into account the fundamental economic policies of the participants, including the balance between their industry and agriculture, and their commercial relations with the rest of the world. Once those essentials have been determined, it should imply a progress towards a lowering of tariffs and the breakdown of economic nationalism generally; it must expand rather than diminish the volume of world trade. While for the time being it may injure third parties it must not be directed against them, and must leave them an opportunity of participating in preferential advantages in exchange for equivalent undertakings. It must not be of such complication or duration as to tie the hands of any party unduly in its trading relations either within or outside the Commonwealth. Above all, it must be based on the principle of mutual advantage and free consent. […]

Trusteeship and 'economic imperialism'

Much of the Round Table*'s portrayal of empire rested on the assertion that Britain was fulfilling a duty of 'trusteeship' towards peoples as yet unfit for self-government. The journal was therefore highly sensitive to charges that Britain was using its position to exploit the colonies economically. Several developments in the early 1930s seemed to give added credence to this latter interpretation, and the* Round Table *was particularly worried by the move towards* *incorporating the colonies within a protectionist trading system, publishing several articles warning of the consequences of such a policy.*

[Reginald Coupland,] 'The Future of Colonial Trusteeship', *RT* 24/96 (September 1934), pp. 732–45

[…] It is sometimes asserted that the theory of trusteeship is a masterpiece of hypocrisy, a cloak to cover the naked selfishness of 'economic imperialism'. It is true, of course, that our occupation of tropical territories was never altruistic. We wanted new supplies of raw materials and new markets for our manufactures; and occupation was the only way to prevent these raw materials and markets from coming under the control of rival foreign Powers. But higher motives were honestly linked with the economic and political. The British humanitarian tradition is an historical fact. We did give a lead to the world a century ago in abolishing the slave trade and slavery; and more than once since then the extension of British rule has largely, and sometimes mainly, been determined by a genuine desire to protect the peoples concerned from those and kindred evils. Not that we have ever admitted that the economic development of the tropics is necessarily injurious to the welfare of the natives, that (to quote the famous jibe) 'philanthropy and five per cent' are incompatible. Wilberforce urged that the expansion of 'legitimate' trade was one of the surest methods of killing the slave trade. Livingstone linked commerce with Christianity as a means of fulfilling our duty to 'civilise' Africa. And it is becoming more and more obvious in these days that the execution of a 'trust' for the welfare of the natives, involving as it does the provision of costly public services for their physical and social advancement, depends for its efficiency on an adequate local revenue, which in turn depends on economic development. […]

But in the economic field there have been changes since the war. The revolution in our economic system at home was bound to affect our economic ideas about the Empire as a whole. Just as in the nineteenth century, after the downfall of protection, we attempted to impose free trade on our 'white' colonies – and were only prevented by the powers of self-government they had already attained – so now the natural tendency is to bring our 'black' and 'brown' colonies within the new system of imperial preference. […]

Already at the close of the war the 'open door' was no longer quite open. Differential duties were temporarily laid on the export of palm-kernels from West Africa in order to foster the manufacture of vegetable oil in this country at Germany's expense. Small preferences were also arranged between Great Britain and the West Indies and one or two other colonies. But it was not till the Ottawa Conference that the preferential principle was extended to cover almost every part of the Empire in which it was not ruled out, as it is for instance in the Congo basin, by the treaty rights of foreign Powers. The Colonial Secretary himself went to Ottawa to represent the colonies, and, speaking in the House of Commons on July 12 last, he claimed that the agreements he had secured there had not only benefited British and

Dominion exporters to the colonies, but had also helped the native producers to fight the economic depression by widening and safeguarding their markets in Great Britain and the Dominions. […]

There has been relatively little discussion of this aspect of the Ottawa policy; public opinion seems scarcely to have realised that, whatever its merits, it was a radical departure from pre-war principles, and that it differentiates the economic status of those colonies to which it has been applied from that of a mandated territory. We can no longer claim to be trustees for the commerce of the world. It should not be forgotten, moreover, that, while the Ottawa agreements between Great Britain and the Dominions were concluded between democratic governments representing their peoples, those affecting the colonies were concluded by the Secretary of State on their behalf, and that, although he doubtless consulted their governments, he was in a position in most cases to put his decisions into effect, whatever local opinion might be. […]

These points require still greater emphasis with regard to the recent imposition of anti-Japanese duties and quotas. […] On the face of it those measures are intended to serve no other purpose than the protection of British exports from Japanese competition: they are a move in the world-wide conflict between this country and Japan. It can be argued, of course, that the interests of the colonies – political, strategic, financial, commercial – are so closely linked with our own that any sacrifices they may make are made in a common cause. But has it been adequately recognised that it is a sacrifice for the poorer natives of the tropics to be deprived of the chance of buying cheap Japanese goods? The Nairobi correspondent of *The Times* reported that East African opinion did not regret that the imposition of the duties in East Africa was barred by the Congo treaties.

> It is felt (he wrote) that the limited native purchasing power has been used, money circulated, and trade kept alive by Japanese goods at a critical time, which would have been less probably the case with more expensive British articles. An example of such indirect benefit comes from Tanganyika, where medical officers declare that the purchase of cheap Japanese rubber shoes has done more to prevent hookworm disease than all the efforts of the health department.[3] […]

A third example of new tendencies may be taken from a different field. The air service provided by Imperial Airways between London and South Africa by way of the Sudan, Uganda, Kenya, Tanganyika and the Rhodesias is aided by a subsidy which amounts this year to £246,000. Of this total Great Britain provides £100,000, South Africa £94,000, and Southern Rhodesia £10,000. The residue of £42,000 is made up by Kenya (£15,000), Uganda and Tanganyika (£10,000 each), Sudan (£5,000) and Northern Rhodesia (£2,000). Those five territories are not, like the first three, self-governing. They are all under 'trust'. One of them is 'mandated'. Their total revenues have averaged in recent years about £10 to £12 million. No doubt they share in benefits that the service confers on all the territories it traverses. No doubt, too, there are political and strategic questions to be taken into account. But the disproportion between a payment by Tanganyika, for example, of over one two-hundredth of its revenue and a payment by Great Britain of less than one seven-thousandth is marked. Sir Edward Grigg went so far as to say in the debate on the Air estimates on March 19 that 'the proportion in which the subsidy is divided is an exploitation of the African taxpayer for the benefit of the taxpayer here'. […]

The point to be repeated and emphasised about these three examples of our recent policy in the colonial field is that the policy is new. It assumes a different relationship between Great Britain and the colonies than that of the pre-war trusteeship, or at least a different conception of trusteeship. The old theory, as defined at the outset of this article, was that the interest of the ward was the Government's over-riding concern. Private commercial enterprise was certainly encouraged, but, broadly speaking, in the belief that it did not injure and should not be permitted to injure the peoples under 'trust'. We were content with the incidental indirect advantages that accrued to us from British rule. We did not ask the peoples ruled to pay for more than the local cost thereof, and when they could not meet even that, we made good the deficiency ourselves. The new policy is on other lines. It can hardly be said, perhaps, to be based as yet on any very definite theory. Things seem to have been done to meet particular needs, or to fit in with other policies, without considering their logical implications. But at least the outline of a new colonial doctrine seems to be taking shape, a doctrine that tends to regard colonial territories less as a class in themselves, and more as an integral part of the Empire, and to identify their interests more closely with those of the Empire as a whole. It suggests that their new path of progress lies in imperial co-operation. […] The conception of the relationship between ourselves and the colonies, in fact, would seem to be no longer that of trusteeship, but rather that of partnership.

In principle, no one can quarrel with that. Partnership in the colonies, as in India, is the natural outcome of trusteeship. It has been said, indeed, that the separate consideration given to the colonies at Ottawa implied a rise in their status, and that the discussion of the new preferences in their legislatures was a step in the direction of fiscal autonomy. There would be more force in that if the majority of most colonial legislatures were not bound to vote in the last resort as the Colonial Secretary in London wished, and if the only important colony that possesses a real measure of fiscal autonomy, Ceylon, had not disagreed with the British Government's proposals. There is danger, indeed, in regarding peoples as partners who in fact are still only wards. It may lead to imposing on wards what partners would refuse. George III's Ministers believed themselves justified in asking the American colonies to contribute to imperial defence. The attempt to impose free trade on Canada in the eighteen-fifties was inspired by a quite genuine belief that it was good for her.

To be a just judge in one's own cause demands a superhuman virtue, and, if indeed such a doctrine as that outlined above is to be adopted, let us take care to define it clearly and truthfully. To talk of 'co-operation' unless we are sure it is voluntary goes far to justify what is said abroad of our national hypocrisy. […]

Monarchy and the Commonwealth

The Statute of Westminster 1931 left the monarchy as the sole constitutional tie between Britain and the self-governing Dominions. Writing after the abdication of Edward VIII and the coronation of George VI, a leading constitutional expert, Kenneth Bailey, explored the nature of 'multiple kingship' in this new era, emphasizing the 'Commonwealth' rather than purely 'British' aspects of the Crown. The article went on to suggest various means for improving the 'Commonwealth' dimension of the monarchy, including more frequent royal visits, royal staff to be recruited from the Dominions as well as Britain, and the appointment of a Governor-General for the United Kingdom, to act in much the same way as those in the Dominions. The idea of a peripatetic monarchy would continue to interest the Round Table *until the 1960s.*

[Kenneth H. Bailey,] 'The King and His Peoples',
RT 27/107 (June 1937), pp. 467–84

The coronation is over. Not only in the Abbey, but throughout the Empire, enthusiastic crowds hailed their 'undoubted King'. The historic formula of the Recognition has never rung more true at a King's coronation. King George VI ascended his throne, in unparalleled circumstances, by the heart-rending but deliberate choice of the whole British Commonwealth of Nations. There has been no uprush of republicanism. The modern kingly tradition has, if anything, grown more precious to us because it had seemed, for a little, to be in peril. The memory of that sharp December week of testing did not mar the 'willingness and joy' of the people's acclamation. Nevertheless, because of that memory many minds have brought to the coronation ceremonies, not only emotional fervour, but also appraising reflection. We have thought of kingship as well as of the King. We have not quite taken it all for granted; we have asked ourselves in concrete and unaccustomed ways what the King should be and should do under the conditions of to-day. […]

When, in her coronation oath, Queen Victoria promised to govern according to law and custom 'this Kingdom of England and the dominions thereto belonging', the formula which had been prescribed for William and Mary still reflected perfectly the character of her empire. Paralysed by the wars and by economic crises, the governing classes of Great Britain had invented no new technique of colonial administration since the collapse of the First Empire. In the first year of the young Queen's reign the old colonial system had, in Canada, again brought a free European population to the point of revolt. Ominously enough, the Patriotic Association in New South Wales threatened to follow its example.

The first great wave of nineteenth-century English liberalism luckily reached the Colonial Office just in time. Presented in 1839, the Durham Report adumbrated a new doctrine of responsible government for the colonies, a doctrine upon which the Third Empire was founded, and which proved flexible enough to make possible a rapid and unparalleled imperial expansion. Colonies became Dominions, and the Dominions took their place among the nations. Autonomy swiftly replaced central control, the co-operation of equals replaced the exercise of authority by Great Britain – a development aptly symbolised by the use of the new term 'British Commonwealth of Nations', instead of the traditional 'British Empire'. Though the United Kingdom retained its primacy of wealth, power, and prestige, that primacy was now a matter of 'stature', not 'status', in relation at least to Canada, Australia, New Zealand, South Africa, and the Irish Free State. After ten years of imperial constitution-making, it was not surprising that for King George VI the ancient coronation oath was revised. What His Majesty was required to swear was to govern the peoples of Great Britain, Ireland, Canada, Australia, New Zealand, and the Union of South Africa, of your possessions and the other territories to any of them belonging or pertaining, and of your Empire of India, according to their respective laws and customs.

In these words is unobtrusively epitomised a great chapter in imperial constitutional history. As other links of empire have been removed, attention has more and more been concentrated upon the Crown, as the point of unity in diversity, the symbol of that free association which is the essence of the Commonwealth. In the new coronation oath, Dominion status is expressed in personal terms. 'British possessions' have become 'the King's peoples'. Nor indeed is the evolution by any means complete. The new special reference to India is no doubt suggestive of that far-seeing attempt, now in full progress, to make over the quondam empire of the Moguls in the image of British parliamentary democracy. There may be other candidates for Dominion status as time goes on – other communities emerging from the older category of 'British possessions' into the happy circle of 'the King's peoples'.

The political evolution of the King's peoples has produced accompanying and remarkable changes in the King's own legal relation to them.

The Statute of Westminster brought the Act of Settlement within the ambit of Dominion legislative powers, and the Imperial and Dominion legislation concerning the succession last December was so drafted as to make it clear that in the Free State at any rate, and perhaps in the Union too, the statutory title of King George VI rests solely upon Dominion law. This fact puts an end to the controversies about what is (rather misleadingly) spoken of as 'the divisibility of the Crown'. Indeed, as the legislation worked out, it chanced that for a day or two Edward VIII was King in some parts of the Empire and George VI in others, and allegiance was temporarily due to two different Sovereigns. But this was only a temporary episode, with no permanent political significance. The common allegiance to the Crown, in which historically the unity of the Empire is expressed, would obviously be at an end if the succession of the centuries through one Sovereign were broken. In order to avoid chaos and the disruption of the Commonwealth, it was agreed in 1931, and the agreement was recorded in the preamble of the Statute of Westminster, that alterations of the succession should not be made otherwise than by agreement among all the members of the Commonwealth. At the abdication of King Edward VIII, this convention was faithfully observed. The episode did make clear beyond doubt the multiple capacity in which the King now acts. But it also expressed and emphasised the will to unity of the whole Commonwealth. […]

The King personifies a wider loyalty, within which political disputes may lose some of their bitterness, and even the extreme partisan displays something of forbearance and the spirit of accommodation. This aspect of kingship has been eloquently stated by the present Governor-General of Canada.

> The King is of no class, being above classes; he is as much akin to the worker in the mine and to the labourer in the field as to the highest nobility. He can have no party bias, for his only bias is towards the whole people. He cannot initiate policies, though he creates the atmosphere that makes policies feasible. … Pinnacled above all, he is yet closer to the national consciousness than even the most famous Minister. His duty is not to act but to be, to represent the ultimate sanctities of the land which endure behind passing fevers and bewilderments. … [The monarchy] is the mystical indivisible centre of national union. It is the point around which coheres the nation's sense of a continuing personality … the symbol of their past achievement and their future hope.[4]

So long as the King fulfils these functions it would be hard indeed for party-worship and führer-worship to take firm root. 'The importance of the integrity of the British monarchy', said Mr. Baldwin […] 'is, beyond all question, greater than it has ever been, being, as it is, not only the last link of empire that is left, but the guarantee in this country, as long as it exists in that integrity, against many evils that have affected and afflicted other countries'. In more direct language, the kingship is one of the most potent influences to-day for the preservation of political democracy in each of the countries of the Commonwealth. […]

This representative character of the King's office is the key also to his function in relation to the peoples of the Commonwealth as a whole. Here, too, as within each of his communities separately, he represents, personifies, symbolises, in his own person makes visible, real and comprehensible, the whole as against the parts. Though between the nations of the Commonwealth almost all the questions are at issue that vex international life generally, nevertheless in their loyalty to the one King these nations are united. The King is king of each of his peoples: but he is also king of them all. By his very existence, he makes it easier for his subjects everywhere to see their own nation against the august background of a wider international community, to which also their loyalty is due. In a world disintegrated by the claims of nationality, this kingship – older than even the Parliament at Westminster – is the last surviving, but the still continuing, organ of a unity that transcends nationality and is deeper than any alliance. […]

The Commonwealth and the dictatorships

During the mid-1930s the editorial board of the Round Table *was deeply split over the policy of appeasement, and editorial writers therefore had to tread a careful line between opposing views on the issue. Nevertheless even the anti-appeasers agreed that appeasement reflected the predominant view in the Dominions, and was therefore perhaps a necessary policy in light of Britain's commitment to Commonwealth co-operation. This cautiousness extended even after the Munich agreement, which in retrospect can clearly be seen as both the apogee of appeasement and the starkest evidence of its bankruptcy.*

[H. V. Hodson,] 'The British Commonwealth after Munich', *RT* 29/114 (March 1939), pp. 238–51

The effect of the crisis of September 1938 on the relations between the different members of the British Commonwealth in foreign policy and defence was much the same as its effect upon their several national defence preparations. It provided a test under conditions that came close to the reality of war. It was a dress rehearsal with all the tenseness of an actual first night. And in each case the general result was the same: to prove strength in some directions and to find flaws in others, and to impel the people of the Commonwealth to repair the weak points before the strain should next have to be taken.

The chief element of strength that was revealed in British Commonwealth relations was the remarkable solidarity displayed among the several member States through the different phases of the crisis. At no moment could a potential enemy have been led honestly to believe in an imminent split in the Commonwealth. There were divisions of opinion in the Dominions, of course, just as there were in the United Kingdom itself. But among their leaders no important voice was raised against the British Government's initial policy of warning the world that France's involvement in central Europe would almost inevitably imply our own […] There was equal official acquiescence in the policy, manifested in the despatch of the Runciman mission, Mr. Chamberlain's journey to Berchtesgaden, and the recommendation of the Anglo-French plan to Czechoslovakia – the policy of seeking a peaceful solution by all possible means, as the alternative to war over an issue of tangled merits, in which none of the Dominions felt its own immediate interests to be involved. […]

The policy of appeasement, which Mr. Chamberlain represents and which he brought to what seemed to be its most triumphant moment at Munich, was the only possible policy on which the public opinion of the different nations of the Commonwealth could have been unified. It had already been unanimously approved in general terms at the Imperial Conference of 1937, and this particular test found it still to be a British Commonwealth policy in the full sense. To risk a more distant possibility of war, for the sake of a present chance that peace may be preserved, is to show a sense of values which is nowhere appreciated better than in the Dominions, anxious as they are to advance swiftly and peacefully towards their destinies as homes of freedom and material well-being.

This solidarity of the Commonwealth in general outlook, however, cloaked certain defects in the working of its internal relations. If the United Kingdom's policy towards Europe can be accused of being vague and dilatory before the crisis, how much more vague and dilatory were the policies of the Dominions. In effect, they had no policy at all towards central and eastern Europe. […]

It may be argued that the Dominions needed no detailed foreign policy of their own towards Europe, being situated so far from that area and being too small seriously to affect its destinies. That may indeed be the conclusion to which the events of last September will lead some minds. It would imply that the Dominions must accept their European foreign policy from others, and confine themselves to problems and areas nearer home. But that is not compatible with the theory of their own status in the world that is held by the Dominions. They insist – and, as free nations, rightly insist – on deciding their own foreign policy and determining their own fate in so far as they physically can. It is impossible for them to have no foreign policy whatever towards Europe, where resides the greatest peril to the peace of the whole world. Either they accept their policy from someone else, or they have a positive policy of their own, or their policy is the negative one of isolationism. Now isolationism is possible only for two classes of countries: for those that are so strong as to be unassailable, and for those that are safe behind the shelter of some powerful State whose clients they are. It is doubtful whether any country in the world comes into the first category; certainly the Dominions could come nowhere but in the second. The role of client State is one that they hotly repudiate. But, if they are not to assume it willy-nilly, they must take up more zealously their responsibilities in foreign policy. A merely negative policy being impossible, their positive policy must be either borrowed or their own. […]

No doubt the realisation that a world war lost by Great Britain would be a world war lost by themselves was at the back of the minds of the Dominion Governments and people when they girded up their loins in the last weeks of September. They were also stirred, it is obvious, by emotional reactions. Whatever their local national interests may be, most of the citizens of the Dominions feel in varying degrees an emotional attachment to Great Britain, some through loyalty to the throne, some through the call of blood, some through belief in the ideals and institutions for which Great Britain stands. But it is as well to remember that roughly half the people of Canada, and the majority of the people of South Africa, have no ties of ancestry with Great Britain, and that even among those of British stock this factor is likely to diminish in force as the generations pass.

Even more important than positive emotional attachment to Great Britain, which must vary so greatly in intensity, is a negative repulsion from those who were on this occasion her potential enemies. No substantial group of people in any part of the British Commonwealth looks upon the philosophy and behaviour of the National Socialist state with anything but disgust. There has not been the same intensity of feeling towards the Italian fascist regime, partly because of its relative moderation in brutality, partly because of the bond between the Roman Catholics of the Empire and any country of the same faith, partly no doubt because Italy is so much less powerful than Germany. But the belief that in the final crisis of September last, which so nearly brought us to war, the forces of evil were ranged against the forces of good was firmly embedded in the minds of the great majority of citizens of the British Commonwealth throughout the world. […]

The first thing that is needed for the strengthening of British Commonwealth relations in the future is the working out of a common scale of values in foreign policy. To elaborate a common scale of values is to establish common principles of foreign policy, indeed to establish a common foreign policy in the only sense in which that is possible within an association of completely self-governing States. In the years after the late war, the solvent common principle was found in support for the League of Nations and collective security. From 1931 onwards, however, this principle, in so far as it remained real at all, conflicted too sharply with the hatred of war to be of effect in practice, except during the period between the imposition of sanctions against Italy and the promulgation of the Hoare-Laval plan.[5] No substitute was found to take its place. The result was that, when the crisis came over Czechoslovakia, only in the white heat of an imminent threat of world war was a sufficient principle restored. […]

The nations of the Commonwealth face a common danger. The danger may perhaps force itself on them through an issue like that of colonies in which the greater number of them, as separate nations, are directly and vitally interested. More probably the test will come over some issue akin to that of Czechoslovakia. The common danger, in any case, is neither more nor less than the overthrow of that system of oceanic power which preserved world peace for a hundred years, which won the victory in the war of 1914–18, which enabled the League of Nations to be established and could alone have made it a successful preserver of peace, that system which above all has assured to the Dominions and India their peaceful and progressive existence while the continents of Europe and Asia and of South and Central America have been racked by wars. […]

Notes

1 I.e. the separate representation of the Dominions and India.
2 Whyte's interpellation.

3 *The Times*, 11 May 1934.
4 John Buchan, *The King's Grace* (1935), pp. 12–13. John Buchan (Baron Tweedsmuir) was a friend of the 'Kindergarten' members, and Governor-General of Canada from 1935 to 1940.
5 I.e. between October and December 1935.

Part 4

The Second World War and its aftermath (1939–49)

War aims

Even after the outbreak of the Second World War the Round Table *was reluctant to condemn those who had sought to appease Hitler – reflecting the fact that several members of its editorial board had been prominent in advocating such a policy. Just as during the First World War, the journal elaborated a set of war aims for the British Commonwealth, re-emphasizing the clash of opposing principles, but this time insisting that only a generous peace could remove the cancer of militarism from Germany.*

[Reginald Coupland,] 'War and Peace', *RT* 30/117 (December 1939), pp. 5–26

The British Commonwealth is again at war, again with Germany, and again in defence of freedom. To most of us, and especially to those who are old enough to remember the last war, this mere fact of repetition must seem the most shocking feature of the whole catastrophe. Only twenty years ago we emerged victorious from a test of strength and endurance far greater than any previous war had imposed on those who fought it. We had lost the flower of our generation. We had dissipated a large part of the wealth accumulated in long years of peace by the skill and labour of our peoples. Our society had suffered injuries, moral as well as economic, which it would take a long time to repair. But for all that there was one deep source of consolation. Most of us believed that the triumph of freedom was final, that the world had indeed been made 'safe for democracy', that the 'war to end war' had ended war. There were few of us, it is safe to say, who did not think, when the bells rang out for the armistice, that there could never be another big-scale war. And, if that were so, our sacrifices had at any rate not been useless. We had bought at a terrible price the chance of making a better and more prosperous world. And then the chance was frittered away. In less than a generation the same ordeal has to be endured again; and, though, of course, the main fault lies with the enemies of freedom, its champions must bear their share of blame. Future historians of this age will marvel at the manner in which the victors of 1918, equipped as they then were with irresistible power on land and sea and in the air, allowed the course of international affairs so to develop as to make it possible within so short a time for their defeated and disarmed antagonist, not merely to challenge the peace settlement they had imposed, but to force them into another desperate fight for their existence. It may be left to those historians to unravel the complex of idealism and selfishness, of good intentions and bad judgment, of illusion and inertia, which accounts for our and our allies' share of responsibility for this catastrophe. This is not the time to define and apportion the blame. All that matters now about our conduct in the last twenty years is the first and simplest lesson to be learned from its result. We start this war knowing that it will not be enough to win it. The fruits of victory must be secured. That lesson does not need teaching twice. […]

The discussion of the peace settlement, it is true, must be provisional. We cannot forecast the situation in which it will be made, and we must not forget, as we are sometimes tempted to do, that it is not only we who will make it. It will be the work of our allies also in the first place; in its final form it ought to be the work of the whole civilised world. Let us keep those provisos in mind in considering the main conditions of the settlement we mean to make as far as it lies with us to make it.

The first is clear. The Nazi régime must be overthrown. *Il faut en finir.* The second is equally clear. This war […] is one of a series of German wars; it is the second German war with Britain, the third with France. There must not be another if we can help it. Germany must be made incapable of challenging the rule of law and liberty again, for as far ahead as we can see. This, it need hardly be said, is far the more difficult of those two conditions to establish or at least to maintain for any length of time. Herr Hitler and his colleagues can be removed by force if it is strong enough, just as Wilhelm II was removed by force. But force could not root out Prussianism from the German mind, and it cannot root out Nazism which, as has been observed, is only Prussianism in more brutal shape. That can only be done by the Germans themselves, and, however we may try to help them do it, they will not find it easy. The tenacity of the Prussian tradition from the days of Frederick the Great is sometimes overlooked. It is not only the making of five wars in eighty years: it is the ready ear accorded for more time than that to a long series of militaristic writers and teachers from the patriots of the early nineteenth century on through Treitschke to the author of *Mein Kampf.* Is there something in the German make-up that cannot be brought into harmony with the spirit of the Western world? Or is it only the accidents of German history that are to blame? Are the Germans so difficult to live with only because, to use the current phrase, they are politically immature? If so, the outlook is more encouraging. There is a liberal tradition, too, in Germany, though it has always been weaker than its foe. Twice liberal governments have been established, for the separate states some ninety years ago, for the whole of the *Reich* the other day; and, though they did not live long, it is something that they lived at all. Those liberal forces, moreover, have been driven into a far more open breach with Nazism than they were with Prussianism. There were no patriotic German *émigrés* in 1914. With such conflicting facts before him no thoughtful man will dare to prophesy what sort of ideas will dominate the German mind when the war is over or ten or twenty years later. But on this question as on others uncertainty is no excuse for doing nothing. Plainly we must do what we can to make it possible for Germans, especially young Germans, to conceive their national destiny in terms of international co-operation rather than of conflict. 'It is no part of our policy', said Mr. Chamberlain on October 12, 'to exclude from her rightful place in Europe a Germany which will live in amity and confidence with other nations'.

That leads us to the third condition of a settlement, namely, that the peace must be a just peace. It must do justice not only to the Germans' victims, to the Czechs and the Poles, but to the Germans themselves. That means a peace which, if circumstances permit, can be negotiated with a liberal German Government; a peace which a fair-minded German admits in his heart to be fair, so fair that it cannot be successfully caricatured as a 'second Versailles'. Secondly – and this is even more important – it must be a peace which at least the great majority of the neutral peoples can approve. For it will need more for its maintenance than the strength and resolution of those peoples who are now fighting for freedom. It will be essentially related to the wider settlement which alone can make freedom safe; and no such settlement is conceivable without the co-operation of all the freedom-loving peoples of the world. […]

It is with the determination, then, as far as in us lies, to win the 'after-war' to-morrow that we brace ourselves to win the war to-day. We do not know how long it will last or how much suffering it will inflict, but that we shall endure to the end there can be no question. Never before has a war been fought on so great an issue. It is for much more than our peace, our safety, our prosperity, that we are fighting: it is difficult indeed to realise how much more. Mankind is at a crisis of its destiny. It has long been recognised that the material power given to men by modern science was in danger of outstripping their moral power to use it right. That danger has materialised in Germany with terrible results. In the last resort we are fighting to save the human civilization, which we have been so long and slowly trying to build up, from suffering the same inhuman fate.

Colonial development

The late 1930s and especially the early years of the Second World War saw an upsurge of interest in the economic development of the colonies, fed in part by Lord Hailey's influential African Survey *of 1938, and finding expression in a series of colonial development acts, beginning in 1940. Writing for the* Round Table *two years later, Hailey set this new direction for colonial policy in the context of the external and internal threats to the empire. While he denied that a new emphasis on economic development was designed to place yet another obstacle in the way of political development, it is nevertheless clear that he did not expect the colonies to reach self-government as quickly as they in fact did.*

[Lord Hailey,] 'Future of the Colonies', *RT* 33/129 (December 1942), pp. 8–16

[…] In normal times the public attitude towards the Colonies appears to be marked by a certain division of sentiment. There is a considerable section which approaches the subject with a sense of embarrassment, if not of actual distaste. There has in the last decades been a strong revulsion from that type of Imperialistic feeling which marked the concluding part of the last century, when so large an increase occurred of our overseas territories. [… These] feelings […] have been accentuated by the teachings of the Marxist school of thought, which professed to see in it at every stage evidence of the sinister promptings of monopolist and capitalist interests. A closer study of the facts of our Colonial economy would have shown them how small, as a matter of fact, has been the attention given to the Colonies by capitalist enterprise, as compared with that shown in other types of overseas investment. Nevertheless this suggestion reinforced their impression that there is something inherently wrong – if not indeed discreditable – in the possession of Colonies. That impression is apt to colour every approach which they make to questions of Colonial policy, and to discount in advance the merits of any achievement it may record.

Those who have spoken to popular audiences on the subject of the Empire have often been surprised to discover the strength of this section of opinion. But it does not, of course, represent the views of the majority of the public. The great mass of people in this country are apt to take the possession of Colonies as a normal feature of British history. They are ready to believe that our record in their administration is creditable to us. But they feel that the problems to which Colonial administration gives rise are not of a class in which their own experiences afford any guidance, and they prefer to leave their solution to those who have made a special study of them. There is, however, an important exception to this rule. They have a genuinely humanitarian feeling towards peoples whose weakness seems to demand protection, and where they suspect that abuses exist they are ready to intervene. This is typically a case in which the ordinary man feels that the credit of Great Britain is concerned. He acts, it is true, on instinct, and his interest is not always well informed; but it has by no means been without benefit to the people whom he has been concerned to protect.

If this represents correctly the prevailing attitude of the British public on Colonial matters, it might seem unprofitable to press on it now the need for a closer study of our relations with our dependencies. The attempt to forecast the position which they may eventually occupy within the Commonwealth must, in particular, seem to raise problems which are distant and even speculative. But these territories represent, as has justly been said, a procession of peoples in which great distances separate the van from the rear. There are some, such as Ceylon or the older 'Colonies of Settlement' in the West Indies, which already enjoy in substance a much larger measure of responsible government than is generally realized, and they are now pressing for a more complete status of constitutional autonomy. There are few among the larger dependencies which do not now contain advanced elements keenly concerned in their political future.

But apart from developments such as these, inevitable in any circumstances, the war has created influences, both within the Empire itself and in the outside world, which must definitely bring the question of our relations with the dependencies within the more immediate range of practical policy. The war of 1914–18, though it caused a significant change in our relations with the Dominions, did not directly produce any issue regarding the status of the dependencies. If their position attracted any attention at all, it was only when we learnt, with a natural satisfaction, that those who framed the Mandates for the ex-German territories had adopted our own doctrine of trusteeship as the guiding principle for regulating their administration. The present war might also perhaps have left the dependencies outside the field of immediate interest but for the Japanese aggression in the Far East. But incidents which occurred in the course of the invasion have brought into question not only the character of the administration of our possessions in the Far East and the Pacific but the policy which has been followed in our Colonial Empire at large. […]

But not only has the policy applied to our dependencies been subjected to frontal attack; the whole scheme of things which permits their existence has now come under indirect fire. In America distinguished personalities have declared that the post-war world can have no place for Imperialism, and a secular tradition seems to have persuaded the American public that the British Colonies provide the most obtrusive instance of Imperialism. The circumstances in which a Peace Conference will meet are not likely to be such as to permit us to disregard views held in America regarding the status to be given to those of our dependencies which she will have taken an active part in recovering from the Japanese. […]

It has accordingly become of some urgency to consider the type of relationship with our dependencies which ought to be commended to the attention of the British public. Up to the present our policy may be said to have been inspired, rather than defined, by the doctrine of 'trusteeship'. That conception was in itself an outcome of the humanitarian impulse which first manifested itself in the movement for the abolition of the Slave Trade, and subsequently extended its interest to questions affecting the welfare of aboriginal and primitive peoples. It has been justly remarked by Professor Hancock that 'the British people can never understand what they have achieved, and what they are, if they forget the hard-won ideas and beliefs which during the last century and a half have guided and inspired them in their adventurous journeys through the wide world – the ideas of Burke and Adam Smith and Durham, of Wilberforce and Fox and Livingstone'.[1] Of the value of the impulses which lay behind the doctrine of 'trusteeship' there can be no question. But the standards to which it appealed were moral, and it did not necessarily afford guidance where no moral issues were involved. The choice of the correct methods to be followed in deciding administrative or economic issues is something more than an exercise in applied ethics. […]

[The] change in the public outlook on the functions of the State, which has exercised so striking an influence over the course of our domestic politics, has been projected also into the field of Colonial policy. The results have been seen in three directions. Opinion in Great Britain has accepted the fact that our responsibilities to people of the dependencies involve a far more effective intervention on our part to promote their development than the traditions of a previous generation had contemplated. It has become apparent that adherence to the established principle of meeting the requirements of the dependencies from their own resources would inevitably condemn some of them to the permanent position of 'depressed' areas. […]

In the second place, there has been a growing agreement that our avowed policy of assisting the dependencies to achieve a self-governing status will lack realism unless we can ensure that there is an adequate foundation of economic and social well-being on which their political institutions can be built up. Political independence can have little meaning to people whose material and intellectual standards of life are so low as those which prevail in many of the dependencies. This does not imply that we must defer any measure of political advance until we are satisfied that the people have attained what we may regard as an adequate social or educational development. The discharge of a progressive measure of responsibility in the management of its own affairs can exercise a formative influence of the first order in the life of a country. If there is any change of view on the subject of political advance, it amounts only to an attempt to place in better perspective the processes through which it must be developed.

In the third place it is recognized that, in regard to some at all events of the dependencies, there must now be a more definite measure of central direction than was contemplated by the older traditions of Colonial rule. In all their earlier history the Dominions and the dependencies were associated under the same political control, and the convention of non-interference, which we were constrained from an early date to adopt in our relations with the former, survived as the principle which in the main determined our relations with the latter. While, however, in the one case this left the initiation of policy in the hands of representatives of peoples who had both knowledge of their requirements and the capacity to express them, in the other it left the responsibility with local officers who had little guidance other than that of their own instincts or personal experiences. The confidence placed in these authorities called forth from them high qualities of self-reliance and of devotion to the interests of the native population. But the earlier stages of development, in which those qualities had their greatest value, have now been surmounted. We have in many territories made very substantial progress in the organization of the social services. The issues of policy which face the administrations now tend more and more to resemble those which in the more highly organized countries occupy the Ministries concerned with the complex problems of social and economic development.

It is inevitable, therefore, as Mr. Amery has pointed out, that there should now be some machinery for giving more systematic consideration to these problems. It is particularly in the field of economic development that such guidance will be required, for it is on the economic side that the Colonial establishments are now weakest. In the long run the raising of local standards of living must depend on the measure in which the people of a dependency can themselves make the best of the natural resources of the country. The need now is for a far greater concentration of attention on the development of the internal economy of these areas. Whatever may be effected by aid such as that which the Act of 1940 will provide, it can do little more than act as 'priming' for the machinery of internal development. […]

The Commonwealth and the postwar world

Written after the unofficial British Commonwealth Relations Conference held in London in February 1945 (the third in a series starting in 1933), Kenneth Bailey's article attempted to square a realistic appraisal of the effects of the war on Britain and its partners with a desire for continuing co-operation. It is perhaps a mark of the extent to which the war gave a temporary boost to 'imperial' or 'Commonwealth' sentiment that he felt it necessary to address the extent to which the Commonwealth could still be seen as a 'power bloc', and the possibility of reversing the trend towards autonomy within the Commonwealth. As before the war, Bailey rested his hopes on the rather metaphysical notion of unity arising out of multiplicity.

[Kenneth H. Bailey,] 'British Commonwealth Relations: The Chatham House Conference', *RT* 35/139 (June 1945), pp. 218–25

The problems that confront the British Commonwealth in the post-war years cannot be solved by any action that the members can take as a self-contained group. The problems of the British Commonwealth are those of the whole world. They can be solved only in so far as the nations of the Commonwealth can be integrated into an effective world organization, for security and for welfare. […]

Though the British Commonwealth in 1945 is a going concern, a living, active, functioning reality, it faces an entirely changed situation as it looks ahead to the post-war years. […] Nations cannot engage in the vast activities, both destructive and constructive, of modern total war on a world scale without making drastic alterations in their reciprocal positions. So far as concerns the British Commonwealth, the war has brought great changes in the internal affairs of each of them, in their mutual relations, and in their relation as a group to the world at large.

Total war on both sides of the world has presented the Commonwealth as a whole and each of its members with a new problem of defence. Australia, for example, has been brought into the defence orbit of the United States to a degree shared hitherto only by Canada. The industrialization of the Dominions means that there must be something like a new balance in world production and trade. Canada has ceased to be a debtor and has become a creditor country. The war effort of India, military and economic, has been on so great a scale that [she] could contend with much show of justice that on every ground save that of political independence she has a claim at least as strong as that of China to a permanent seat in the Security Council of the United Nations.

The changes brought about by the war in the world position of the United Kingdom itself have been perhaps the most striking of all. How much her will to victory has cost her begins to stand out clearly even from the unemotional pages of the White Paper giving the official statistics relating to her war effort. On the one hand the disposal of a large fraction of her capital assets overseas, and the loss of important overseas earnings by reason of hostile action at sea and in her colonial territories, have seriously weakened her capacity to regain and maintain her traditional standard of living. On the other hand the development necessitated by the war in the huge military and industrial potential of the United States and the Soviet Union, with populations three and four times the size of Britain, has already shifted the balance of world power. She will not, in her own right, dispose in the post-war world of forces even roughly equivalent to those of the other two members of the Big Three. Only if one included the resources of the Dominions and Colonies would there be something like a balance between them. […]

The Commonwealth has been evolving hitherto by creating autonomous national units within its membership, dissolving one by one all the mechanisms of central organization and control. The process is still going on. Has the time not come to get into reverse gear, as it were – to draw the units closer together, to re-establish some means of unified decision and direction? Under the existing system of free co-operation there is always the risk of divided opinion and action, even on vital issues. Eire's decision to remain neutral in the present war is a clear case in point. The narrow majority that decided South Africa's entry into the war suggested again how real the risks were.

In a good many authoritative quarters the suggestion had been current for some time that it would be well to avert the possibility of such dangers as these by devising methods for reaching a single British Commonwealth decision, expressed in a single voice. Lord Halifax had publicly ventilated ideas of this kind. So also had General Smuts. Opposition had immediately been expressed, particularly in Canada. Nevertheless, the general idea had found a good deal of acceptance. Sometimes only half-consciously, it formed the assumption on which many people approached the problem of Britain's future, and that of the Commonwealth.

Views of this kind were by no means confined to, nor were they by any means universal in, the United Kingdom. It was not a simple case of a British view against Dominion views, the Great Power outlook contrasted with the outlook of the lesser States. Advocacy of 'one voice', too, did not always mean at all the same thing. Sometimes – as in Mr. Curtin's proposals of 1943–44 – it meant only more effective and constant consultation: better methods of reaching agreement, not a method of reaching a single majority decision, even in the face of disagreement. […]

Plainly, however, the opinion prevailed that the now traditional structure and methods of the Commonwealth are best; that to depart from them would prejudice the effective functioning of the Commonwealth in world affairs and would even endanger its present unity. The case for the present system of the Commonwealth was thus put on grounds both positive and negative. Negatively, the claim was that for a majority of the Commonwealth to assert the right to overrule a minority of the member nations would drive some of the members out of the Commonwealth altogether. Positively, the case rested on the fundamental proposition that the Commonwealth cannot solve its own problems by its own sole action. To form blocs is to create counter-blocs. If the member nations were to keep their heads down, so to say, in a kind of private scrum, they would lose the support of other free nations. The very freedom of their association makes it easy for them to enter into individual relationships with other nations, which are of the utmost value to the whole of the Commonwealth. Canada's close relations with the United States are only one example of this. The strength of the Commonwealth has resided fundamentally in the large measure of willingness to agree that exists among the members, a willingness that springs not only from their close and constant contact and consultation but from common traditions and ideals, and a common sense of purpose. […]

Committed to the task of renewing the attempt to organize collective security through international co-operation, united by fundamental community of purpose, the Commonwealth nevertheless enters the World Organization, not as one, but as several legal entities, not unitary but multiple in its policies and in its decisions, but still a Commonwealth.

Indian independence

That India would eventually be self-governing had been a cornerstone of Round Table *analysis of the sub-continent since the journal's inception, and that it would achieve independence soon after the war had been clear since the Cripps Mission of 1942. Even so, the speed of events which led to the partition and independence of India and Pakistan in 1947 took many by surprise, and the* Round Table *reflected this feeling. The author of this article, H. V. Hodson, went on much later to write what for many years was regarded as a definitive account of these events,* The Great Divide *(1969).*

[H. V. Hodson,] 'Valediction to India: The Last Phase of the British Raj', *RT* 37/148 (September 1947), pp. 330–38

The imprint of recent events in India upon the mind of the world has been the less for their swift succession. Any one of the major phases in Anglo-Indian relations in the first eight months of 1947, if it had happened at the pace of nineteenth-century history, would have no more needed recapitulation a few weeks or months later than Queen Victoria's Proclamation of 1858, or the outbreak of the Mutiny in the Bengal Army in the previous year, needed to be recalled to memory two or three generations after their occurrence. At the time of writing it is less than six months since the British Cabinet's declaration of February 20, which began the rapid chain of events by setting a time-limit upon British withdrawal from the government of India, and by entrusting the carrying out of the new policy in India to a new Viceroy, Viscount Mountbatten. It is barely two months since Lord Mountbatten sought and obtained the assent of the chief Indian politicians to the partition of British India into two nation States and to an immediate transfer of power under the constitutional convention of Dominion status – that is to say, national independence within the British Commonwealth. Yet February 20 and June 3 have been almost erased from the tablets of public impression by the even more memorable date of August 15, when by her own will and action Britain ceased to be the overlord of India, and two great new independent nations were born.

As astonishing as the speed of these events was the virtual unanimity with which this self-termination of British rule was accomplished, a unanimity all the more remarkable in view of earlier dissension. The announcement of February 20 had its severe critics, not confined to those British Conservatives who saw in it a disgraceful resignation from Britain's responsibilities to the Indian minorities, and generally to the Indian people, to refrain from handing over power until a new constitution had been established by agreement in India, capable of guaranteeing peace and justice for all. There were also many non-party well-wishers of India who disliked it for a different reason. They foresaw the fifteen months' time-limit running out, with agreement among the Indian parties actually baulked by the British declaration itself, since none would agree with his political neighbour in India if he could hope to get more from the British when they were obliged by their own promise to hand over power; so that in the end Britain's retreat from the government of India would have to be conducted under the most dangerous conditions of three-sided political strife. However necessary the declaration may have been to create the conditions for a fresh policy, the new Viceroy's later actions reveal clearly that, once on the spot, he instantly recognized the force of this criticism. The time-limit could not be allowed to run to its appointed end. At all costs it must be anticipated.

Lord Mountbatten perceived equally clearly that the declaration of February 20, in terms of practical politics, was a promise of Pakistan in some form or other – articles of surrender to Mr. Jinnah's seven years' campaign. Fortunately, Indian political opinion, including that of the Congress, had at once drawn the same conclusion, and accepted it as the preferable alternative to a violent struggle in which the present right-wing leadership of the Congress would almost certainly be submerged. Putting these two propositions together, Lord Mountbatten devised a plan which at any other period of Indian politics might have been execrated, but which, matched with supreme skill to the moment, was instantly accepted both by the main political parties in India and by almost every section of British public opinion. The magic formula was immediate practical independence for two Dominions, the decision on India's partition being taken, not arbitrarily by the British Government, but by vote of the areas affected, in such a way that while partition was a foregone conclusion it would cost the Muslims the sacrifice of large non-Muslim-majority sections of the key provinces of Bengal and the Punjab.

Lord Mountbatten's policy represented in effect a reversal, not only of the February 20 policy, but also of a certain trend in British policy towards India, already apparent in 1940, but strongly accentuated by the Cripps Mission of 1942 and by the Cabinet Mission of 1946, with which Sir Stafford Cripps was again prominently associated. British policy appeared to be based on the belief that what chiefly interested Indian political opinion was the ultimate constitutional settlement; all efforts must accordingly be bent towards devising a watertight scheme for evolving such a settlement, while immediate policies would emerge naturally once the long-term future was assured. Lord Mountbatten reversed the priorities, with such instant success that one is tempted to wonder how much happier might have been the course of Indian affairs if Sir Stafford Cripps had been able to offer in April 1942 not a clockwork-smooth piece of post-war constitutional mechanism but a rough-and-ready plan for sharing power during the war; or if the Cabinet Mission had given to the immediate tactics of shifting the load of governmental responsibility as much careful skill and effort as they gave to the long-term strategy of constitution-making under the plan of May 16, 1946.

Another piece of wisdom-after-the-event provoked by the Mountbatten scheme is the conclusion that the Pakistan issue was bound in the end to be settled by the British. Left to themselves, the two Indian parties could never agree, because their respective policies of unity and partition of India were logically and for ever irreconcilable. Mr. Gandhi's mesmeric formula about the absence of the third party should be turned upon its head. In this respect at least, only in the presence of the third party was Indian agreement possible in practice. After the opportunity was lost, before 1945, of saying once and for all that Britain would not take responsibility for handing over India in pieces, eventual decision of the third party in favour of partition became more and more certain. So utterly uncompromising upon the principle of Pakistan has Mr. Jinnah been that those who were not against him were in the end bound to be for him; only head-on conflict might have broken his will or disunited his supporters.

Since unity was the first and greatest benefit of British rule to India, so the division of India is the first and crucial fact about the plan for ending the British raj. Historical judgments cannot be made on short views, and no more can be attempted here than some interim reflections upon the creation of Pakistan. First, it does not solve the communal problem in India. Minority rights in either of the two nation states will be as difficult to reconcile with the claims of the communal majority as they would have been in a single Indian union. Each will have to face its own problems of electoral weightage, communal registers, representation of minorities in executives as well as legislature, guaranteed proportions in public employment, and all the rest. Cow-killing and music before mosques will continue to be the signal for communal rioting in Pakistan as well as India. Nor is there any substance – or, if there is substance, any comfort – in the theory, often advanced by Mr. Jinnah in the past, that the minority in each country would serve as a hostage for the minority in the other. […]

How Pakistan will fare in practice when it really stands on its own may be a matter of doubt. It is industrially and financially weak, and is left with the major burden of frontier defence without the advantage formerly enjoyed by the Punjab of being heavily subsidized by the rest of India as the main source of military recruitment. Detachment of the Eastern Punjab is a serious blow to its wealth in produce and in people. Nevertheless, in other respects it is stronger than is commonly recognized. It is self-sufficient in essential foodstuffs – a vast advantage over the deficiency areas of the rest of India. Its provincial finances are sound, and with a proper use of its water power and the development of its ports it has great opportunities of industrial and commercial advance. If Pakistan can have a peaceful start it should be able to survive and prosper.

At the same time it is manifest that the first task of the two new States in their external affairs must be to regulate their mutual relations in a fashion far more intimate than those that normally subsist between foreign States. Wherever the frontiers may be eventually drawn, they can have little natural defensive meaning, and must cut across the lines of trade and communications which have developed freely over all India under British rule. A European type of frontier barricade would be strangulation and folly. While national sovereignty will be jealously cherished, the two new nation States must clearly, in their own vital interests, set up some common organs of administration for defence, customs, communications and currency. On a basis of equality and a free veto it should not be impossible to devise such organs which will work, however defective their theoretical structure. […]

There is still a strong section of British opinion which feels it a defeat and betrayal of the highest national duty to have passed over our responsibility to hands less practised at least, and perhaps inherently less capable, than our own: some would say, a betrayal of India to the politicians. There is much that is sound as well as noble in this view, so often mocked by those whose political motives are far baser. If British will and British resources were still matched to the task, another decade of British rule, with all the lessons of economic as well as political experience thoroughly learnt, might well leave a more united, peaceable and prosperous India than is likely to emerge after ten years of independence. But neither the will nor the resources are to-day so matched. And the tasks of reconstruction in India are such that an alien power, inherently feeble in imposing the necessary social revolutions, is under a serious handicap by comparison with one supported by the people's suffrage. Indians, far more easily than British, can enforce agrarian reform in India, upset ancient social customs and religious usages, take the powers and the property needed for national economic policy, defeat the rising force of Indian Communism, and do all else that will be necessary for India to catch up with the middle decade of the twentieth century. […]

Commonwealth citizenship

The Canadian Citizenship Act of 1946, followed by the British Nationality Act of 1948, delivered a fatal blow to the previous notion of a common British subjecthood linking the peoples of the empire/Commonwealth. In this article (written while the British legislation was still in the process of passing through parliament), Hodson highlighted the benefits of the old system and deplored the fissiparous tendencies of the new. Nevertheless his remarks on the monarchy make it clear that by this stage he (and the Round Table*) acknowledged that there were now no legal bonds tying countries into the Commonwealth, which could only be based on free, willing and equal membership.*

[H. V. Hodson,] 'The British Subject: Personal Loyalties in a Changing Empire', *RT* 38/151 (June 1948), pp. 655–63

The nature of the Commonwealth will manifestly not be found in constitutional structure or constitutional formulae. Such formulae are false if they imply the existence of any constitutional bond in the true sense; and, if they do not, they are part of a symbolism which, however valuable, expresses the nature of the Commonwealth rather than determines it.

That is the position even of the Crown. The existence of the common Crown vastly eases the practical problems of law, personal status, international representation and so forth in a community which is something more than an *ad hoc* collection of nation-States. But it does so as a symbol, not as a political or judicial authority. The King reigns but does not rule; and even as a constitutional mechanism without independent power his rights and functions as King of England give him no rights and functions in, say, the Union of South Africa, where they derive from his South African Ministers and Parliament. The common allegiance of all British subjects to His Majesty is a symbolic expression of a common personal status; but each of the independent nations of the Commonwealth is free to legislate both as to whom it admits as citizens and what practical meaning allegiance has in respect of rights, duties and punishment within its jurisdiction. […]

Thus we must regard the Crown and the legal formulae deriving from it as no more than clues to the underlying nature of the Commonwealth connexion, not as the nature itself. We may even have to consider whether some parts of the existing recognized symbolism may no longer accurately represent the facts, and whether their retention may not actually work against the cohesion of the Commonwealth.

The nature of the Commonwealth is essentially pragmatic. It is what it is because it does what it does. Having emerged from history as a group of associated nations having common interests and purposes, it serves them through collaboration in many ways that may differ in form or intimacy from its members' relations with foreign countries. Commonwealth relationships are 'un-foreign' relationships.

The proposition on which the nature of the Commonwealth connexion rests, that in the Commonwealth we are not foreign to each other, implies two things. First it implies that, in the context of State affairs, we not only reserve the right to deal with each other more intimately than with foreign countries, notwithstanding 'most-favoured nation' or other such principles of general international relations, but also exercise that right through mechanisms of our own in the diplomatic, political, economic and military spheres. The second implication is that there is a common substratum of personal status, so that individual as well as national relations within the Commonwealth are un-foreign. Those two characteristics obviously interact. Especially does the second support and often enable the first: for example, collaboration in the sphere of defence is greatly facilitated by the fact that no question arises of disclosure of military secrets to persons of foreign nationality.

In some form, both characteristics are essential to the Commonwealth connexion. The lapse of all strict constitutional bonds makes it all the more important that these practical elements should be strengthened. If they become feeble the nations which are not attracted by the same motives of sentiment and race as the older self-governing members will find little practical value in the Commonwealth connexion to offset what they may regard as its symbolic distastefulness. Indeed, the value of the Commonwealth as such in the world of to-day may be called in question. […]

In respect of the common personal status […] a lack of vision in high places seems to have been displayed in the promotion of the British Nationality Bill. This Bill was sprung without warning on the United Kingdom Parliament, as if it were an uncontroversial measure for serving a universally agreed purpose of strengthening the Commonwealth. In fact it may well do the opposite; and if this is so it is presumably because Ministers and officials have failed to grasp the true nature of the problem to which the legislation is addressed.

The nationality laws of the United Kingdom, and of all countries whose legal systems derive from the common law of England and the statutes of what used to be called the Imperial Parliament, have been bound up with the concept of British subjecthood. This has been the common status of all subjects of His Majesty wherever within his dominions they were born or resided. No other domestic nationality was known to the law of this country, nor indeed until recently to that of other self-governing countries of the British Commonwealth, though all of them – including in practice the United Kingdom itself – reserved and exercised the right to prescribe what qualifications were required of British subjects for local rights such as immigration or the franchise.

This system had, and has, great advantages. It gave substance to the proud boast *Civis Britannicus Sum*. It enabled citizens of different parts of the Commonwealth to intermarry without problems of losing or changing nationality or complications as to the nationality of their children. It fostered the growth and work of unofficial all-Commonwealth associations for professional and the like purposes confined for good reasons to British subjects. It made possible official and military collaboration which would otherwise have encountered fatal legal or administrative obstacles. It opened the door of opportunity in the public services of the United Kingdom – civil, diplomatic, colonial, military – and in the professions, too, as widely for citizens of countries of the Commonwealth overseas as for British subjects in these islands. It was of great importance in the working of the diplomatic and consular system abroad, which is available to protect the interests of all British subjects and British-protected persons in the absence of a representative of their own national Government. […]

Hitherto the operative nationality in the Commonwealth generally has been British subjecthood. If this Bill is passed, and followed by like measures in the Dominions, the operative nationality in each Commonwealth country will be its own local citizenship. Otherwise there is no point in passing these measures. In the United Kingdom, in particular, there can be no reason for introducing the Bill unless this totally new concept of citizenship of the United Kingdom and Colonies is going to have some practical meaning; unless, that is, holders of such citizenship are going to have privileges and duties in the United Kingdom and Colonies more extensive than other classes of British subjects; unless, to be plain, a fatal injury is to be done to the old system of the common status, full of practical meaning and not a mere name, as British subjecthood will become under the system now threatened to be substituted. […]

As this is being written the Government have yet to defend the Bill in Parliament. No doubt the debates will reveal what overmastering reason could be held to justify such an attack upon the old beneficent tradition, which is even more important to the modern Commonwealth, with its weaker political bonds and its new facilities for intercourse, than to the old. Lacking such an explanation, we can only guess that Ministers have been bamboozled by the notorious plea from 'experts' for uniformity. Uniformity is an object-in-itself for officials, not for statesmen. In this case, it does not involve a levelling up to the wise and generous practice of the United Kingdom; it must in practice involve a levelling down to the narrower nationalism of which in this field Canada has been the chief exponent. But what the most nationalist of the Dominions think good for themselves is not necessarily good for the United Kingdom or for the Commonwealth as a whole. […]

Note

1 W. K. Hancock, *Survey of British Commonwealth Affairs*, Vol. II, *Problems of Economic Policy, 1918–39*, Part II (London: Oxford University Press for RIIA, 1942), p. 300. Hancock was briefly a member of the editorial board of *The Round Table.*

Part 5

The era of decolonization (1949–65)

The London Declaration

In 2009 the Commonwealth Secretariat celebrated the 'sixtieth anniversary' of the Commonwealth, highlighting the significance of the London Declaration of 1949, which allowed India to remain in the Commonwealth as a republic (and thereby removed what since 1931 had been thought to be the sole legal bond between Commonwealth members, a shared allegiance to the British Crown). At the time, the Round Table *detected no such revolutionary significance. Arguably, the* Round Table *underestimated the Declaration; then again, the journal was perhaps right, that the Declaration merely stated what had in fact been understood for some time, that membership of the Commonwealth was symbolized but not constrained by any remaining legal bonds.*

[Dermot Morrah,] 'Crown Without Sceptre: A Republic Within the Commonwealth', RT 39/155 (June 1949), pp. 203–07

The declaration of the London Conference of Prime Ministers has surmounted a great crisis in the constitutional development of the British Commonwealth by the practical, and indeed traditional, resource of saying in effect that no crisis exists. A sound political judgment decided at the outset, in the manner of the courts of Common Law, to limit discussion strictly to the circumstances of the particular case that had arisen, and to eschew any attempt to lay down a general rule. India came before the conference with two clear intentions to define. First, as had been foreseen for many months, she was firmly resolved to set up for herself a republican constitution in which there would be no place, even symbolic, for the Crown. Secondly, as had not been foreseen with any confidence until recently, she desired to retain her association with the other nations of the British Commonwealth on terms as intimate as before. The question to be decided was whether these two intentions could be reconciled with one another. The declaration rules that they can; and it says very little, if anything, more than this. India wishes to remain the permanent associate of her seven present partners in the Commonwealth; and all the seven declare that she is a welcome member of their brotherhood. This is the substance of the relationship it is desired to maintain; and no questions of constitutional form can be allowed to stand in the way. It is true that the forms centred upon the monarchy have been found by the older members of the Commonwealth the indispensable means of preserving the association; but if India finds them not a help but a stumbling-block, then the partnership between her and the rest must in some way be sustained without them. The King will continue to be 'the symbol of the free association of the independent member nations and as such the head of the Commonwealth' to which India belongs. Yet although the King is the symbol for all, India's relation to him will be different from that of any other member nation; at the same time it is laid down that there are not two classes of members, but only one. All are free and all are equal.

The declaration has been rightly applauded in all countries of the Commonwealth, and by most of its leading statesmen, for it makes in the structure of the Commonwealth as a whole the least possible change compatible with India's exercise of her undoubted right to renounce a system of symbolism which in her case could not serve its essential purpose, because the monarchy carries an historic connotation for Indian sentiment which is quite other than that which makes it a bond of social cohesion for other nations. […]

It has already been suggested that the status now accorded to India would have had attractions for Burma at the time of her secession; but although the doors of the Commonwealth are certainly open for her return, it is easier to imagine such a movement after a substantial course of years than in the immediate future, when it might be misinterpreted to the diminution of the prestige of her independence. Ireland, on the other hand, is in an altogether different position; for there the republic has been set up for the sake of separation from the United Kingdom, rather than separation endured for the sake of the republic. […]

Since 1931 we have been accustomed to say that the monarchy is the sole formal link on which the unity of the Commonwealth depends. If pressed to expand that statement we should probably say that the Crown binds us together because each individual state in the Commonwealth has at the head of its government the same person, His Majesty the King. We cannot, however, continue to regard the King as the link in that sense; for he is not the head of the Indian government, and yet he is the symbol of association for all members of the Commonwealth alike, of whom India is one. It is clear that we have to learn to think of the Crown as the symbol of association in some other aspect than that implied by its political headship of the individual member nations.

It may be noted that in that part of the declaration which relates to the status of India the reference is not to the Crown but, following a line of thought suggested by Dr. Evatt, to the King. Nevertheless it is useful to reflect upon the significance of the popular instinct which, from the many emblems of majesty with which the King is invested after his unction, has chosen the Crown as the pre-eminent symbol of the royal office. For the Crown, as the liturgical formulae of its imposition make clear, is not an emblem of power. That position belongs to the Sceptre, the rod of justice, descending no doubt from the first bough torn from a tree by prehistoric man as a weapon to impose his will upon his fellows. The Crown stands, according to the liturgy, for glory and for righteousness.

Now India has chosen to remove the King as bearer of the Sceptre from her political system. But she still participates in the glory and righteousness of the Commonwealth, that is, in the ideals and the way of life for which it stands, and in that sense continues to pay respect to the King as wearer of the Crown. But if that is so, it becomes necessary for India's partners in the Commonwealth to see their own mutual association symbolized by the same aspect of the monarchy. If the Sceptre is not a link with India, and India is constitutionally equal with all the rest, then it cannot be a link between these others. To dispense with the metaphor, the element of authority is now wholly removed from the apparatus by which the unity of the Commonwealth is sustained. Neither the authority of one privileged nation over the others, nor the authority of the corporate whole over its parts, now has any function in holding the Commonwealth together. […]

Apartheid

> *The* Round Table *originated in South Africa, and some of the editorial board's closest allies were to be found in the United Party in that country, led by Jan Smuts (whom in the interwar period the journal's writers seemed almost to revere). Hence – despite its commitment in general terms to multiracialism and progressive self-government – the journal was, to later eyes, frequently and almost bafflingly reluctant to condemn racial discrimination in that country while the United Party was in power. It was more forthright, however, in condemning the Nationalist policy of* apartheid.
>
> [Edgar Brookes,] 'The Doctrine of *Apartheid*: Nationalist Native Policy in South Africa', *RT* 39/155 (June 1949), pp. 208–13

Ever since the Nationalist party brought the term *apartheid* into current use in South African politics, earnest efforts have been made by seekers after truth to find out exactly what it means. As a general outlook on life, as the expression of a deeply felt emotion, the term has a meaning which is as significant as it is vague. All attempts, however, have failed to get from members of the Government a clear statement of its exact application in every sphere of national life. We are therefore driven to undertake the prosaic task of analysing its meaning point by point in the light, not merely of Nationalist election propaganda, but of what the Nationalists have done, refrained from doing, or threatened to do since Dr. Malan came to power. Before doing this it may be as well to glance for a moment at those few supporters of *apartheid* who have taken this election slogan seriously, and endeavoured to work it out logically. These, as might be expected, consist mainly of university professors, and appear to fall under the definition of Edmund Burke, 'those good souls whose credulous morality is so invaluable a treasury to crafty politicians'.

They have faced the possibility of *apartheid* in the sense of the literal separation of White from Black, and have envisaged a great Bantu State or group of States to which at least one ingenious thinker has affixed the term 'Bantustan', somewhere in the fastnesses of southern Africa. This State or group of States is to have some measure of self-government, although apparently the suzerainty of the White man must always remain. The issue of labour is faced, and the European community is exhorted to learn to do with less African labour, although indeed there are crosscurrents of thought which seem to favour the entrenchment of the migrant labour system – in which case Bantustan would be something unique in history, a dormitory State.

This unofficial 'solution' leaves a number of questions unsolved. The simplest and perhaps the most important of them is that of the geographical boundaries of Bantustan. The supporters of *apartheid* appear to have a distaste for maps. Up to the present it has not been possible to get any authentic map showing the proposed redivision of the country, in spite of challenges, pleas and plaintive requests for it.

In the second place, the professors do not seem to have settled, for themselves or anyone else, the question of the future of the non-Bantu elements in South African society. So far as the Indians are concerned, the simple solution of expatriation to India is sometimes put forward by those who have no political responsibility and occasionally by some who have. But what of the large and increasing Cape Coloured population, over 750,000 of whom live in the western part of the Cape Province in the most intimate economic contact with the Europeans? There is no equivalent of Bantustan for them, and although they are sometimes exhorted to develop in their own areas, they have no areas of their own. If these were created, they would have to be carved out of some of the richest farming land of the whole Union.

It would perhaps be best to say that *apartheid* represents rather an emotion than a policy. It is none the less a critical issue for that reason. Built up into it is much of the feeling which has been the strength of South African Nationalism in the past – the appeal to history, a history much of which is composed of inter-racial war, White against Black; the appeal to tradition, stabilizing the tradition of the Afrikaner more or less as it stood in 1899, or earlier; the appeal to fear. What is this fear? It is the not unnatural fear of a large number of Afrikaners that their hard-won nationality, so sore beset by alien contacts, their own way of living, their own outlook on life, should be lost in the rising tide of colour. To them liberalism in any of its forms is the removing of the dike which keeps this sea of colour out of the territory so hardly wrested from it. […]

So far as the Africans are concerned, the land question is the crux of the policy of *apartheid*. By it the Africans will test the validity of the conception. Most of them are not inhibited by liberal or socialist theories. If the Nationalists had come forward with a clear, extensive and generous policy as regards land, they might have carried a good deal of African opinion with them. Many Africans are realists in these matters. The majority of established leaders would, on general principles, have been against the apartheid policy, but they would have found their followers slipping away from them if Bantustan had appeared on the map, and if its exponents had been practical surveyors rather than meditative theorists. All possibility of this has disappeared. Bantustan, which had a certain limited usefulness during the election campaign, has now outlived its usefulness. Nationalist Ministers are now using the argument that the increasing urbanization since 1936 means that it is doubtful whether they ought really to carry out General Hertzog's promise to buy the 7/4 million morgen (approximately 14,500,000 acres) provided for in the Natives Trust and Land Act, of which a little over 4 million morgen have been bought. This kind of argument is better calculated than anything else to condemn *apartheid* in African eyes. […]

As to Parliament, the Indian franchise, existing only on paper under the Act of 1946, has been abolished. It is now proposed

a to remove Native representation from the House of Assembly, where three Members elected by the Cape Natives sit among the total of 153;
b to separate the Coloured vote in the Cape Province from the European vote, and to give the Coloured people a limited number of European representatives with restricted voting power – that is, a lower type of representation than that which it is now proposed to abolish as regards Africans;
c to limit the voting power of Senators elected by Natives, so that they may not vote on certain specified matters.

The third of these suggestions is the least likely to be implemented. As regards the first and second, it is almost impossible to prophesy. […]

The constitutional issue raises also the question what effective undertakings can ever be given by a South African Government if and when the time comes for the taking over of the High Commission Territories.[1] If it is legally impossible to bind the Union Parliament, the only guarantee that can be offered is South Africa's good faith in keeping her word. This is an important consideration, for the forcing through of the abolition of the Native franchise and the limitation of the Coloured franchise by small majorities, in defiance of the clear intention of the Constitution, must have the same effect in the political world that the repudiation of public debt might be expected to have in the financial world.

Only a very small number of political thinkers take the orthodox liberal line of 'no differentiation on the grounds of race or colour only'. The differences between the Nationalists and the United party on some of the issues discussed do not in fact seem to be very great. There is, however, a great difference of spirit. The real need of South Africa at the present time is not so much for a recasting of its system as for the interpretation of the system with kindliness, tolerance and common sense, and the creation of a sufficient number of exceptions to make more possible the transition towards the uncertain future.

All this the United party has been prepared, and is prepared, to give: judged by the measures they have passed and the attitude they have displayed during their first year of office, the Nationalists seem to wish to harden practice into law, and general custom into a rigid caste system.

It must be added here that there are differences between Nationalist and Nationalist too, and that the whole party system of the Union at the moment is in a condition more fluid than it has been for many years. Underneath this confused and confusing parliamentary position there are the voteless millions, on whose reactions the future of South Africa so largely depends. What most South Africans fail to see is that the chance of winning co-operation from the large non-European groups is diminishing every year, and that if present policy is persisted in, the danger of failure and tragedy for South Africa becomes greater and greater. The next ten years are a critical time in the country's history, and the electoral victories of *apartheid* may well turn out to be, viewed from the perspective of subsequent history, delusion and disaster.

Decolonization in Africa

The speed of decolonization in Africa and elsewhere in the 1950s and 1960s took many commentators by surprise. Most Round Table *articles followed the orthodox British government line of welcoming independence, and portraying it as the culmination and logical outcome of British rule. The author Elspeth Huxley, however, took a more critical view, identifying several obstacles to the successful implementation of democracy in the newly independent countries. While her approach was undoubtedly tainted by racism and deliberate neglect of the negative effects of British rule, the questions she raised were ones which the journal returned to in the decades which followed.*

[Elspeth Huxley,] 'African Independence and After: Some Reflections on "SG"', *RT* 46/181 (December 1955), pp. 17–26

[…] For some years the British people have been watching the development of a love affair between the colonial peoples and the spirit of independence – 'SG' as Gold Coasters call it (for self-government). This has been, and is, taking place simultaneously in many parts of the world. The courtship has had its ups and downs, of course, but everyone has hoped that, sooner or later, the bride would be led to the altar and the pair live happily ever after.

Now that the marriage has been consummated in some places, and is about to be solemnized in others, it is becoming clear that the altar is no more the end of the road for a people and their 'SG' than it is for any other bride and groom. Just as novelists now probe eagerly into the post-marital situation, so must public opinion be prepared to take an interest in the probable post-independence affairs of the erstwhile colonies. […]

A question constantly asked is: 'Are Africans ready for self-government? How will they manage when the Europeans withdraw?' Point is given to such questions by recent events in the southern Sudan. What happened when the Europeans withdrew is becoming painfully clear. The southern Sudanese refused to accept their new masters, the northern Sudanese, and revolted; and the country reverted to its previous condition of latent disorder. Normal administration has, for the time being, been replaced by an uneasy, limited and (in places) harsh military rule.

The southern Sudan is a special case, however, because the conditions of the marriage were not fulfilled. The southern Sudanese did not obtain self-government, they were simply handed over to the northerners. The fact that educated southerners had worked with the northerners in various branches of government did not really affect this position. They were learners still. Now they are victims of the British fiction that the Sudan is one nation, not two. Through this we can perhaps arrive at one proposition: fitness for self-government presupposes a political unit which is, so to speak, self-governable. It is no good drawing lines on a map (as was done when Africa was partitioned) which pay no regard to race, tribe, economics or geography and saying, in effect: 'That is a country, and it must now govern itself.' Those ancient tribal loyalties, history's half-hidden fears and memories, the pulls and thrusts of trade, the barriers of faith and language will reassert themselves. Countries are not made by cartographers but by the people who live in them. It was the failure to remember this that may have put the clock back by many years in the Sudan.

To see that powers are handed over only to a self-governable country, to a viable political unit, is the responsibility of the colonial Power – the father (to continue the metaphor) who gives away the bride. Other responsibilities lie on the bride's own shoulders. She has got her man; the vows are to be taken; can she be sure that she has the moral and domestic training to make him not merely an ardent mistress but a good wife?

In one sense, no community that has survived and even prospered can be called unfit to run its own affairs. Africa, before the European advent, was full of independent kingdoms which managed very well. Some had achieved a high degree of political cohesion, military strength and social organization. Africans could, and did, govern themselves, and could no doubt do so again today.

The real point is, of course, that we do not merely wish to see them self-governing, we wish to see them operating a certain type of government, known as parliamentary democracy. That system of government is as much a European invention as the internal combustion engine or the dynamo; and, like these, it needs a certain grasp of technique, a certain experience, to make it work. Any one of us can run a motor-car, perhaps even tend a dynamo, until it begins to go wrong. We then need some understanding of the principles and practice of engineering. If we lack this, the car or dynamo will stop and we shall have to go back to walking, and to lighting fires. So, when we ask the question about fitness, what we really mean is: 'Are Africans sufficiently trained in the principles and practice of parliamentary democracy to operate it by themselves?'

Put like this, it can be seen to be a very reasonable question. Parliamentary democracy as we know it, with its universal suffrage, its party system, its incorrupt hard-working bureaucracy, its freedom of speech, its centralization, its high taxes, and its many social services is a very new thing, so new that we have had it in its present form for less than forty years – too short a time to be sure that we can work it ourselves, let alone pass it on intact to pupils. To ask whether Africans are 'fit' for self-government is only to ask whether they have had long enough, and thorough enough, training in our alien system of parliamentary democracy to be able to carry on without help: always provided (and this is a question that we never do ask) that this is the system they themselves really want, in their heart of hearts, to adopt as their own. […]

We have seen that the first condition for success in SG is that some firm balance shall have been struck before the transfer of power between the fissiparous tendency of all cartographer-countries and the need to maintain a viable self-governable unit. The second condition is that the country which attains its SG shall have enough men soundly trained in the technique of parliamentary democracy to carry on at a reasonable level of efficiency.

No one can be certain just how large a cadre is needed of these trained men, just how thorough their training has to be, and how to define efficiency. Two kinds of people are needed: politicians and civil servants. And here we are on slippery ground. Why should not African politicians and civil servants be just as good as other peoples'? Britain prides herself on the high quality of her public servants. Perhaps she overestimates herself – a regrettable national trait. In any case there are countries other than Britain. Cannot Africans produce politicians as able as most French deputies and civil servants as efficient as the average official of one of the less-advanced of the United States? It may be that we are too apt to set our hearts on a series of Utopias and to shrink back from anything falling short of standards to [*sic*] which few, if any, Western countries do in fact attain.

Some Africans counter with an accusation that we cannot free ourselves of the habit of considering ourselves to be members of a superior race. At one time we used to say that African brains were inferior. This has been disproved. We now admit that Africans can hold their own, or beat us, in examinations but impute to them a moral inferiority. And beyond this lies a third line of defence – that Africans lack experience. There are too few Africans, far too few, who know how to administer things, whether government departments, health services, police forces, banks, treasuries, co-operatives, marketing schemes or trading firms. With all these complex activities handed over to inexperienced amateurs, only one result can follow: a breakdown of the machinery, followed by confusion and distress.

Certainly it is a valid point that administration is far more difficult and complex than most Africans are ready to believe. There is a tendency to think that almost anyone with a secondary education can sit at an office desk drawing a large salary and cause schools to be built, or taxes to be collected, or crops to be sold. There is tragedy in the shortness of the time permitted for the training of a whole generation in the running of things. Even another fifteen or twenty years would have made a great difference. Fifteen years! It is like an age in the modern time-scale of political advance. It was only in 1947 that the Nigerian legislature first acquired an unofficial majority and that the first Houses of Assembly were set up in the three Regions. Four years was the life of that constitution; the next one lasted two years, and 1956 will see the end of it, and full SG for Houses of Assembly less than ten years old. […]

In days gone by, under their own system, kings and chiefs waxed fat and were expected to do so; a poor chief was merely an unsuccessful one. Like everyone else, Africans respect success and measure it in terms of material goods. To make money out of a public position, therefore, is not to go against the grain of society but with it. It may be questioned whether there is a deal of difference, in this respect, between the attitude of Nigerians and that of many Americans towards state (if not federal) politics.

Nor is it traditionally wrong to use such influence as you have been able to attain in order to help on in the world your less fortunate relatives. It is unnecessary here to expatiate on the African family system: on its strength and complexity, on the tight bonds of kinship, on the right of which every child learns to claim the protection of his kinsmen, and the duty each man owes his kin. These are not light feelings, they are ingrained into the bone of every African and they have a religious base. And they have been but little weakened by the impact of the West. It is true that the outgoing British have set up a system, modelled on their own, designed to keep the public service clear of such practices through examinations, commissions and so on. These will act as a brake; so, too, will the judiciary.

It is true also that many individuals disapprove of bribery and nepotism, but they are not the bosses of political parties and are not in the least likely to be. They are therefore impotent, politically. If you transfer to Africa lock, stock and barrel an alien scheme of universal suffrage, ballot box and party system, and offer as reward to the successful an almost unlimited power over the public purse, in advance of universal education, of local government and of the building of a tradition of public morality; and if at the same time the indigenous plan of government by chief-in-council, together with the power of the ruling class, is destroyed, it would indeed be astonishing if the result were not a welter of political skulduggery. […]

It would be wrong to overestimate the danger. Things will find their own level; Africans will evolve a system that suits their needs. The austerity underlying British ideals, derived from that puritan spirit which is an enduring element in British life, strikes but a feeble spark from the African soul. Puritanism, self-denial, austerity, atonement – these are not at home under hot skies. An East African, asked what he thought would happen if the Europeans left, replied with a smile: 'We should revert to more human standards!' […]

What, then, shall we be left with? A series of Liberias, a number of unstable States resembling the minor South American republics? Possibly: yet is there not too much vigour, too many hopes, too close and eager a penetration of European thought and energy, too strong a sense of being on their mettle in the eyes of the world, to allow them to relapse into inertia? […]

Commonwealth membership

Decolonization resulted in a rapid expansion of Commonwealth membership, and seemed to many commentators to threaten the cohesion and usefulness of the organization. In this article H. V. Hodson took issue with the prevalent assumption that Commonwealth membership was the automatic right of all newly independent countries, or was in the gift of Britain, and suggested that membership still carried with it obligations (in particular the obligation of mutual consultation) as well as privileges. In fact, Hodson would live to see the Commonwealth expand to include more than fifty independent nations, while debate over the extent and nature of the obligations that membership implied would remain unresolved.

[H. V. Hodson,] 'The Future of the Commonwealth: Its Membership and Its Obligations', *RT* 46/183 (June 1956), pp. 215–21

Like a familiar landscape, the British Commonwealth changes gradually, almost imperceptibly, but in the long run radically. Trees are planted here, cut down there, a house is built, a road widened, a stream dammed: no single event, even if noticed when it happens, is more than a passing wonder, yet in a couple of generations the changes may leave only the broad contour of hill and valley to recall for the returned exile the scene of his childhood.

So it is with the Commonwealth. Its last recognized ideologist, the last who set down the full panorama in one definitive picture, was the late Lord Balfour, whose famous report on imperial relations, with its Athanasian subtlety, was penned exactly thirty years ago. Only because the hills and valleys are still there is the present prospect still recognizable as the same.

The decisive novelty was the creation, less than ten years ago, of three great self-governing Asiatic nations, to join the Dominions and the United Kingdom in equal partnership. At a stroke, a Commonwealth which was still a European empire divided and modernized became a multi-racial community of diverse nations. That was one aspect of the Commonwealth revolution of 1947. The second was made more manifest when two years later India was accepted as an equal member of the Commonwealth, though a Republic owing no allegiance to the Crown, acknowledging the Sovereign only as Head of the Commonwealth.

India, Pakistan and Ceylon were not only of different race, colour and religion from the countries whom they joined in equal partnership: they did not share the same history beyond the relatively brief period of imperial domination; the legends, myths, loyalties and evocations of their folk-memories were entirely different; they sprang from ancient – indeed much more ancient – civilizations of their own. The establishment of the Indian and Pakistani Republics – to be followed soon, it seems, by Ceylon[2] – was a natural expression of this underlying difference. The retention of those Republics in the Commonwealth, on the other hand, confirmed the fact that the Commonwealth itself had changed, both in their eyes and in those of its other members, and was still changing. (It must not be supposed that the change was sudden: it was the Commonwealth formed by the nationalism of the older Dominions, especially Canada and the Union of South Africa, into which the new Asian member nations so readily fitted.) […]

All this provokes a number of questions, some of them immediate or imminent in their impact, others for the future, but to be pondered by thoughtful people now.

What conditions is it necessary for a country to fulfil to become a full member of the Commonwealth? What authority is to apply them and determine such a country's status? Will the machinery of Commonwealth co-operation which is appropriate, or at least workable, for a group of seven or eight countries be suited to a group of double that number, of such various sizes and kinds as the Commonwealth group would comprise if it included new independent units from Africa, South-East Asia and the West Indies beside its present nation-members? What does that machinery set out to do, and what relationship does it express? What, in fact, is this modern and arising Commonwealth? Is it really something worth while? […]

The Commonwealth, once but another name for the Empire, is certainly the name of the whole congeries, and includes the Empire. There are both self-governing and non-self-governing countries in the Commonwealth. The existence of self-government, or the degree of it, is a question of fact, not the testimony of a diploma: not necessarily coincident with the fact of membership of the special circle of countries for whom the term Commonwealth is sometimes reserved. Thus pre-1947 India, though not fully self-governing, was a full member of the Imperial Conference. Conversely, attainment of full self-government does not automatically admit a country to participation in the less formal present-day machinery of Commonwealth Prime Ministers' conferences.

This reasoning clears away at least one possible misconception. The extension of self-government and independence to a country now subordinate concerns only that country and the imperial power to which it was formerly subject: it cannot be questioned by other nation-members of the Commonwealth on the ground that its completion will make that country 'one of them'. The question of admission to Prime Ministers' conferences is quite separate, and there the principle of equality, *prima facie*, gives everyone a say, if we are to regard these conferences as a formal apparatus defining a certain community of equals. […]

It will at once be recognized that mere additive expansion of the present arrangements cannot for ever be pursued. Conferences of more than half-a-dozen or so members soon become too unwieldy to do good work, at least in a short period. Moreover we are thinking here not of officials whose time is at command but of Heads of Government with many duties to discharge. Even now that air travel reduces the time factor to a minimum, it is a matter of arduous negotiation to arrange a conference at a time acceptable to all of eight men whose preoccupations at home include daily administration, parliamentary sessions and general elections. These material difficulties alone suggest that as the number of its members expands the full and inclusive Commonwealth Prime Ministers' conference will become less and less frequent, more and more the stage piece for rare and special occasions.

If personal contact at this high political level is not to be lost altogether, more workable plans have to be envisaged. There is no reason why there should not be regional or other limited Prime Ministers' conferences. One obvious possibility is an African conference or council. There might be meetings of those Prime Ministers who were specially concerned with migration, or with particular aspects of defence. Such mechanisms ought to grow out of practical need, not be created for their own sake, though the formation of an African Council might valuably anticipate an emerging need, and a Mediterranean Council might deflect the need for some of the desperate expedients conceived for Malta and Cyprus.

This brings us to the real crux of the matter. Is there anything which the Commonwealth does that cannot as well be done without it? Groups of its countries, obviously yes – Britain and the developing African colonies must, for example, hang together and have special non-foreign relationships for a long time to come, in their own essential interests – but is that true of the Commonwealth as a whole? Has it still a meaning and is it still worth while?

The question has already been, in part, implicitly answered. No conceivable organization or connexion other than the Commonwealth can provide the right system within which countries of widely different stages of political and economic advancement and widely different degrees of national viability, such as the British territories in Africa, can proceed and develop, giving each other mutual aid and support. […]

It may, however, rightly be said that adding together a lot of special interests of particular members does not create a value for members who do not share those special interests, nor make their membership valuable to the rest. If there are such members, India perhaps might be reckoned the first of them. What is the Commonwealth worth to India, and what is India's membership worth to the Commonwealth? […]

It may be assumed that if India were not now a member of the Commonwealth she would not wish to join or rejoin. That is the corollary of the inert-acceptance view of the Commonwealth. Consider the matter in another way: if India were not now a member would the rest of us wish her to join or rejoin? It is very doubtful. The argument that her neutralist policy, her discard of more and more relics of the British connexion, had left us with too little in common, too little to expect of her membership, would surely prevail.

Yet, as things are, the majority of informed people both in India and in the rest of the Commonwealth regard her actual and continued membership as a desirable thing. Why? Because, when we come down to the truth, the Commonwealth expresses a fact which in these days people are almost afraid to acknowledge: that complete national independence is an illusion, that we are all members one of another, and that if we do not work together we shall perish separately. Pandit Nehru can hardly say that openly, for it pricks the bubble of neutralism as a principle, but he can tacitly admit it by keeping India in the Commonwealth; and the rest of the Commonwealth admits it by agreeing that it is worth while modifying our own several views by the process of discussing them with India under the Commonwealth shelter, because she and we belong together. Having come together, then, we should stay together. If the Commonwealth is no more, it is at least a protest against the falsehood of extreme nationalism and neutralism, the common names of blind selfishness in world politics.

The politicians, of course, neither speak for nor control all the facts of the situation. Beneath the surface of the constitutional position, interdependence is constantly exemplified in practice. In trade and business, of course: the decline of tariff preference has far from obliterated the special character of economic connexion within the Commonwealth, including its Eastern nation-members. Even more fundamental are the inter-relations of a cultural, professional and private kind. These are tough, and hard to destroy. They are the grass-roots of the Commonwealth, little affected by the political mowing-machine. […]

The Suez crisis

The Suez crisis led to extensive discussion and disagreement within the Round Table*'s editorial board, as it did in Britain and the Commonwealth more widely. Perhaps surprisingly – given the journal's previously stated views on the importance of Commonwealth consultation – the Conservative interpretation prevailed, and Hodson was deputed to write for the journal defending the British government's actions. While he took comfort from the fact that the crisis had not destroyed the Commonwealth, his remarks on the stances adopted by the Canadian and Indian governments amounted to a tacit admission that in future national and regional interests would tend to prevail over those of the Commonwealth as a whole.*

[H. V. Hodson,] 'Commonwealth and The Crisis: Bonds Strained but Unbroken', *RT* 47/186 (March 1957), pp. 114–20

A writer in the June 1956 issue of *The Round Table* on 'The Future of the Commonwealth'[3] observed that

> when two ideologies are so flatly contradictory as that of neutralism and independence and that of the Commonwealth – belonging together – one or other must be preferred and win. The time is coming … when the question will need to be put to the constituents of the Commonwealth: do you, or do you not, accept that this belonging-together involves both rights and responsibilities? At least the responsibility of consultation as the obverse of the right to be consulted?

This problem has been illustrated in a most vivid and realistic way by events that have since occurred.

The *Round Table* writer evidently had in mind that the newer Asian members of the Commonwealth would be the ones that would hesitate to answer 'Yes' to the question about rights and responsibilities. But the second question, about consultation, might suggest to some minds, in the light of the Suez crisis, that the older, 'white' members may themselves be unwilling to fulfil the responsibilities of 'belonging together' if these require consultation before deciding upon any international action or policy. For one of the many charges of mishandling levied against the United Kingdom Government for its conduct in October–November 1956 is that it failed to consult even its fellow member governments of the Commonwealth before acting, outside previously declared policies, in a way that intimately concerned their interests, and might have provoked war.

In order to weigh this charge justly we must consider the facts as they occurred. In the situation that confronted Britain and France in the last days of October there were certain new factors, but a great deal also that was not new. The Arab–Israeli conflict had been bitter and violent ever since the foundation of Israel in 1947. Egypt and her other Arab neighbours had never accepted her legitimacy, and talked freely of a 'second round' in which they would eliminate her by force of arms; and the 'second round' prospect was also deeply and hopefully embedded in the Jewish outlook. The Tripartite Declaration pledging British, American and French support for Israel against aggression was six years old. In the Arab countries latent anti-Western mass feeling had been steadily seeping to the surface: it was on March 2 last, as one of many portents of this, that the King of Jordan dismissed Lieutenant-General Glubb.

On June 13 the last British troops left the Suez Canal base, ahead of the time fixed by treaty engagement, to the sound of boastful and hostile Egyptian propaganda. Egypt was now receiving arms from Russia and the Communist countries on a big scale, and a catastrophic arms race between the Arab States and Israel was threatening, despite the pacifying policies of the Western powers. Such was the Middle Eastern scene that confronted the Commonwealth Prime Ministers when they met in London at the end of June for their seventh post-war conference. At least up to that point we may assume that there had been the fullest Commonwealth consultation.

On July 26 Colonel Nasser seized the Suez Canal, which had always been regarded as a life-line not only of Britain but of the Commonwealth itself, and whose security had repeatedly figured as a declared common objective of its members' defence policies. […]

Such was the background to the dramatic events of the last days of October. It may be well to summarize how matters then stood, as seen by any Commonwealth member thus kept informed.

1 Egypt and the Arab League countries had sworn to exterminate Israel, to whose defence all Commonwealth members were bound under the United Nations Charter, and the United Kingdom specifically bound under the Tripartite Declaration.

2 Both sides were breaking the Israeli–Arab truce with provocative and retaliatory border raids.
3 Egypt was receiving arms from Russia and Czechoslovakia on a large scale with the open object of securing a preponderance over Israel.
4 Egypt, having already acted persistently in breach of the 1888 Canal Convention and in defiance of the United Nations by stopping the transit of Israeli ships or cargoes, had seized the Canal from the international concessionaires.
5 The British Government had repeatedly declared that a situation in which the control and management of this international highway remained in the hands of one country was 'intolerable'.
6 Since the rape of the Canal a mobile Anglo-French force had been assembled in Cyprus and at other Mediterranean bases, against eventualities that might require its use in the Middle East.
7 It had also been a cardinal point of British policy, explicitly emphasized to Messrs. Bulganin and Krushchev when they visited London in April, that Middle Eastern oil was a literally vital interest for Britain, which she would defend as she would her own territory.

A realistic view of these facts must have led inexorably to two prognostications: that sooner or later there would be large-scale war between Israel and her Arab neighbours; and that when that happened the British and French would intervene under some banner or other, and in so doing would seek to safeguard their interest in the Suez Canal. It must be assumed that every Commonwealth government was as cognizant of this as were intelligent newspaper-readers everywhere. Military plans – which would have to take account of various possible events – would not, of course, be exchanged. But again certain known facts spoke for themselves. […]

The actual reactions of the various Commonwealth members suggests [*sic*] that even with all the expert advice and inside information available to them they had not drawn the inferences as to probable British policy that in retrospect seem so obvious; for there is in them a strong element of puzzlement and surprise. Thus even Mr. Menzies, while announcing the Australian Cabinet's unanimous support of Britain's action, found it desirable to excuse her – on grounds of great emergency and vital interest – from blame for having decided to use force without first seeking the consent of the Commonwealth countries and the United States. And Mr. Holland, the Prime Minister of New Zealand, giving equally loyal support, used language about disturbing features in the situation, having 'full confidence in Britain's intentions', and hopes that in due course there would be wider understanding of her motives, which plainly suggests that he was taken aback, and himself felt greatly in need of explanation. […]

The Canadian Government's reaction was quite different. So hostile was it initially to the Anglo-French action that when Mr. Lester Pearson, the Minister of External Affairs, said that the crisis threatened to cause a split in the

Commonwealth (and Mr. St. Laurent, the Prime Minister, used similar terms) it was widely understood both in Canada and in Britain and elsewhere that he referred to the possibility of Canada's seceding. Much later he explained that he was thinking only of the position of the Asian members. Canada was, of course, powerfully affected by her position as a North American power: it would have been surprising to find Ottawa completely contradicting Washington on such an occasion. […]

As to the newer, Asian members, the obvious truth is that their Asian and 'anti-colonial' connexion had the upper hand. There is nothing surprising, and certainly nothing reprehensible, in this prevailing of the one influence over the other. On occasions the United Kingdom, or Canada, say, has been moved by a regional interest to the detriment of a Commonwealth interest, or has found the Commonwealth interest divided and has chosen that part of it which conformed to her regional or similar motives. (A classic example is the Washington Conference of 1920, at which the United Kingdom, under pressure from the United States and Canada, accepted a Far Eastern and disarmament policy which Australia and New Zealand thought inimical, and which certainly was not a Commonwealth policy as such.)

What is interesting, and more surprising, is the firmness and zeal with which the leaders of those Asian countries – Mr. Nehru, Mr. Suhrawardy and Mr. Bandaranaike – defended their policy of remaining in the Commonwealth notwithstanding their acute differences with Britain and her friends. Mr. Nehru had to repel a particularly strong demand for India's resignation from so 'colonialist' and aggressive an association.

That the Commonwealth in its present multi-racial form should have withstood this assault on its coherence, its sense of 'belonging together', is itself a remarkable tribute to its viability. Its bonds, slight as they appear to be, have evidently a tenacity that may have surprised many outside observers. In particular, the reactions are proof of the worth that the experienced leaders of the Asian member countries attach to their membership. We in Britain who speak of the value to ourselves of keeping this peculiar and irreplaceable link with countries of Asia, as a bridge across the gulf between races and continents, often forget that the bridge renders the same service for those on the other side of it. […]

The Central African Federation

In 1953, in an attempt both to perpetuate colonial rule and to create a counterbalance to South Africa, the British government created the Federation of Rhodesia and Nyasaland (better known as the Central African Federation), joining together white-dominated Southern Rhodesia with Northern Rhodesia (Zambia) and Nyasaland (Malawi). Discontent among Africans particularly in the latter two colonies led the British Prime Minister, Harold Macmillan, in 1959 to appoint a commission under Lord Monckton to investigate the future of the

Federation. Its report, in October 1960, proposed a weakened Federation with a legislature in which an equal number of seats would be reserved for 'whites' and 'blacks', voting on communal rolls. This arrangement inevitably failed to satisfy African opinion. In December 1963 the Federation was dissolved, and soon afterwards Zambia and Malawi became independent.

[Garfield Todd,] 'The Monckton Report: African Awakening in the Federation', *RT* 51/201 (December 1960), pp. 22–28

Viewed from the midst of the Central African Federation, the Monckton Commission's proposals seem to conceal two grave flaws: compromise and transitoriness. These flaws are grave because anguish among both races has already become acute. To prolong this present state of mind would be tormenting – and dangerous.

The members of the Commission left the Federation in May. Since May so much has happened, above all in Southern Rhodesia. There, Africans have begun to awake to consciousness: it is a rapidly multiplying process and there is no returning. Meanwhile, partly through mischance (a great bubble of unemployment), there have been riots and death from police bullets in the three major cities of Southern Rhodesia. The African population has been blooded for the first time since the last Matabele revolt, in the reign of Victoria. These recent events have been spectacular, and inflated rumour has rioted through African townships. Now that there has been a taste of revolt, there is a need for it.

It has been also since the Commissioners left the Federation that there has taken place release of the African pressure that had been building up in the two northern territories since 1959. The Nyasaland constitutional conference in the summer indicated to both territories the route by which they would achieve self-rule under African governments: and Mr. Macleod, with his secret touch, has convinced the two significant leaders of both territories (Mr. Kaunda of Northern Rhodesia and Dr. Banda of Nyasaland) that Britain is in absolute earnest in guiding the territories along that route.

Thus, the African awakening in Southern Rhodesia is taking place in the conflicting contexts of approaching independence for the two northern territories and of entrenched European mastery in Southern Rhodesia itself. Because of the former, visions of long-forgotten dignity have been touched and aroused. But the latter immediately restricts self-esteem; the fear of inferiority intrudes and almost every man is a potential rebel because of the thing inside him.

The recent developments have deepened Southern Rhodesia's isolation from her fellows. It is the African leaders now who matter in the two northern territories, and there is little to attract them to marry their countries with a white-dominated Southern Rhodesia. Rather let Southern Rhodesia slide into ruin without the wealth of Northern Rhodesia and with African labour from Nyasaland under Nyasaland's control. Southern Rhodesia, with its 210,000 whites among two and a half million blacks, could hardly go the way of

South Africa: it would be too late to embark on an official policy of *baaskap* now. The revolt of Southern Rhodesia's Africans – the northern territories' Africans are prepared to argue – would be delayed rather than hastened by retaining it within the Federation; the considerable benefits of Federation to Southern Rhodesia would merely serve to uphold the white regime and preserve the Africans in helotry. […]

In the situation at the moment, therefore, the Africans of the northern territories are pulling away from Southern Rhodesia, and the whites of Southern Rhodesia pulling away from the northern territories. Meanwhile, whites and blacks alike in Southern Rhodesia are approaching a sullen desperation in their separate camps.

It is an indication of the appalling failure of the ideal on which the Federation was founded that Sir Edgar [Whitehead]'s territorial United Federal Party should now be so gravely threatened from the right. It is not as if seven years of supposed progress towards partnership had produced any basic changes that might have disturbed Europeans. After seven years there is not even multiracialism in hotels. Yet in their despair and fright the political attitude of the whites has hardened.

The failure of the liberal approach since the founding of the Federation in 1953 must be ascribed primarily to the reluctance of the two Federal leaders, Lord Malvern and Sir Roy Welensky, to put to the electorate what the meaning of partnership really is. No one else in Central Africa besides these two men could have carried the white population into the new concept called for by Federation, as it was genuinely envisaged by the British Government. It is hard to believe that neither Federal Prime Minister grasped what Britain intended by partnership. Yet neither has showed any appreciable inclination to project it as anything else than a useful word. Lord Malvern, in fact, spoke in Salisbury of partnership between 'the rider and the horse'. Sir Roy spoke of it as something to be achieved over the next two hundred years. […]

It is in this scene of apparently irreconcilable forces, in which the local liberals find themselves without any remaining function, that the Monckton Commissioners have stepped forward to play the liberal role. How do their proposals fit the situation? Apart from the secession clause – a magnificent red herring – their three basic suggestions are the reduction of the federal realm of authority, the widening of qualifications for the vote, and parity between the races – thirty seats each – in the Federal Assembly. This last proposal has been powerfully attacked by Sir Roy Welensky and others in the Federation as an abandonment of the principle of non-racialism in the method of selecting parliamentary representatives. Indeed it is; but the proposal is the more realistic for all that, since it is a principle that has rotted to nothing for lack of use (only about 2,000 Africans considered it worth using their vote on the present franchise at the last Federal election).

The retreat from non-racialism as a principle is emphasized by the Commission's proposal for common-roll elections to be preceded by selection of candidates on communal (i.e. racial) rolls. The effect of these proposals might well be to create two racial blocks in the Assembly, precisely balanced and equally obdurate. A majority government could be formed only if a member selected by his own race ratted to the other side. This probability of a deadlock vividly illustrates how futile it has become to attempt any longer to reach the perfect compromise.

The majority of the Commissioners reached this formula, however, because they were aware that anything less evenly matched would be rejected out of hand by one side or the other, and either Southern Rhodesia would secede or the Federation would continue under the impossible conditions of full-scale non-co-operation by the Africans of the two northern territories. Since the Commissioners left the Federation, as has been shown, the new authority of the northern territories' African leaders and the final failure of conciliation by the Southern Rhodesian white government have made it unlikely that either side can now be brought to accept even the thirty–thirty compromise offered. […]

A choice, therefore, must be made, the risk taken; and as with single colonies, the broad direction that the Federation should follow from now on must be indicated firmly and irrevocably by the British Government, and provided for constitutionally. The Commission admits that it is not possible – if only from the point of view of security – to clutch the territories in association against the will of the majority of inhabitants. Thus, three courses, singly or in combination, remain open to the British Government.

First, an African majority could be provided for in the Federal sphere in the near future. This would be to risk Southern Rhodesia's secession, but it would go far to allay the fears of the Africans in Northern Rhodesia and Nyasaland.

Alternatively, or in addition, the British Government could – even by some extreme form of coercion – ensure the fundamental liberalizing of the Southern Rhodesian Constitution, so as to bring the future of that Colony, however approximately, into line with the northern territories. Reaction among many of the whites would be sharp and bitter; but as has been suggested earlier, acknowledgement of the reality and even inevitability of the African awakening is beginning to seep into the settler mind.

Or, thirdly, the process advised by the Commission of stripping the present Federal powers to economics, defence, and foreign affairs should be carried further, leaving only broad economic co-ordination between the territories in the hands of a High Commission for the foreseeable future.

Whichever choice is made, it is essential that it be followed through with decisiveness and courage. A temporary solution would aggravate widespread unrest. […]

South Africa departs

Having adopted a republic, in order to remain in the Commonwealth South Africa had to gain the assent of the other Commonwealth members. At the

Commonwealth Prime Ministers' Meeting held in London in March 1961 it became clear that this was unlikely to be forthcoming, and the application was withdrawn. South Africa's departure from the Commonwealth was a matter of particular regret for the Round Table, *given its historical links. Fifty years on, the editor's assertion that there was nothing inherently wrong with ideas of an 'aristocracy of race' strikes an ill note (as does his talk of Britain and the former Dominions as 'seniors' within the Commonwealth), even if he was at pains to emphasize the difference between the traditional British policy of 'equal rights for every civilized man' and the new doctrine of* apartheid.

[Dermot Morrah,] 'A Leaf Falls: South Africa Outside the Commonwealth', *RT* 51/203 (June 1961), pp. 219–23

The decision of Dr. Verwoerd's Government to withdraw the Union of South Africa from the family of nations that has sheltered its growth to maturity, and go out alone into a manifestly antipathetic world, should be a matter for regret to the whole Commonwealth, and in a peculiar degree to those who have tried to serve the Commonwealth through *The Round Table.* The genesis of this review was in the Closer Union Societies, which fostered the movement to unite the four colonies of British South Africa into a single nation destined to early sovereignty; and some of its founders believed that in the process they had discovered a model for the future development of the British Empire itself. The march of events soon proved that hope to be illusory; but *The Round Table* has never ceased to take a particular interest in the fortunes of the country in which its roots were struck, and will not soon or lightly learn to think of it as an alien land. […]

Whatever doctrine of extreme democracy may be proclaimed by the more recently emancipated States of the Commonwealth in Asia and Africa, their seniors have never thought it an intolerable anomaly that one of their number should be constituted as an aristocracy of race. Many nations have passed through such a phase, not excluding England. Admittedly that was long ago; but that should be a reminder that for the Transvaal and the Orange Free State the date corresponding to 1066 is 1838, and that it is unfair to expect of a nation so young a mental and emotional outlook identical with one that has forgotten for seven centuries that it once had a problem of integrating a conquering with a subject race. In carrying racial privilege into the twentieth century South Africa is not by any means unique. It is as normal in a Commonwealth of nations as in a family of human children that some are more mature than others. Throughout the half-century of association between the Union and Great Britain it has been frankly recognized that South Africa is a country in which the races are socially segregated and politically unequal. It was as known representatives of such a society that the South African forces were gratefully welcomed as brothers-in-arms in two world wars, both fought professedly in defence of liberty and human rights. In full recognition that this was a legitimately organized community the fruitful intercourse of peace has been founded, and a close-knit web of friendship and kinship preserved between the peoples. That inequality of the races was inevitable for their time was taken for granted by all responsible South African statesmen from Rhodes to Smuts; and none of their colleagues in other sovereign regions of the Commonwealth as it then existed saw in this any obstacle to collaboration with them. So long as inequality meant that the white man led along the path of advancing civilization and the black followed, but the path itself was open to all, there was no irremediable clash of principles.

The great change can be exactly dated to the general election of 1948, when the Nationalist Party triumphed on a programme of *apartheid*, which they explicitly declared to be something different from, and more fundamental than, the old *segregasie* which both the principal parties recognized. The new term was at that time criticized by its opponents as vague and ambiguous; thirteen years of Nationalist rule have since filled out its content. Even after a decade of increasingly harsh discriminatory legislation, it is still possible to interpret the theory of *apartheid* in the comparatively favourable terms to which the old friends of the Union should be predisposed. The project of Bantustan, for example, the idea of disentangling the races so completely that the question of equality or inequality between them would not arise, is in abstraction morally unexceptionable. For economic and demographic reasons, however, the abstraction cannot be made concrete. It is impossible to challenge the judgment expressed in Parliament by Lord Brand, speaking with continuous knowledge of South Africa from days before the Union came into being:

> While *apartheid* in South Africa is not, in my opinion, wrong in principle, if it could be worked out with justice to both races, the trouble is that it is quite impracticable and cannot be achieved. For both black and white races are now too dependent on one another.

This is the essence of the matter. *Apartheid* in theory merely acknowledges that indigenous and European-descended Africans belong to different races, have different needs, and may have the best chance of attaining their fullest natural development if they are kept apart; *apartheid* in practice necessarily involves injustice to those of the dark-skinned races who have to live or work in the areas where the white man is supreme. The black man is not regarded as a being who will, in his own person or his descendants, rise and be helped to rise without limit; he and his are denied in perpetuity any escape from the status of inferiority. In contrast with Rhodes's 'equal rights for all civilized men', each individual of the race is born with an inherited curse, which cannot be lifted whatever his personal qualities or attainments. If this is not the meaning of *apartheid* – and it must be said in all fairness that it is denied not only by some of its advocates but by some friends of South Africa who do not share the creed – Dr. Verwoerd undoubtedly failed to convince the Prime Ministers in conference that it was a misrepresentation. Their reaction, and especially the reaction of those representing nations in Africa and Asia, was not against racial discrimination as a phase through which South African society is passing, but against the belief, out of which they could not be argued, that this discrimination is held by the Nationalists to be good in itself and intended to be maintained in perpetuity. This, as Lord Hailsham said for the United Kingdom Government in the debate already cited, is the change that has come about in the Union's prevailing doctrine of race in the decade since Smuts died:

> It is not that a social convenience, a temporary but unavoidable evil, has been tolerated, but that it has been advertised as a permanency, erected into a social philosophy, lauded as a virtue, almost exalted as a religion.

If that image of *apartheid* could not be dispelled, it was scarcely conceivable that African and Asian Ministers could be persuaded to make positive affirmation of their desire to renew association with the country in which it was professed as a fundamental philosophy […]

The remaining nations of the Commonwealth are bound to watch the progress of the new republic with the active hope that their help may some day be welcomed in working out some better mode of life between the races than that which finds favour with its present rulers. Though a breach has opened between us and the Nationalist Government, it is more important to remember that the people of the Union, of all races, remain our friends – a large section of them our kinsmen. Without reservations, we wish them and their country well. Perhaps the outstanding mission of the Commonwealth in the latter part of the century is to take the lead in drawing Africa into the main stream of world civilization. On that work the Union, in or out of the Commonwealth, cannot fail to exert a powerful influence. We need to maintain communication with those elements in the country which are able to think and work in harmony with the more liberal thought of the Commonwealth. Though henceforth we can speak to these only across the gulf of political separation, we shall look forward to the day when they win over the majority of the electors to their side. […]

Federation in the Caribbean

Federation was also seen as the way forward for Britain's Caribbean colonies, although in this case in order to create a viable candidate for independence rather than to perpetuate colonial domination. However, the West Indies Federation was even shorter-lived than the Central African Federation, coming into existence in 1958 but collapsing by 1962 as a result of internal political rivalries and local nationalisms. Jamaica and Trinidad and Tobago thereupon became independent. At the time, the Federation's collapse was thought to preclude independence for most of the smaller islands as separate units, and further, albeit fruitless, efforts were made to perpetuate Federation. In fact most became independent as separate states, although in some cases not for many years (St. Kitts and Nevis only achieving independence in 1983), while Montserrat, the Cayman

Islands, the Turks and Caicos Islands, and Anguilla all remained UK overseas territories.

[Lady Huggins,] 'Failure of a Federation: Causes of Breakdown in the West Indies', *RT* 52/207 (June 1962), pp. 273–78

[…] For longer than most people realize, in fact since 1922, it has been the view of successive British Governments that Federation of the West Indies should be brought about, but that this could only be done with the concurrence of the majority of the inhabitants of the territories concerned.

Why, with their background of education and culture, was nationalism not the urgent matter which it is in the African colonies? Why did the demands for self-government not come sooner? The reason is mainly because of the insular habit of mind natural to islanders, which has always stood in the way of closer relations between the different units. The islands, in addition to having their collective population of 3,153,000 very unequally divided, suffer from two grave disadvantages, one physical, and one traditional. They are widely dispersed over the Caribbean, Jamaica being over 1,000 miles to the west of the Eastern Caribbean, which stretches northwards from Trinidad to St. Kitts for a distance of over 500 miles. On the traditional side, they have had a long history of separate governments and resultant insularism.

As a result of these two factors, there has been little to link the ordinary people of the territories together, and even in racial make-up each island shows some variation. Under Colonial Office rule, each of the units was kept quite separate, with different governors, legislatures, taxation, economic development. Was this the earliest mistake of all, and the reason why Federation failed, because when we did have the power over the different areas, under Crown Colony Government, we kept them apart, rather than try to bring them closer together?

Gradually though, since the war, and during it, popular opinion was influenced towards a closer association by a number of factors. There were the common difficulties faced by the West Indies during the war, there were institutions for the whole area, such as the Imperial College of Tropical Agriculture in Trinidad, founded as early as 1924, and the University College of the West Indies, started in Jamaica after the war. The University has taught the young West Indians from all the territories the meaning of West Indian nationhood as apart from local patriotism, and the tragedy is that this feeling could not have been more widespread.

The idea slowly spread among the people of the West Indies that the linking together of the islands would improve efficiency, and inter-island trade, through the establishment of a Customs Union and unification of some branches of the Civil Service.

All this led up to the famous Montego Bay Conference, held in Jamaica in 1947, and very ably presided over by the then Secretary of State for the Colonies, Mr. Arthur Creech Jones. […]

Why had all these representatives from the various units come with such enthusiasm and interest to that first conference? It was not only that the leaders of the various territories felt that the time had come for closer consultation and association between the territories: it was because the individual units felt that alone they themselves could never become fully independent. Here was the beginning of national feeling and unity, which sadly enough was not fostered and nurtured as it should have been, when the actual Federation of the West Indies came into being. It seemed then, that the only way for them to reach a viable status was by coming together in some form of Federation, and thereby securing Dominion status. […]

One of the most vital and probably the most disastrous decisions taken was that there should not be dual membership of the Federal and local island Legislatures. Were there really enough West Indian leaders with real political experience, character and personality, to man both the Federal and Island Legislatures? This especially in islands where the personality of the politician is of such tremendous importance.[4] […]

Added to this, was the appointment of Lord Hailes as Governor General really the right one? Everyone who knows the West Indies well, and has watched events since the inauguration of the Federation, will pay a tribute to Lord and Lady Hailes. They have done a tremendous job, worked very hard, showed a splendid understanding of the racial set-up in the West Indies; but all the same, how could they know the intricacies of West Indian politics, and the characters of the West Indian politicians they were dealing with? Was this the third mistake? Should Sir Hugh Foot, now one of our Ambassadors at the UN, have been given the appointment? He had a great understanding and a great affection for the West Indies, and might have been better able to deal with the rivalries between Jamaica and Trinidad and the smaller units, or the Little Eight, as they are now being called.

In addition to this, there were other factors which certainly contributed to the breakdown of the Federation, and the fact that Jamaica seceded, to be followed by Trinidad, thereby making the Federation as founded in 1958 impossible to work.

With Jamaica 1,000 miles away from Trinidad, and with more than half the population of the entire Federation, surely there should have been enough foresight to give them either the Federal capital, or the Federal Prime Minister? As it was, the Federal capital was sited in Trinidad, and the Federal Prime Minister came from Barbados. With the insularity bred for centuries, the ordinary men and women in the street felt the Federation was very remote from their everyday lives. […]

Jamaica becomes an independent nation within the Commonwealth on August 6 this year. Much more than many already independent countries in the Commonwealth, Jamaica is well able to govern itself. There is an efficient Jamaican Civil Service, a strong two-party political system, a great many well-educated and cultured people, a booming economy, with revenue from bauxite added to agriculture, many new factories and industries, and a strong sense of Jamaican nationhood.

The colony of Trinidad and Tobago is making moves now for independence, and will also be viable like Jamaica. […]

What of the future of the Little Eight? A Conference took place in May in London with the Colonial Secretary, Mr. Maudling, and the Ministers and their advisers of the Little Eight. It was agreed that there should be a Federation of Barbados and the Windward and Leeward Islands, to be called the West Indies Federation, with its capital in Barbados. The form to be taken by both Federal and Unit Legislatures will be set out in a White paper, which will be referred to the Unit Governments for full discussion and approval, after an interval for full public discussion in the territories. This is most important, for the people themselves, from the ground up, must show real desire and decision to federate. Final decisions about the form of the new Federation and the date for Independence will be reached at a later date. The most important factor is that the new Federal Government, when it is set up, should be strong, in both political and economic matters. […]

One can foresee in the future that the independent nations of Jamaica and Trinidad, and the Federation of the Little Eight, if this takes place, which seems nearly certain, will get together eventually of their own free will to form some kind of Union. These are a sensible people, and it must make sense for them to be one nation, perhaps joined by British Guiana and British Honduras.

It may not be too long before we see the West Indians themselves decide the time has come to become one nation, one people, with a great future lying ahead of them.

The Commonwealth under attack

On 2 April 1964 The Times *published an article entitled 'Patriotism Based on Reality Not on Dreams', by 'A Conservative' (widely rumoured, and subsequently revealed, to be Enoch Powell). In this, Powell described the Commonwealth as a 'gigantic farce': a mere 'ghost' of the British empire, but one which constrained British policy on immigration, trade, defence and other matters, and which therefore exercised a positively deleterious effect on Britain. The article was but the most striking expression of a view increasingly common in Britain. In the 1960s and 1970s, the* Round Table *expended much ink attempting to counter such views, although, as in this article, it tended to do so elliptically rather than head-on.*

[Timothy Raison,] 'Is the Commonwealth a Farce? An Answer to "A Conservative"', *RT* 54/215 (June 1964), pp. 215–21

During the past year or two Britain has been involved in a reappraisal – searching if not agonizing – of her institutions, her economic vitality, her education and, above all, her role in the world. This reappraisal, which will undoubtedly shape the result of the forthcoming general election, was responsible for our unsuccessful bid to enter the Europe of the Six. Today, one of its focal points is the future of the Commonwealth.

Looking back, it seems clear that the British negotiation with the EEC [European Economic Community] and the Commonwealth Prime Ministers' conference which took place during that negotiation in September 1962 caused many people in the Commonwealth countries to ask the question which was raised so dramatically by the writer (or writers) who signed himself (or themselves) 'A Conservative' in *The Times* of April 2: is the Commonwealth a farce? 'A Conservative', whose identity is still a subject of speculation, had no doubt of the answer: the Commonwealth is not merely a farce but a 'gigantic farce' at that. But the readers of *The Times* scarcely seemed to agree, for this particular article provoked a vigorous and overwhelmingly hostile response.

Nor, it is becoming increasingly clear, do the leaders of the two major political parties in Britain accept that view. Ever since Mr. Gaitskell's famous speech at the 1962 Labour Party conference, Labour has increasingly been seen as a defender of the Commonwealth connexion. Though there are some passionate and able 'Europeans' in the party, the majority of Labour's leaders have been keen to emphasize the potential of the Commonwealth in helping rich and poor and in bringing different races and colours closer together. […]

But what of the Conservative Party, traditionally the party of the Commonwealth? The position here is more confused. Undoubtedly, Mr. Macmillan and Mr. Heath saw entry into Europe as the overriding aim of British policy, and were prepared to risk annoying the Commonwealth countries to achieve it. (In fairness to them it must be said that they believed that Britain in Europe, strong economically and politically, might be able to do more for the Commonwealth than she could if she remained outside the EEC.) Undoubtedly, too, the attraction of the EEC lives on, whether in the Conservative parliamentary party, among some influential conservative intellectuals or in business; while part of the press – notably *The Economist* and perhaps the *Daily Telegraph* – remains as strongly as ever committed to British membership of the Common Market. Yet the fact remains that the curious lack of regret felt in Britain as a whole at de Gaulle's termination of the Brussels talks applies to many Conservatives, who still feel that if Britain has a destiny in the world it lies in a wider setting than the continent of Europe alone. […]

In these, as in other ways, there is a good deal of evidence that it is too sweeping to say, as a New Zealand broadcaster, Alexander MacLeod, suggested not long ago, that Britain is bored with the Commonwealth. Yet it must be admitted that he had some grounds for his assertion that 'if there is one single lesson to be learned from Britain's year of exile, it's that Britain herself shows little sign of recognizing, of her own accord, the importance her partners attach to belonging to a great, though perhaps dying, association. Without being reminded, I fear, she won't regain her own enthusiasm. And she won't understand the enthusiasm and needs of others'.[5] The view which Mr. MacLeod attributed to some people in Britain – that the Commonwealth was conjured up to save British self-esteem while the Empire dissolved and the country got used to being Little England – is one with which the *Times* 'Conservative' at least would undoubtedly agree. Nor would he be alone, for all the signs of resurgent interest in the Commonwealth which may be detected. […]

But what *is* the modern view of the Commonwealth? What *are* the answers to the *Times* 'Conservative'? What is the bond that means or might mean something in the face of such stresses as those which exist between neutralists and westerners, different colours and races, rich and poor, India and Pakistan, one-party State and Westminster democracy and so on? What can there be in common between nations spread across the five continents and a wide ideological spectrum? […]

But there is much to be done if the full potential of the Commonwealth is to be achieved. Some ideas were listed recently in a broadcast by S. C. Leslie. They may not all be right, but they are worth considering.

> On the political side, the machinery of consultation could be extended and the tempo quickened. There could be a Commonwealth consultative assembly with a standing secretariat; prime ministers could meet rather more often; other ministers could hold functional gatherings as finance ministers do now – ministers of commerce, transport, education, what you will; conferences of civil servants in various spheres could be developed. On the economic side, the proposals that have been responsibly put forward include an export council with regional subdivisions – and remember that business attitudes can be at least as potent as fiscal mechanics in increasing trade; a development council to analyse, discuss and co-ordinate plans for growth; a Commonwealth bank, or more positive banking policies by Britain as the manager of the Sterling Area; more collaboration in maintaining the central reserves and more co-ordination of balance of payments policies among its members; long-term bilateral trading arrangements not involving tariff changes; the appointment in member countries of ministers for Commonwealth trade; the adoption and active promulgation of a more ambitious programme of financial and technical aid, with specific targets; and finally, and in the long run perhaps the most important of all, the resolute development and extension of the network of educational links, exchanges, and assistance programmes, which are part of the very fibre of the partnership: a Commonwealth university has been mentioned.[6]

But in some ways it is not on developing institutions that the Commonwealth ultimately depends; it is not even on the development of a spirit of unity. The essence of the Commonwealth should be above all that it is a relaxed association. In a world where many pressures lead towards conformity, rigidity and the formation of tight blocks, the Commonwealth can help to ease tensions, to make life both more pleasant and more fruitful. It does this through the blend of friendships and common language, systems, traditions and communications which characterize it; and through the fact that its members have so much to give to each other.

An understanding of the last point is essential if the true potential of the Commonwealth is to be achieved. The Commonwealth is a fine instrument for aiding the poorer nations. But at the same time the poorer countries have also a good deal to give to their fellow members of the Commonwealth. Their coffers may be empty but their cultures have riches which we are beginning to appreciate – the gaiety and spontaneity of West Indians or West Africans, for example, or the subtlety and fairness of Indians. We must exploit the fact of relationships between free peoples, while aiming not for a forced cohesion but for the frankness of maturity. In this sort of way, we can demonstrate that it is not the Commonwealth which is a farce but A Conservative who is a farceur.

Notes

1 I.e. Basutoland (Lesotho), Bechuanaland (Botswana) and Swaziland, which at the time came under the authority of the British High Commissioner in South Africa, but whose control the white politicians in South Africa coveted.
2 In fact, Ceylon only became a republic (as Sri Lanka) in 1972.
3 Hodson himself: see previous extract, pp. 99–102.
4 In particular, Norman Manley chose to remain premier of Jamaica and Eric Williams chose to remain premier of Trinidad.
5 New Zealand *Listener*, 13 March 1964; MacLeod subsequently joined the *Round Table* editorial board, in 1975.
6 *The Listener* (UK), 6 February 1964; Leslie also subsequently joined the editorial board, in 1966.

Part 6

The modern Commonwealth (1965–2010)

The Commonwealth Secretariat

Since the 1920s the Round Table *had argued for a secretariat independent of the British government to organize Commonwealth meetings and co-ordinate Commonwealth diplomacy. This idea was opposed, however, by successive British governments, who wished to retain the leading role in the Commonwealth. When finally the proposal was agreed, the British government initially viewed the Secretariat with some suspicion, as the memoirs of the first Secretary-General, Arnold Smith, make clear. While the Secretariat was to prove rather more than the 'clearing house' advocated by Kwame Nkrumah, it was nevertheless rather less than the 'confederal institution' hailed by the* Round Table.

[Dermot Morrah,] 'A Commonwealth Secretariat: The First Confederal Institution', *RT* 55/217 (December 1964), pp. 3–5

When *The Round Table* first set out to pose the dilemma of Empire – the question how liberty and self-government in the Dominions could be reconciled with their involvement in the foreign and defence policy of the mother country, in formulating which they had no voice – its founders insisted at every turn that a solution should not, and probably could not, be imposed from the centre. It should come by the initiative of the oversea [*sic*] dominions themselves, shouldering their share of the burden of imperial defence, and claiming their right to participate in its control.

The particular solution most discussed in the early days of the review was that of federation or organic union, on similar principles to those embodied in the Constitution of the United States of America. Any hope of winning general consent to such a degree of centralization foundered, as we can now retrospectively see, in the First World War. The Dominions, led by Canada, their sovereignty internationally recognized when they signed the peace treaties as high contracting parties, set their faces for many years against the creation of any central institutions of government; for every such proposal was suspected to conceal an insidious hankering of Whitehall after the reintroduction of United Kingdom control. Now that after half a century the Prime Ministers meeting in London have at last consented to set up a Commonwealth

Secretariat, it must be regarded, not as an approach to federation, but as the first Con-federal institution. But the early argument of *The Round Table* is to this extent vindicated, that the new body has been projected on the initiative of the oversea members themselves. Even Canada has ceased to be suspicious; and the many younger members emancipated in recent years show their confidence and political maturity by being quite free of the fear that, by asking for a common organ of co-operation, they are in any way jeopardizing their new independence.

Although the location of the new secretariat in London is a practical necessity, for the Commonwealth must have a centre, it is important to maintain in its working the same impulse from oversea to which its foundation responded. […] The secretariat is to be conceived as a joint organ of the oversea members of the Commonwealth, linking them to one another as well as to the United Kingdom; and it is placed in London solely because that is at present the most convenient node of Commonwealth communications. […]

The mode of its recruitment has yet to be defined. There is no visible governing body short of the Prime Ministers' Conference itself. It is reasonable to suppose that, through the current channels of consultation while the Conference is not in session, some committee of officials will be set up charged with general supervision and with selecting at least a Secretary General and his Deputy. After that it would be desirable to allow these heads of the organization the principal voice in choosing their subordinates. The secretariat is hardly likely to offer its staff a career for life, nor is it desirable that it should, for then there would be a danger of their becoming in effect immigrant denizens of the United Kingdom and losing their capacity to represent the Commonwealth. It would be more natural for them to be enlisted for a term of years by secondment from the civil or diplomatic services of their respective countries. They will need to be drawn from all its widely separated regions; but it would be a mistake to insist on a mathematical distribution. Every state of the Commonwealth should, over the years, contribute some of its subjects to the staff; but it is not necessary that each and all should be represented at any one time. It is far more important that the Secretary General should be free to select and lead a small team, whose personal distinction will command the confidence of the authorities with whom he has to deal. […]

The great function and value of the secretariat is to provide, what has often been found defective, lines of communication running, so to speak, round the rim of the Commonwealth wheel, rather than along the spokes leading to and from the centre. This function is quite distinct from any hitherto discharged by the Commonwealth Relations Office [CRO], although there are also some aspects of the work of that office that it will be natural for the secretariat to take over. It needs, incidentally, to be kept constantly in mind that the operative words are 'take over', not 'duplicate'. […]

One function that must certainly be taken over by the secretariat is the organization of the Prime Ministers' meetings themselves. This was for long the business of the British Cabinet Office, which at one time tended to exclude the CRO, though not so much in 1964 as on some previous occasions. Whether through the one office or the other, Great Britain has borne the responsibility too long, and its transfer to the collective shoulders of the Commonwealth should be warmly welcomed. Even the attempt to keep British control of the agenda for the meetings is a temptation to be resisted.

There have been three main lines of criticism of the project in the United Kingdom. To some it seems a manifestation of ingratitude for the services of the mother country to the Commonwealth in the years of tutelage. Undoubtedly at the last meeting there were signs of resentment by the visiting Prime Ministers at what they thought was their British colleagues' desire to score political points – perhaps reflecting dissatisfaction with their relationship to the CRO. But this, if it existed, was an ephemeral sentiment: the lasting reality is the sense of maturity among the junior members. There is nothing ungrateful or unfilial in the wish to be recognized as adult.

Secondly, there is the fear that the new organization will grow without limit; and that undoubtedly is a danger to be closely watched – perhaps most vigilantly by the score of Commonwealth Treasuries. And thirdly, there is the fear that the secretariat will become a begging agency. As to that, the days of central support and, in one form or another, subsidies to the less prosperous Commonwealth peoples are certainly not over. Having pride in our imperial tradition we should be glad to be munificent, and must rely on the Commonwealth secretariat to keep us informed of what our more needy fellow-subjects want.

Finally, the secretariat should be ready to fortify the Commonwealth at one of its points of potential weakness – the difficulty of securing combined action in time of urgent emergency. It is not only between Washington and Moscow that a 'hot line' is necessary. In this special department, unlike diplomacy, relations for the Commonwealth are not bilateral. They are multilateral by nature, and an organization is required for quickly securing multilateral decisions when danger threatens. This could be the most vital, though the least frequent, of the many services to be expected of the Commonwealth Secretariat.

UDI in Rhodesia

As was the case with South Africa, the existence of white minority rule in (Southern) Rhodesia was the cause of bitter arguments within the Round Table *editorial board. The minority regime's Unilateral Declaration of Independence (UDI) in November 1965 to an extent resolved the issue, since the challenge to law as well as to Commonwealth principles was overt. Unlike the British government the* Round Table *favoured a robust response. Nevertheless it was as yet unwilling to endorse the principle of immediate majority rule, and instead argued for a period of direct rule by Britain, during which African capacity for self-government could be built up.*

[Leonard Beaton,] 'A Policy for Rhodesia: Direct Rule by Britain',
RT 56/222 (March 1966), pp. 107–11

The Rhodesian Government's decision to seize independence was both comprehensible and disastrously wrong. Mr. Ian Smith has forced on his country the British rule which it has never really had before. How that rule will come and after what suffering remains to be seen. But there can be no choice open to the British Government but an establishment of its own authority in Rhodesia and a substantial period of direct rule. This may not appeal to the proud and independent ruling minority in Rhodesia who have played so great a part in making it a prosperous country; but it offers them their best hope of moving towards a system of national government which will sustain and develop all that they have achieved.

The strong belief in Rhodesia that direct rule is out of the question is eloquently expressed in this issue of *The Round Table* by Rhodesian and South African correspondents.[1] It is rapidly becoming doctrine among British Conservatives. Many who have visited Rhodesia since the Smith declaration believe that British rule is out of the question. They argue that Britain has not taken any serious part in the rule of the country for 43 years; that the military facts are such that British intervention would be exceedingly difficult (and has in any case not been tried); and that the legalities must catch up with the facts of power after a greater or lesser pause.

The British Government cannot and should not accept this line of argument. Local Rhodesian rule has been an undoubted fact since 1923: but it was rule on certain conditions which have become more explicit as the objectives of colonial rule have become more clearly defined. The fact that law and power had become divorced was an unpleasant one with potentially dangerous implications. Since these dangers have now been realized, the British Government must make a choice: will it stand on the facts of law or will it stand on the facts of power as they now are? It has no option but to stand by the legal position and bring the facts of power into line. There are two main reasons for this. First, it has been openly and blatantly humiliated in territory which the whole world considered to be under British authority. The attempts by Mr. Harold Wilson to head off a declaration of independence by making concessions constituted a sufficient humiliation. When these were rejected, a people worthy of the world's respect had no choice but to bring the situation under their control. Secondly, it would be wrong to leave the territory under the control of a small minority, however much they may represent the most advanced elements of the population. Government on the basis of race is bad government and can only endure by becoming steadily worse. To embark Rhodesia on independence on the basis of its present system of government would be bad for Rhodesia, bad for Africa and bad for the world. It would solve nothing and would be most unlikely to get rid of the problem. There is no basis for an enduring political system in Rhodesia at present: and in these circumstances, Britain should not abandon her responsibility.

All this has been argued at length by the African Commonwealth countries and by many on the left in Britain. But generally speaking they seem to be as little interested in national government in Rhodesia as Mr. Smith's followers. They talk of majority rule by which they seem to mean that all power should be transferred at an early date to elective institutions. They can hardly be blamed for thinking that Rhodesia should go the way of Algeria. Like Mr. Smith, they are assuming that British rule must soon end and they are asking the British Government to see that its heirs are Black. The rebellion (or UDI) was caused ultimately by the conviction of Rhodesians that while legality remained in London they were faced with a serious danger of Black African rule with the British Government as the agent. These fears are being reinforced by the belief that Britain's attempts to get control of Rhodesia are aimed exclusively at this objective. Any suggestion that British policy is governed by the views of the African Commonwealth countries helps to reinforce this conviction.

There are two fundamental reasons why it is no more justifiable for the British Government to turn over Rhodesia to the majority than to leave it in the hands of the present minority. The first is that in the present circumstances this would lead to a break up of White Rhodesian society and the ruin of the economy. It is on this economy that the prospects for African education and progress depend. The sheer wealth which is generated by the Rhodesian economy is quite as fundamental to the future of Central Africa as the constitutional arrangements. The second reason is that a rapid transfer of power to one group in so divided a society would mean that the White minority would be denied their reasonable rights. Britain's ultimate responsibility for Rhodesia – now so clearly reaffirmed before the world – cannot be surrendered to any group which can be expected to deny any substantial part of the population its proper rights.

There is therefore no good alternative to direct British responsibility for the government of Rhodesia for a substantial period of time. How long that is will be determined by the speed with which the true basis for national rule is laid. It could be a generation. […]

The two objectives of British rule in Rhodesia must be to develop the existing political and economic order and to ensure that all rights and opportunities are totally non-racial. Full self-government will be possible and desirable when the African middle class has grown to such proportions that partnership is easy. The key to this is education and job opportunities – and, of course, the wealth to make both these possible. It is in these decisive areas of government that British authority must be exercised when and if direct rule can be achieved. There is no inconsistency between the interests of White Rhodesians and the interests of Black Rhodesians in developing a strong and prosperous economy and an educated population. Their only clash is about who is to be master. Once it can be asserted that neither is to be master the great work of developing a single country with a strong economy can begin again.

The necessary constitutional and administrative arrangements should be given careful and urgent study. They are by no means obvious. It is possible that the anomaly of British sovereignty without power might recur in the form of nominal British rule without an administration able and willing to give it effect. Difficult problems must be faced about the status of the Governor, the character and powers of his executive and the kind of parliamentary institutions which are desirable in the next few years. Clearly, the idea of direct rule does not mean Whitehall rule over domestic Rhodesian issues. What must be constructed is a system of political control which maintains an equal system of law and justice; in which economic growth and education progress to the greatest possible extent; and in which all races enjoy the fruits of this progress equally. […]

One of the most remarkable aspects of the Rhodesian situation has been the moderating influence of the Commonwealth. The vigorous use of Commonwealth machinery by Mr. Wilson has helped enormously in maintaining trust in the British Government's intentions on the part of African states. It is not the machinery which has been particularly important – though it has enabled such Prime Ministers as Mr. Lester Pearson to play a constructive part in reaching compromises. It is the trust which lies behind it. The decision of the late Prime Minister of Nigeria, Sir Abubakar Balewa, to call a Commonwealth Conference in Lagos was an act of statesmanship of the highest order in the face of the intolerant and hostile views of the Organization for African Unity. It was, of course, also a wise action from the African point of view because it created a context in which the maximum influence could be brought to bear on the British Government. If all African states had responded as intemperately as Ghana and Tanzania and had broken off diplomatic relations with the one country which can do anything for the Black African population of Rhodesia, all African influence on the situation would be distant and indirect. […]

A South African correspondent writes of Rhodesia in these pages as a tragedy.[2] It has certainly been a tragic story through the great failures in partnership of recent years. But tragedies end and the curtain comes down. In the history of a country, there is no end. It is a continuous story with its happy periods and its disasters. To say that partnership is impossible in Rhodesia is to say that the Whites must leave or that the Blacks must be a subject people. Either of these is possible but either would be a disgrace to those who have been and are responsible. Partnership will take many years to achieve, but the alternatives are unacceptable. Rhodesia marks the end, at least for the present, of imperial withdrawal. The whole world is asking that Britain should herself provide the country with the government which is domestically impossible. The responsibility cannot be avoided. First White Rhodesia and then Black Africa must accept the fact that there is no basis for a transfer of power to Rhodesians in the next decade at least. […]

The Commonwealth in the 1960s

How far from being a mere relic of empire the Commonwealth was by the mid-1960s is made clear in this article by the organization's first Secretary-General, Arnold Smith. His emphasis on the Commonwealth's diversity and its potential role in bridging the divide especially between economically developed and economically developing countries were themes which at this time appeared frequently in other Round Table *articles. Indeed, Smith's approach encapsulated much of what was written in favour of the Commonwealth at this time.*

Arnold Smith, 'The Need for Commonwealth: Resisting a Fragmented World', *RT* 56/223 (July 1966), pp. 219–27

The Commonwealth association as we now know it has its links with the British Empire and all that this past represents to what are now the 23 states of the Commonwealth. But its formal existence was a product of something different: the series of forward-looking decisions by hard-headed statesmen in Africa, Asia, the Mediterranean and the Caribbean which expanded the old close grouping to something much larger and more varied.

Australia, Britain, Canada and New Zealand worked out methods of easy consultation and practical co-operation without rigid commitments. They were an apparently homogeneous group. Whether or not they were really homogeneous, there can be no doubt that the present Commonwealth group is important precisely because it is not homogeneous. Indeed, it can fairly claim to be a typical cross-section of all mankind with important peoples from virtually all of the main races and virtually all continents. It includes the very big, such as India, Pakistan and Nigeria, and the very small, such as The Gambia, Trinidad and Singapore.

That we are varied, no-one can deny. Certain other negatives must also be stated. The Commonwealth is not a power-bloc. Membership does not involve any legal obligations to other members. There is no written constitution. If one thinks of political activity and institutions in terms of social engineering or architectural blueprints, it is easy to conclude that the Commonwealth has no real existence.

The engineering and blueprint approaches have their valid place in politics, though if over-emphasized they can be dangerous. But there is another and more profound approach to politics and history, which can be conveyed by the metaphors of gardening. The gardener's approach is organic rather than static. It has more humility, seeking to guide rather than control. It also recognizes that when we are dealing with life and growth, the intangible is even more important than the tangible. In politics as in other aspects of relations between men, the key factor is the human spirit. The laws of economic or geographic determinism can sometimes help us discern the conditions in which the human spirit has to operate; but it is the psychological factors that really shape the future. What matters most, in shaping history, are such intangibles as attitudes, values, intuitions, motivation, faith. It is in this field that the Commonwealth operates.

During the 1920s and 1930s and even 1940s, there were many proposals to make the Commonwealth into a sort of power-bloc, with unified policy in the key fields of foreign affairs and defence. In those days, the proposals to set up the central machinery of a Secretariat were linked with this concept. The

Commonwealth then consisted of a few countries, all relatively rich, essentially of European and mainly Anglo-Saxon origin. […]

Today, no-one can realistically think of the Commonwealth as an Anglo-Saxon club, or a rich man's club. Nations of significant Anglo-Saxon origin are a very small minority – some 10 per cent of the people and four out of the 23 member countries. The decisions of Jawaharlal Nehru and some other Asian leaders to join the Commonwealth, and the similar decision 10 years later by Kwame Nkrumah, soon followed by many other African leaders, were not based on backward-looking sentimentality. On the contrary, they represented a courageous and conscious transcending of their own and their people's natural resentment at years of colonial subjection, racial discrimination, political struggle and, in many cases, personal experience of jail. The decision was taken because these leaders saw practical value for their countries in building on the positive aspects of an association that linked races and continents, and in forgiving past injustices. […]

The potential significance of the Commonwealth association in world politics must, of course, be measured by assessing the trends and major problems in world affairs, and the relevance of Commonwealth members to these problems. Here there are several points worth noting. In the first place the world is rapidly becoming smaller and more interdependent. With technological developments in man's ability to travel quickly, to exchange news and views, to trade or to hurl weapons, the planet is rapidly becoming one neighbourhood. That is merely a fact; but a comparable development of good neighbourliness would be a moral and political achievement. It cannot yet be taken for granted. Indeed, our greatest problem is how to make our progress in this moral and political field keep pace with that of technology.

There is another factor worth considering. This is that the line between the white races and the other races coincides (not completely, but much too close for comfort) with that between the affluent industrialized societies on the one hand, and the poorer developing or under-developed societies on the other hand. This coincidence, coupled with the growing gap between the haves and the have-nots, enormously increases the scope for malice, uncharitableness, fear and even hatred between major segments of humanity.

It is against all this background that the potential significance of the Commonwealth needs to be assessed. In the first 40 years of this century, the most dangerous problems in world politics were, I suppose, those involved in relations between the nation states of Europe. It was these that led us into two world wars. For eighteen years or so after 1945 the most dangerous and difficult problems may have been those involved in Western relations with the Soviet Union. But I think that in the decades ahead the most important, the most difficult, and if we mishandle them potentially the most dangerous problems in world politics, are in the broader sphere of relations between different races, different civilizations, between the industrialized countries and the developing or under-developed nations, between the rich and the poor.

And it is precisely in this area that Commonwealth relationships can help. The Commonwealth represents on a scale that is more than that of a pilot plant, but nevertheless much smaller and more manageable than that of the United Nations, a fair cross-section of humanity and of its problems. It is about a quarter of mankind. And there are a number of common factors which can make co-operation and understanding easier to achieve among this group. Though only a minority of Commonwealth citizens have English as their native tongue, the members of governments, senior officials, businessmen, pressmen and educators, can use English easily as a working language. There are a number of relatively similar political, administrative, organizational and educational traditions in fields as varied as the rule of law, military staff procedures, the concept of nonpartisan Civil Service, and the ideal (if not always the practice) of freedom of the press. Above all, there are habits of frank, informal and private consultation. […]

Among other things, the Commonwealth is an instrument for taking political leaders and officials from a wide range of countries, and rubbing them together every now and then. Over a period of time intimate contacts and friendships are built up between influential people in various fields and these can prove invaluable. Often, of course, the meetings discuss problems on which agreement is not reached nor even sought. Even so, the discussion can prove tremendously important. It can, for example, lessen self-righteousness, which has proved so dangerous and unlovely an emotion throughout history. It can broaden horizons. The transcending sense of fellowship makes it less likely that disagreements on certain topics will rub off to hinder co-operation in others: and usually views and policies, even on thorny subjects, are at least somewhat harmonized. This is not the same thing as co-ordination, but it is no less important if our aim is to make the world safe for diversity, as I think it should be.

Julius Nyerere, a great African revolutionary, and now President of Tanzania, described the Commonwealth in the following terms:

> Stronger than treaties, less selfish than alliances, less restrictive than any other associations, the Commonwealth seems to my colleagues and myself to offer the best hope in the world today of lasting peace and friendship among the peoples of the world. … More than any other group of nations in the world today, the Commonwealth binds together in friendship and in like-mindedness an astonishing variety of nations great and small, without distinction between them and without discrimination amongst them.

This emphasis on equality of members is, of course, very important. The fact that such limited central machinery as the Commonwealth possesses is now in the hands, not of the British Cabinet Secretariat or its Commonwealth Relations Office, but of a mixed-manned secretariat headed by an official selected by and responsible only to the Heads of Government of all the

Commonwealth countries collectively, illustrates and symbolizes this equality. Britain is one member among the others. The establishment of a Commonwealth Secretariat also illustrates, I think, the desire of the member governments to be able to co-operate more closely in the future, in fields where this seems pragmatically desirable, without sacrificing any of the flexibility of the association. Contrary to the fears of those who in previous decades opposed proposals to set up a Secretariat – that it would involve centralizing power in the hands of Downing Street – the establishment of the Secretariat has marked a further stage in the devolution of the Commonwealth away from Anglo-centrism toward the equality of all the members. […]

It is, I suggest, only the blind who see in the Commonwealth the Emperor's new clothes. Those who have eyes to see will perceive in the Commonwealth a device for broadening the horizons of its members, and for getting international co-operation on the problems revealed by this stretched awareness. The Commonwealth association is based not on sentimentality about the past, but rather on intimations of a possible and desirable future.

British entry into Europe

Britain's applications to join the European Economic Community were interpreted by many (mainly among their opponents) as evidence of a shift away from the Commonwealth; indeed, Hugh Gaitskell, leader of the British Labour Party, had in 1962 cited Britain's obligations to its Commonwealth partners as the primary reason for opposing British membership. Despite a number of editorial board members opposing British entry, in general the journal was more favourable. Amongst the points put forward in editorials were that the EEC and the Commonwealth dealt with different matters; that British membership would actually benefit its Commonwealth partners (for instance, by putting a brake on the tendency towards protectionism in the EEC); but above all that Britain should no more be constrained in pursuing its national interests by its membership of the Commonwealth than any other member would expect to be.

[Michael Howard and Robert Jackson,] 'Britain, the Commonwealth and Europe', *RT* 61/244 (October 1971), pp. 431–45

[…] The effects of economic and military interdependence, and of the beginnings of the transformation of popular attitudes to authority and national identity have been particularly felt by the States of continental western Europe. Their prosperity since 1945 has been a sudden and rapid growth. The close proximity of national economic centres in the Continent has sharpened the sense of interdependence. And their individual weakness over against the United States and the Soviet bloc has helped to articulate their consciousness of vulnerability and mutual dependence. The 'European' forms taken by this sense of mutual dependence were largely determined by political factors. The United States […] gave active encouragement to the movement towards a European regional identity. At the same time the authority of the continental European States was weakened by the experience of defeat in war, which exposed their institutional weaknesses and shattered the charisma of tradition. The two new States in Germany had no authority that was not conferred upon them by their victorious enemies, and by the continuing success of their economic arrangements. The French State preserved a damaged legitimacy by the personal intercession of General de Gaulle, and it was twice reconstituted by the sovereign people after 1944.

In nearly all of these respects the experience of continental Western Europe has differed from that of Britain. In the nineteenth century she had accustomed herself, at first with relish but later with increasing unease – reflected in the foundation of *The Round Table* – to a relationship of economic interdependence with the world outside the British isles. Her people had long reconciled themselves to their dependence upon the Commonwealth system and their special relationships within the English-speaking world. While the States of western Europe had become accustomed to regard one another as rivals, the British people had built up a partnership with a large part of the world outside Europe. After the United States entered the Second World War Britain shared – but with some imperialist reservations – in her globalist aspirations. She certainly did not see herself as merely an element in an emerging regional entity in western Europe. The legitimacy of the British State had not been undermined but was reinforced by the events of the war and eventual victory. During the conflict and its after-glow, the authority of tradition and that of rationality seemed to have achieved in Britain a unique unity, so that every development of British policy, even under the Labour government, was best defended as a development of the past.

But British history since the early 1950s demonstrates that she also has been increasingly affected by the processes which have sapped both the actuality of national independence and the will to be independent in the nation states of western Europe. And the historic reversal of British policy which has occurred since 1957 is almost as much a measure of this as it is of the dynamic magnetism of European developments and of the weakening of other relationships outside Europe.

For as western Europe has been moving into a post-national era, the Commonwealth has almost completed its evolution towards the national self-expression of its constituent parts in sovereign States. […] The historical process implicit in the British principle of nationality destroyed the 'first' British Empire in the late eighteenth century, and overtook the worlds of its 'second' and 'third' successors in the nineteenth and twentieth centuries. The global system of economic and strategic interdependence which constituted the Empire in its last stages was dissolved by the efforts and effects of the Second World War. Together with the British sense of being a world-power this system had made up the bony structure of the Empire–Commonwealth. Today it is mainly the nervous system that remains.

But a comparison between the presently existing mutual relations of the members of the European Communities with those of the members of the Commonwealth should remind us of how much survives in the Commonwealth and how much further 'Europe' has to go. With respect to formal institutions the Commonwealth has a single Head and a common citizenship; but it has no operative supranational institutions comparable with the agencies which exist within the European Communities. Most members of the Commonwealth share a common reserve currency, and they have in common the recent memory of operating as a tightly-knit monetary bloc. These attributes of unity still lie a long way ahead for Europe. The EEC countries have a common foreign and defence policy – but only within the framework of NATO, from which France has partially excluded herself. The countries of the Commonwealth made it clear between the two world wars, in which nevertheless they fought together with Britain, that the Commonwealth had no common foreign or defence policy. Since the last war, however, the Commonwealth has supplied the framework for a wide range of alliances and security arrangements. Within the EEC there has been some progress towards the freeing of investment; within the Commonwealth the free flow of investment, at least from Britain, has only recently been curtailed. The European countries have just achieved the freedom of migration which was abandoned by Britain within the Commonwealth only eight years ago. But the 'post-entry' barriers to immigration, including access to civic rights and the interchangeability of professional qualifications, continue to be greater within Europe than inside the Commonwealth. Similarly, freedom of trade within the Commonwealth is subject to only slightly greater tariff obstacles than are to be found within the Common Market. Europe has been able to achieve a greater harmonization of social policies than exists within the Commonwealth – outside the even more highly developed relations which exist between the more advanced countries of the Old Commonwealth. The Community's approach to a common legal framework has encountered obstacles that do not exist within the Commonwealth. […]

To the extent that its members feel that the Commonwealth has been able to confer freedom only at the price of incoherence, the Commonwealth experience suggests that it will indeed be difficult for Europe to construct a multinational order which is at the same time liberal and democratic. A sustained political effort will be required to build 'Europe', effort of a kind which must inevitably distort and deflect the internal life of the member states from the channels of national self-expression. Whatever solutions may be found to the problems of 'democratic representation' at the highest levels in the European Community, this deflection of national purposes will probably be subjectively perceived as a loss of liberties – if not worse. The Commonwealth experience suggests that part of the price of internal cohesion is sustained external pressure. He who wants Europe to succeed must pray for bad weather.

Meanwhile, the Commonwealth continues: and it is probable that once the effort of Britain's entry into Europe has been accomplished there will be a welcome revival of concern for the future of the Commonwealth relationship, both in Britain and in the other countries who have suffered with her in the Gaullist antechamber. This revival will probably be assisted by the interest in the countries of the Commonwealth that will certainly be shown by Britain's new partners in Europe. […]

We must continue to reaffirm the continued value of the Commonwealth both as an example and as a living experience. Beside its value in improving the quality of international communication – of which only one element is communication between governments – the Commonwealth continues to offer a set of relationships which transcend national self-assertion, racial arrogance, and regional parochialism. It provides a *connexion* (perhaps an eighteenth-century word serves best) within which a wide range of national States, including the United Kingdom, can define a role which is not merely regional in character. The Commonwealth both as a fact of history and as a continuing aspiration helps to keep open human relationships which can only become more valuable as the years pass.

In a purely practical way the countries of the Commonwealth must adjust to British membership of the European Community just as they adapted to the special relationship with the United States. They must be prepared to exploit it in the same way. Often the best route to Brussels may be by air through Frankfurt; but there will be many occasions on which it will lie through London. While the European embassies continue to coexist with the art galleries and motor-car showrooms of fashionable Mayfair, the High Commissions will still stretch out from Trafalgar Square towards Fleet Street and the City. As a great trading and investing country the United Kingdom will continue to have interests that generally coincide with those of her partners in the Commonwealth. They will want to assist her in ensuring that those interests are accorded their full weight in the formation of Community policy in world trade, aid, money and investment. Some of them may even want to secure her assistance in engaging the European States in the tasks of providing security and stability outside Europe. There will still be many occasions in the future when the countries of the Commonwealth will be able to reflect with Cardinal Newman, that 'in a higher world it is otherwise, but here below to live is to change, and to be perfect is to have changed often'.

Taking stock

After a brief demise in 1982, the Round Table *reappeared in 1983 under a new editor who, over the next twenty-one years, would preside over a striking revival in its fortunes. In this, his first editorial, he set out some of the key themes which would be explored in the journal during his editorship: the loosening of the bipolar, Cold War world in which the Commonwealth operated, the importance of issues relating to democracy and development, the increasing significance of the 'unofficial' Commonwealth, the need for greater clarity of thinking about the Commonwealth amongst both governments and analysts, including of course about its limitations, but above all, perhaps, the need for the Commonwealth to act boldly and not to hide its light under a bushel.*

[Peter Lyon,] 'The *Round Table* Revived and the Contemporary Commonwealth', *RT* 72/285 (January 1983), pp. 3–10

[…] The Commonwealth, especially since 1965, has become a unique post-imperial international organization. What is the potential of this association? Must it remain prudently low key or could it be more active and influential than it is? These are not easy questions to answer and they need to be asked – and answered – afresh every few years. As it now has 47 member countries there is a danger that its plenary proceedings will become unwieldy and suffer from some of the more pernicious aspects of 'UN-itis' – excessive rhetoric and collective inaction. In general, so far, the Commonwealth has succeeded in avoiding these diseases, but it is not immune from them by some law of nature. […]

The Commonwealth is not, of course, just an affair of governments and officials and of intergovernmental organizations (IGOs), but embraces societies, professions, indeed peoples. Games, festivals, exhibitions, carnivals, associations, clubs, groups – all these, and more – are part of what comprises the present day unofficial Commonwealth. There is thus a rich, diverse, active and expanding, unofficial, non-governmental (NGO), peoples' Commonwealth. And, yes, it is expanding. […] It is still, however, remarkable and regrettable how little is generally known of the unofficial Commonwealth, or serious questions asked of its general purposes and potential. […]

We come to Britain and the Commonwealth, a subject not much discussed seriously in Britain nowadays. In part this relative silence is welcome if it means that the premature obituarists have ceased to be active. But silence might also imply indifference. As Britain is just one member state (not the automatic permanent chairman and self-appointed leader) and it is no longer appropriate to speak of the 'British' Commonwealth, this does not mean that Britain's role and input into Commonwealth proceedings are clearly conceived and well understood in Britain. […]

The considerable differences between Empire and Commonwealth are probably more easily mistaken or confused in Britain than elsewhere, for three main reasons. The first is the sheer time-lag of opinions, attitudes and ideas catching up with not only events but general arrangements and dispositions. The fact that functionally the Commonwealth still has some considerable London-centricity has camouflaged for many observers the real change which began to occur when Whitehall gave up the management, and from 1965 the main managerial and functional centre became Marlborough House and its associated offices. Secondly, in Britain the vexatious issue of immigration and the tendency to discuss this matter under the heading of 'Commonwealth immigration' gave a tendentious and generally opprobrious twist to the Commonwealth connection in many a Briton's mind. Thirdly, as the issues of the Falkland Islands, Gibraltar, and Hong Kong have become so topical lately, there have been acute reminders that, willy nilly, Britain does have residual colonial responsibilities. It should be added, however, that the Commonwealth connection here is an asset and a help to Britain in handling these issues, much more than it is a hindrance or embarrassment.

To mention these three matters central to the contemporary Commonwealth is not to deny that there are many other matters of importance […] or that these three will always be the most prominent or controversial. […]

The African dimension of the Commonwealth is bound to remain important, not least because at present 14 members (more than one quarter of the overall membership) are from that continent. Namibia is still a danger spot, its international status and independence unresolved. South Africa – not least in its sporting aspects – having five of its immediate neighbours within the Commonwealth, is a major Commonwealth concern. Commonwealth interests and involvements in the Caribbean and in the Pacific are also currently being revalued and retested.

The settlement which led to the independence of Zimbabwe was the latest, but surely not the last, major intra-mural preoccupation for the Commonwealth and one in which its own proceedings played a major part. In the past, regarding Indo-Pakistan relations, or Cyprus, for example, the Commonwealth on a number of occasions has been unwilling or unable to make a decisive contribution to improve a situation. The Commonwealth, in fact, is not an agreed blueprint for a better world, nor some magic elixir to produce instant solutions for the world's ills. It is itself undoubtedly a political body operated by politicians who, despite occasional flights of fancy and rhetoric, are usually practical people – which is not to deny that the Commonwealth is many other things as well. It is important therefore to be practical and clear sighted about the contemporary Commonwealth, and not woolly, airily philosophical or pseudo-historical. The Commonwealth today politically and organizationally is generally in good heart and good condition and should not be too timid. Not over-exertion but excessive hypochondria is its most likely debilitating disease. […]

From the late 1940s until at least the early 1960s the two superpowers undoubtedly presided dominantly over their respective alliance and economic systems (NATO and the Warsaw Pact, OECD [Organization for Economic Co-operation and Development] and Comecon), thus giving credibility to the claim that this was a basically bipolar world. Furthermore, it was a world in which the Commonwealth seemed to be either little more than a reversionary of the British Empire or else an adjunct of the *Pax Americana*. Thereafter, the eruption of the Sino-Soviet Cold War, the growing economic strength of Germany and Japan, and much decolonization, as North–South issues cut across and complicated East–West relations, altogether produced a much more pluralistic, polycentric, loosely structured, more volatile international system. As the Commonwealth shed its Anglocentricity, it gradually showed a capacity to persist as a unique post-colonial international organization and in the late 1970s and early 1980s to be an interlocutor, promoter, initiator or ginger-group for North–South relationships.

With skilful steering by Sonny Ramphal, its Secretary-General since 1975, the Commonwealth has sought to give real meaning to two of his maxims: that the Commonwealth cannot negotiate for the world but can help the world to negotiate, and that there is for humanity today and in the future not so much North and South, East and West, the third world, but 'One World to Share' – albeit, it should be added, one in which recent events strongly indicate that it would be a mistake to discount the so-called superpowers. […]

Britain and the Commonwealth

Mrs. Thatcher's government frequently found itself at odds with its Commonwealth partners in the 1980s, especially in relation to proposed sanctions against South Africa. Though written for public consumption rather than the edification of his Prime Minister, the following extract shows clearly that her third Foreign Secretary was mindful of the benefits of the Commonwealth connection to Britain.

Sir Geoffrey Howe, 'Britain and the Commonwealth Today', *RT* 73/289 (January 1984), pp. 7–16

[…] The key foreign policy objectives of this and preceding British governments are to provide security, to enhance prosperity and to promote stability. But Britain's role has changed and is changing from that of a global power. Inevitably this has meant that to achieve our objectives our diplomatic activity has concentrated more on regional issues. Our commitments to the European Community and to the Atlantic Alliance have become the twin pillars of our foreign policy. Both have a vital role in achieving security, prosperity and stability. But […] our membership of the Community has not meant a renunciation of old ties. Rather it has provided a new context for them. […]

If Britain is now more of a regional power, then it is one with worldwide interests and responsibilities. We have our commitments in the Falklands, Hong Kong, Gibraltar and the other overseas territories under the protection of the Crown. We derive a considerable proportion of our national income from overseas activities: much higher than most other industrialized nations. We import many of the raw materials for our industries. We export across the globe. We have extensive foreign investments which need protecting.

And we have a vital role as a responsible Western ally in helping to deny opportunities outside Europe to the Russians and their satraps. If then we are looking at the Commonwealth in these hard-nosed nationalistic terms, in terms of what we get out of it, its value to us is inextricably linked to our worldwide interests. Much of the benefit to British interests from the Commonwealth is invisible or intangible. This makes the task of the sceptic easier.

But there are concrete and visible benefits too. The existence of the Commonwealth gives us an immediate and privileged *entrée* to the governments of 30 per cent of the membership of the United Nations. And to markets with a quarter of the world's population: markets which are growing in purchasing power. In 1982, Commonwealth countries took nearly 13 per cent of our exports. Nigeria alone bought well over £1 billion of exports and is one of our three largest markets outside the industrialized world. In 1981 Commonwealth countries accounted for some 35 per cent of our income from non-oil investment overseas.

But the advantages are not only economic. Commonwealth membership has been of direct political benefit to Britain. I regard the Lancaster House settlement which ended a civil war and brought independence to Zimbabwe as one of the very important achievements of Mrs. Thatcher's first government. I very much doubt whether Britain would have achieved that settlement if it had not been for the agreement reached at the CHOGM in Lusaka in 1979. And the role of the Commonwealth of course did not stop there. The Commonwealth monitoring force and the Commonwealth observer group played an important role in the run-up to independence in Zimbabwe. They helped to ensure that power was transferred peacefully and smoothly. Britain's reputation was enhanced as a consequence. And so was that of the Commonwealth. And wider Western interests were served because opportunities for meddling outsiders were reduced.

The Commonwealth saw it as their duty in Zimbabwe to help us to discharge a British commitment. It was the same with the Falklands. Many of you will remember Mr. Ramphal's speech at the height of the Falklands conflict. Its title was 'Not Britain's Cause Alone'. Another clear example of a situation in which the Commonwealth came to the aid of Britain in dealing with what was technically a national responsibility. The great majority of Commonwealth states gave us strong support after the Argentinian invasion. New Zealand lent us a frigate, others took economic sanctions. Some gave us quiet support for military logistics or open political support in the UN. I am convinced that Commonwealth support for Britain among non-aligned countries was a significant factor in deterring the Soviet Union from vetoing SC [Security Council] Resolution 502.

And I can cite other examples where the Commonwealth has helped to promote stability, thereby serving our political and security interests directly or indirectly. The achievement of independence for Belize was due in no small way to the support which the Commonwealth drummed up in the UN. And the Commonwealth Declaration on Belize gave reassurance to the people in their dispute with Guatemala. The Commonwealth also helped to promote stability in Africa when it sent observers to monitor the Ugandan elections in 1980 and later a military training team. And in general the existence of the Commonwealth provides a highly effective means for Britain to play a responsible part alongside other Western nations in aiding the development and stability of the Third World. Certainly many of the smaller states feel that their membership of the Commonwealth and its regional bodies makes them much less exposed in a hostile international climate. […]

So much for the direct and visible benefits to Britain from the Commonwealth. But many are more intangible. To speak of shared values in the context of the Commonwealth is to use a truism. But the fundamental characteristic of truisms is that they are true. The Declaration of Commonwealth Principles adopted in 1971 is perhaps the clearest expression of the values which we hold in common. One has to acknowledge that not all members are successful in practising these principles. But they do provide an ideal, a benchmark, towards which all the member states can strive. And the Commonwealth countries generally compare favourably with their counterparts elsewhere in preserving and practising the independence of the judiciary, a key foundation stone for a fair society. In the political sphere Nigeria has just demonstrated anew that parliamentary democracy can work in Africa. In a subtle way, all these shared values work in our national interests because they help to spread a way of life which has worked for us and which can enhance stability.

I also see the Commonwealth as a unique channel for developing contacts and understanding between the industrialized and developing world. This too serves our interests. In particular our Commonwealth experience puts us in a good position, along with Canada, Australia and New Zealand, to act as a fulcrum in international financial negotiations. And the Commonwealth in general provides a valuable, possibly a unique forum, free of polemic and bitterness, in which the developing and the industrialized countries can gain a better understanding of the constraints and needs of the other. […]

And finally, in this 'accountant's approach' to the Commonwealth, we must not forget the edge in trade which the English language gives us. Nor the advantage we gain from the direct experience which many Commonwealth leaders have of British institutions – schools, universities, the Bar and, for some – happily very much a thing of the past – our prisons! […]

Foreign policy is not of course susceptible to accurate cost–benefit analysis. But in terms of the Commonwealth the visible and invisible balances of costs and advantages do appear to leave us in substantial political surplus.

The Commonwealth, however, means much more than that to us. We cannot ignore the more human and emotional factors. That is what distinguishes our society from that of the Communists. There is deep sentiment in this country in favour of the Commonwealth. The ties of kinship and blood to the old Commonwealth are now strengthened and enriched by the links between the ethnic minorities here and their families in the Caribbean, the sub-continent and West Africa. And then there is the unofficial Commonwealth, that benign mafia of everybody from Commonwealth architects to athletes. […]

It is not always going to be 'sweetness and light' inside the Commonwealth. In such a diverse body there will be occasional differences of perception and interest. The Grenadian intervention showed that even within a small region of apparently similar states, Commonwealth members can differ sharply on what needs to be done. But any differences are temporary and soluble. They will not detract from the underlying value of the Commonwealth for multinational co-operation and mutual help. […]

The Commonwealth is in short a body of which Britain is proud to have been the midwife. And it is clear that the attractions of the Commonwealth endure for others. Since the last CHOGM Antigua and Barbuda, the

Maldives and St Kitts and Nevis have all joined. Brunei is planning to do so when it gains full independence next year.

The continued growth in membership is welcome in itself. But it also means that the Commonwealth has a better chance of sharing its experience with the wider world. And in particular for demonstrating that co-operation between peoples of different races and backgrounds can help to solve world problems. […]

A Commonwealth without Britain?

Such was the anger in other parts of the Commonwealth at the British government's stance on sanctions against South Africa that thirty-two Commonwealth nations decided to boycott the 1986 Commonwealth Games in Edinburgh. There was also, as this extract shows, serious discussion of the possibility of Britain withdrawing or being expelled from the Commonwealth. The author, a distinguished Caribbean diplomat, was not in favour of such an outcome; but it is a mark of how far the Commonwealth had developed from its imperial origins that, as he argued, a British withdrawal was not likely to spell the end of the Commonwealth.

Ronald Sanders, 'Is Britain Indispensable to the Commonwealth?', *RT* 76/303 (July 1987), pp. 366–77

[…] Last year, a number of Commonwealth governments decided to withdraw from the Commonwealth Games in Edinburgh. Nigeria began the process. According to Mr Duro Onabule, the Press Secretary to the Nigerian Head of State, Nigeria's withdrawal was 'in response to Britain's policy on South Africa'. Mrs Thatcher, in an interview with columnist Hugo Young in *The Guardian*, had said that 'sanctions are immoral', and that she 'found nothing moral' about those who called for sanctions, 'sitting in comfortable circumstances, with good salaries, inflation-proof pensions and good jobs'. What offended Commonwealth sentiment even more, however, were her remarks that 'South Africa should never have been isolated by the world' and that there should have been more contact with the government.

Not even the *Sunday Telegraph*, usually a strong supporter of the British Government, upheld these remarks by Mrs Thatcher. In an editorial, it described as 'unfortunate' what it called Mrs Thatcher's attempt 'to turn opposition to sanctions into a moral crusade'.

In the event, not all Commonwealth countries agreed with Nigeria that they should withdraw from the Games. Indeed, the compelling argument was that the Games were the Commonwealth's games not Britain's and to boycott the Games would do as much harm to the Commonwealth as it would to Britain. […]

I believe that 1986 was the year in which the separation of Britain from the Commonwealth emerged in the minds of many. While the older Commonwealth members, Canada, Australia and New Zealand, have always made the separation, a similar attitude developed among the smaller states. For instance, Dominica's Prime Minister, Eugenia Charles, said that she saw no value in damaging the Commonwealth to make a point to Britain. The influential Trinidad *Guardian* said in an editorial that 'attacking South Africa is one thing, weakening the Commonwealth is another'.

Let us step back a moment to consider the background to the emergence of this feeling.

The British Government's attitude toward sanctions against South Africa had demonstrably put it out of step with Commonwealth opinion. For many, it became unbearable to be part of a 'voluntary association' with Britain in which fundamental differences existed only with Britain. This situation reached boiling point at the Review Meeting of seven Commonwealth heads of government. Britain was clearly divided from the others. Bob Hawke, the Australian Prime Minister, summed up their attitude by saying that the leaders were faced with a choice between unity with Britain and the credibility of the Commonwealth and they chose credibility. […]

In these circumstances, it is possible to envisage a situation in which Britain's continuance in the Commonwealth could be reviewed both by Britain herself and by the other Commonwealth countries.

For instance, if the British Government felt that the nature of its disagreement with Commonwealth countries over sanctions against South Africa was harmful to its own interest, it could simply withdraw. A distinguished legal expert, Sir William Dale, points out that 'it follows from the voluntary nature of Commonwealth membership that it is open to a member to withdraw from the Commonwealth if it wishes'. He also emphasizes that the Republic of Ireland withdrew in 1949, South Africa in 1961 and Pakistan in 1972 without any formality. […]

Of course, it is also possible that consideration could be given to the suggestion by Ghana's Dr Busia in 1970 that Britain could be expelled. S. A. de Smith argues in the 'New Commonwealth and its Constitution' that 'there is no precedent for expulsion of a member, but reference to the facts of the South African case and to the Commonwealth's history of pragmatic innovation suggests that expulsion cannot be dismissed as a constitutional impossibility'.

De Smith stresses that what happened in the case of South Africa in 1961 was that it had applied for continuance in the Commonwealth as a Republic and the opportunity was taken by heads of government to denounce its racial policy. The South African Prime Minister resolved not to alter his policies to satisfy Commonwealth opinion and decided not to proceed with the application. But this sequence of events did not rule out the possibility of a motion being put forward for the expulsion of South Africa. Therefore, technically, it is possible, though highly unlikely, for Britain to be expelled from the Commonwealth.

There is perhaps one other element which could be raised as evidence that Britain is imperative to the Commonwealth – and that is the Queen in her capacity as Head of the Commonwealth.

The present relationship of the British Monarch to the Commonwealth was agreed in 1949 when the question was raised of India's continuing membership after becoming a Republic with a separate Head of State.

A great deal of negotiation went into arriving at a formula which could accommodate India's republican status. This was helped considerably by the strong desire of the King himself that India should remain in the Commonwealth. It was agreed that the King would be 'the symbol of the free association' of the independent member states and 'as such, Head of the Commonwealth'. Two points are important about this declaration – the first is that it was the 'King' who became Head of the Commonwealth and not the 'Crown'. […]

As 'a symbol of the free association of the independent member states' does the Queen's position as Head of the Commonwealth derive exclusively from her being Head of State of Britain? At least in technical terms the answer would seem to be 'no' – whatever the real politic of the situation. She is, after all, Queen of 17 Commonwealth countries other than Britain.

I suspect that because of the Queen's greatly appreciated role as Head of the Commonwealth, every member state would welcome her continuance in that role. Of course, if she felt that she could no longer carry out this function, member states might agree with S. A. de Smith that 'it would not necessarily be appropriate to retain the concept of a Head of the Commonwealth'. In other words, the position would fall away. […]

If Britain is not indispensable to the Commonwealth, it is Britain herself who is the biggest contributor to that state of affairs. In the early days of the new Commonwealth, British governments found it very useful and worked at making Britain indispensable. But her policies on South Africa have alienated her from other Commonwealth countries and her policies on fees for Commonwealth students and the manner in which she has implemented her immigration and nationality laws have further distanced her from the Commonwealth and weakened her opportunities for maintaining contacts.

The question that now has to be addressed is what would happen to the Commonwealth if Britain were to withdraw or be expelled. Let me do this by posing a series of questions and attempting to provide the answers:

Would other countries leave the Commonwealth in sympathy with Britain? A great deal would depend on how and why Britain's membership ended. In general, however, I believe the answer is 'no'. For Canada, Australia and New Zealand, the Commonwealth has become an important forum for political consultations with countries in the Third World which they would not wish to lose. Further, Commonwealth countries are important markets for their products. In any event if Britain were to be expelled from the Commonwealth, it would have to be with the concurrence of these countries. Moreover, it is significant that Britain's departure from UNESCO was roundly criticized by Australia and Canada which remained in the organization and, to a large extent, assumed Britain's place. Other Commonwealth countries would remain in the Commonwealth for its political role in advancing their cause as developing countries and for the assistance they receive in advancing their economic welfare.

Would the activities of the Commonwealth Secretariat be affected? Obviously they would, for Britain is a significant contributor to the Secretariat's budget. But a reduction in the budget would not be fatal. When the USA withdrew from the ILO [International Labour Organization], the organization continued to function quite well and, eventually, the USA returned. Similarly, after the withdrawal of Britain and the USA, UNESCO has trimmed its programme but has maintained a high level of activity.

Would the Commonwealth lose a voice in the councils of the developed countries such as the OECD and NATO? No. Canada and Australia are members of OECD. Canada is also a member of NATO and is respected in the IMF and World Bank. In this context, the Commonwealth could still exert influence in these organizations.

Would the Commonwealth lose a friend in the EEC? In effect, yes, but the reality is that the negotiations between the developing countries and the EEC have demonstrated that there may be countries in the EEC more sympathetic than Britain to the aspirations of developing countries. On sanctions against South Africa, for instance, several EEC countries were more willing than Britain to act.

But, of course, while the Commonwealth would not wither because of a separation from Britain, it is considerably stronger for counting Britain among its members and, indeed, among its greatly valued members. There could be no Commonwealth government, nor nation, except in rare moments of anger – and we have counted only five such occasions in 30 years[3] – which would seek a divorce between Britain and the Commonwealth. For there is no doubt that the Commonwealth is enriched by the membership of all its states and is particularly so by the quality of membership by Britain, which has given to each Commonwealth country and to the Commonwealth as a whole some of its finest and longest lasting traditions.

And I believe that despite occasional rumblings from a few politicians, fewer journalists and even fewer academics, Britain does value the Commonwealth. […]

Human rights: the Harare Declaration

Human rights have been increasingly central to the Commonwealth's agenda, as evidenced by the Singapore Declaration of 1971, whose principles were given further substance by the Harare Declaration of 1991. Writing shortly after the latter, Sir Dawda Jawara, President of the Gambia and a leading exponent of democracy and human rights, addressed the importance of human rights for his own continent, although the points he made were clearly of wider relevance to the whole Commonwealth. Sadly, Jawara was himself overthrown by a military coup in 1994.

Alhaji Sir Dawda Kairaba Jawara, 'The Commonwealth and Human Rights', *RT* 81/321 (January 1992), pp. 37–42

[…] In the past, some Africans have argued that the restrictions of political rights and its corollary, the one-party state, is [*sic*] appropriate to Africa as a safety measure against ethnic tension and internal friction. It was further claimed that one-party rule would provide stability through centralized control during the process of nation-building. In effect, multi-party democracy was seen as an instant recipe for national disaster, on account of the centrifugal forces that were so pervasive in the early stages of our nationhood. This view became even more entrenched as the multi-party experiments in the immediate post-colonial era were marred by confusion and bloody interethnic rivalry and violence.

Still, I am also aware that there were those who tended to qualify their support for democratic principles with a big '*but*' or, even more preposterously, to suggest that we sacrificed a little bit of our hard-won liberties in order to allow our economies to grow faster. Worse still, some even went to the extent [of claiming] that we could not have democracy with rampant illiteracy. Others claimed that democracy was a long-term process and Africans have not got time enough to pave their way through social change. We in The Gambia have rejected these short-sighted arguments in the past and we continue to reject them now.

The dangers of national fragmentation are indeed real enough. But there is very little evidence to suggest that one-party rule in Africa diminishes ethnic rivalries and tensions. Indeed, the imposition of one-party rule, often based on one or few major ethnic groups, has kept ethnic friction alive and not the reverse. In some cases, as you all know, the one-party state was akin to the tyranny of the majority, whereby stronger and more dominant groups have attempted to dominate and control minorities and disregard the need for national consensus. This has inevitably led to dictatorships, for even if the leaders started with good intentions, the possibilities that absolute power allowed were soon realized. Tyranny, bureaucratic paralysis, weak judicial systems, arbitrary decision making and a siege mentality quickly became the norm. Under these conditions, African governments became more preoccupied with day-to-day political survival and the accumulation of power. Societal needs and concerns were quickly discarded.

At any rate, if the justification of one-party rule were to provide stability for economic development, then it has been a disaster. It has led not to sustained economic development, but in most cases to blatant economic failures.

There is enough evidence to suggest that those countries around the world that are economically successful on a sustained basis are those that are democratic and free. Those that are economic disasters are those that have allowed one-party dictatorships or systematic violation of human rights to take hold. In other words, the linkages between political stability, democracy, popular participation and socio-economic progress are now more clearly seen than a few years ago. It therefore requires no great leap of the imagination to realize what must be done.

The starting point must be to reaffirm our strong commitment to the respect for human rights and the rule of law. These may be self-evident but in a world in which human rights' protection and the spreading of democracy still leaves much to be desired, they need to be stated and re-stated. If the basic human rights of our citizens are to remain inviolate then a firm knowledge of those same rights must become a vital element in the political ethos of our societies. The key elements in this regard, are knowledge by the individual citizens of their basic rights and how to protect them.

Institutions and measures have been established in some African countries to create an enabling environment for sustained economic development. But the most crucial enabling factor for human progress is a full and unequivocal endorsement of the democratic spirit. In this atmosphere of debate and dissent, breakdowns in the body political will become fewer, course correction faster, and discontinuities will be avoided, rather than when there is unquestioning conformity.

In order to respond effectively to the preferences of our citizens and to ensure their basic political rights, the following conditions are absolutely necessary: freedom of expression (implying media and public fora free to raise and debate political issues and to criticize government) and freedom of assembly; a strong and independent judiciary enforcing the rule of law; and an opportunity on the part of the public to change the political leadership through periodic, free and fair elections. It would be impossible to fulfil these conditions under a one-party state. […]

There should be increased knowledge and awareness of international human rights standards among public officials, particularly those whose work has direct implications for human rights, as well as among the population at large. After a long period of standard-setting and the development of procedures and mechanisms, greater attention now needs to be given to inculcating a culture of respect for human rights through public awareness campaigns. Attention should also be given to encouraging all African and indeed Commonwealth states to become party to the main international instruments on human rights and for them to take the necessary measures to discharge the obligations they will assume under those instruments.

More importantly, future action should concentrate on education, training and technical assistance. There is at present lively debate on the increasing tendency to impose conditionalities of a political nature for assistance to developing countries. It is important to add that these conditionalities are not allowed to run the risk of compounding developing countries' current problems. It is feared in some circles that the issue of political reform could be used as an excuse to simply cut back aid. However, in this respect, we would expect aid donors to deploy part of their aid to support some of the measures that are useful in promoting democracy in developing countries. Training and technical assistance programmes geared towards strengthening national institutions whose efficiency and respect for human rights and fundamental freedoms – i.e. the judiciary, law enforcement agencies, the legal profession, the public service – are crucial to the maintenance of a democratic system of government under the rule of law.

In this regard I cannot but refer to the reaffirmation of the strong commitment of the Commonwealth to the principle of good governance embracing justice and human rights, the rule of law, the independence of the judiciary, equality for women and accountable administration. The Commonwealth is now ready, as underlined at the Commonwealth Heads of Government Meeting at Harare,[4] to support these objectives. In this regard the Heads of Government agreed to strengthen the Human Rights Unit of the Commonwealth Secretariat through, among other things, the creation of a voluntary fund to finance some of these activities. […]

I would emphasize the need to find a formula for making human rights enforceable, because one of the reasons for the failure of human rights protection is the absence of effective machinery designed to ensure that the rights guaranteed will be respected. In the absence of a controlling machinery and the vesting in it of the function necessary for its effectiveness, it is futile to elaborate rights and duties.

The establishment of such machinery and the vesting in it of the functions, powers and procedures necessary for its effectiveness is too often proposed by adherents of an extremist view on state sovereignty. It is unfortunate that we in Africa have tended for too long to overstate the principle of non-interference in the affairs of other African states in relation to violations of human rights, when it is obvious that the question of human rights should be of universal concern and not only of that state within whose borders the gross violations are allegedly occurring. […]

It is my hope that the efforts being deployed by the Commonwealth of the 1990s and beyond, coupled with those of the wider international community, will bring nearer a state of affairs which, to quote Professor Maurice Cranston, will ensure 'positive rights for everybody everywhere'.

South Africa returns

Through the work of the Eminent Persons' Group, the sports boycott, and various other means, the Commonwealth played an important role in the international campaign to end apartheid *in South Africa, and one of the first acts of the post-*apartheid *government was to rejoin the Commonwealth, which South Africa had left in 1961. The* Round Table*'s editor (who observed the first democratic elections in South Africa as part of the Commonwealth Observer Group) reflected in this article on the changes which had occurred in the Commonwealth during the time South Africa was not a member, and emphasized the extent to which the Commonwealth, as well as South Africa, had changed.*

[Peter Lyon,] 'South Africa and the Commonwealth', *RT* 83/331 (July 1994), pp. 275–87

[…] South Africa's past, present and future are entwined in the Commonwealth (not excluding the years 1961–94 when South Africa formally was not a member).

The Commonwealth has been different things at different times. Sequentially for South Africa over the last forty years the Commonwealth has been (a) a British-run club to which she belonged virtually as a founder-member; (b) a rapidly changing association whose membership was expanding as a result of decolonization and it is this body she left in 1961; (c) the principal international body which sought to mount and maintain comprehensive sanctions, especially from the mid-1980s onwards; (d) an agency for encouraging the transition from apartheid to a democratic system based on universal adult franchise; (e) a helpful witness and certificator – with other international organisations – of the country's first comprehensive democratic election based on universal adult suffrage; and (f) an organization the re-modelled post-apartheid South Africa has rejoined (no longer a pariah) as it seeks to play an active constructive part in the international community.

The Commonwealth that South Africa left in 1961 was still basically a British-run club of Britain's former Dominions and dependencies. In 1961 it had eleven or twelve members (there was some ambiguity as to the precise status of the Federation of Rhodesia and Nyasaland). Its Prime Ministerial meetings were always held in London, chaired by the British Prime Minister supported by a phalanx of other British ministers and civil servants in total making up almost half the complement of those present. Press briefings were few and generally anodyne or perfunctory. Final communiqués at the end of each meeting usually were brief and unrevealing, as if to confirm Napoleon's advice regarding constitutions: that they should be short but obscure. By 1961 decolonization had already brought some new members recently into this club – Ghana and Malaya (from 1963 Malaysia) in 1957 and Nigeria and Cyprus in 1960[5] – and these new members, soon to have their ranks augmented by many more, began to question the established verities regarding Britain's permanent chairmanship and always meeting in London. […]

In the same year that South Africa withdrew from the Commonwealth Britain applied for membership of the European Economic Community (as it was then called) avowing that its entry was in no way incompatible with its continuance within the Commonwealth. President de Gaulle disagreed and said so in characteristically lofty tones at a press conference on 14 January 1963 though it is true that he then said much less about the Commonwealth as a barrier to British entry than voicing his fears of 'a colossal Atlantic community under American domination'. Henceforth leading British politicians, officials and entrepreneurs decided in effect that it would be prudent to lower Britain's profile in the Commonwealth even whilst continuing membership. By 1965 this coincidence of new members wishing to shape the future Commonwealth and Britain's desire to lower its profile and to circumvent the French veto, led to the launching of the Commonwealth Secretariat. The

Commonwealth of 1994 thus is recognizably the heir of what was re-modelled in 1965 much more than it is a descendant of what this association was in 1961. […]

The April 1994 general election in South Africa was only an episode, albeit an important one, in the life of this reconstituted polity. The election was an expression of choice which has been accepted as constitutionally binding; it conferred legitimate authority. Ahead lie the tasks of drawing a new permanent constitution and the perennial many-sided day-to-day tasks of governance. The overall task can be simply stated (though achieving it will be no simple matter): it is to induct a genuinely civic culture for this 'rainbow nation' and to achieve and sustain an expanding economy which will enable economic redistribution to proceed without inflicting heavy pain on all involved in these processes.

The ideals that the Commonwealth collectively avows no less than the practical ways in which it seeks to tackle and surmount common problems mark it out both as a distinctive international agency devoted to co-operation rather than conflict and in some respects as an exemplar to the rest of the world; but these are inherently different roles which it almost always seeks to reconcile.

It is in this company, in several ways significantly different from the association it left in 1961, in which the 'new' South Africa now resumes its membership. In the complex world of the mid-1990s South Africa and the Commonwealth henceforth will be steering some courses together.

A global role for the Commonwealth

The second Secretary-General of the Commonwealth, Shridath Ramphal, was a man especially noted for his vision as well as his political shrewdness and administrative ability. In this article – written some seven years after he had left the Commonwealth Secretariat – he took issue with the then increasingly prevalent idea that the Commonwealth could only aspire to play a 'niche' role in international relations. Instead, he offered the prospect of a large and increasingly important role for the Commonwealth in the late twentieth and early twenty-first centuries, based in particular on its potential contributions in the areas of development, democracy and human rights.

Shridath Ramphal, 'The Commonwealth in the Global Neighbourhood: A Distinctive and Enlarging Role', *RT* 86/342 (April 1997), pp. 175–85

[…] In recent years it has been my privilege in the Commission on Global Governance to share in a wide-ranging examination of global relationships and global trends. We called the Commission's Report *Our Global Neighbourhood*.[6] Its title is its message; a message of realism, not piety. It was our conviction within the Commission that the world had become a global neighbourhood, interlocked, interactive, interdependent human community. We had 'entered the global phase of human evolution' to recall those prescient words of Barbara Ward and Rene Dubois way back in 1972.

Neighbourhoods are not just places with well-trimmed hedges – neighbourhoods are people living together in a great variety of conditions; people who may not even like each other but are still neighbours, people who must live together, like it or not. Essentially, neighbourhoods are congregations of people whose fate depends on each other, people who come to recognize that the neighbourhood cannot be good for any if it is not good for all. It leads in the end to discovery of the riches that lie buried in the neighbourhood's variety – the 'otherness' within it.

It is in this 'global neighbourhood' that the Commonwealth must function. It must be distinctive and its role must be an enlarging one; but it must be an integral part of the neighbourhood, seeing itself and being seen as such – and helping the neighbourhood by its own example to live by neighbourhood values. The Commonwealth must have its quota of service to perform for its members, its mission to both people and governments of the Commonwealth; but it must have an ethos that informs its works, values that guide it and for which it stands – a Commonwealth ethic that is as distinctive as its role within the larger neighbourhood. […]

The Commonwealth is the commingling of a quarter of the world's people and a quarter of the world's countries. It need not be an insignificant player; it owes it to itself, it owes it to the global neighbourhood to help it meet those needs by itself having that vision and by informing its every act by that global civic ethic. A Commonwealth that gives that lead in the world need never worry about its role. The world's greatest imperfection today is the absence of enlightened leadership. We said as much in *Our Global Neighbourhood*. The Commonwealth has a great opportunity to provide it. I believe that it can; but, more to the point, I believe that it must. […]

Nowhere in the spectrum of international forums is there anything like the Commonwealth Summit, and when you add to that the character of a Commonwealth of over 50 countries bridging several divides, then it becomes a very significant occasion. Having said that, it is right that I should underline my own perception that the true character, and I would say the true value of the Commonwealth, derives not from likeness or even like-mindedness, but from variety. It derives from the fact that this family facility is a commingling of the world's diversity. What the Commonwealth tries to do is to harmonize difference over a wider range and to a further degree than any other grouping in the world. And as we look to a distinctive and enlarging role for the Commonwealth, it is that quality that is significant because it means there is at least one facility of a functional kind that reaches across these divisions and can from time to time find common purpose and a common basis for action.

A part of this variety is the gap between rich and poor, between developed and developing, between countries that are industrialized and those that are not. There are wide variations within the Commonwealth in that respect. Of course, not everyone is among the poorest; there are some middle-income developing countries like Malaysia; but, by and large, the Commonwealth of the future to which we are looking for this distinctive and enlarging role, is a Commonwealth of nearly 50 developing countries and four developed countries. That is the fundamental reality, a preponderance of poor countries in a community of a billion and a half people – and just a few countries on the other side of the rich/poor divide. These countries are members of the rich countries' club, the OECD, and Britain and Canada are in the more exclusive Group of Seven. That Group, if it has its way, will be meeting at the Summit each year, well into the future, playing a role they perceive as being managers of the world economy. But for many other countries, the future could be a kind of marginalization. When I go to developing countries, in the Commonwealth and outside, people do not now talk to me so much about economic domination, but about being forgotten, about dropping off, about being marginalized; and that I suspect is right. That anxiety is valid.

So the Commonwealth, if it is to remain relevant, must place economic development and poverty alleviation at the centre of its concerns. If not, it will lose credibility and it will lose relevance. Therefore in devising a distinctive and enlarging role for the Commonwealth, this dimension of development must remain fundamental. And that is so not just because so many of its members are developing countries; it is not just a matter of numbers. The issue of those disparities in the world is now important as well to the rich as to the poor, to Canada, to Britain, to New Zealand and to Australia. It is important to them that the prospects for real development should be enlarged; and in the Commonwealth there is a real chance to work together to advance development because it provides a setting in which industrial countries can interact with developing countries in an atmosphere of cordiality and friendship. […]

I suppose if there is one notion, one concept, which is the touchstone of so much that is happening in our own times, it is democracy. What can the Commonwealth do, what should it do to help to strengthen democracy within its member countries and in the world? In my last report as Secretary-General to Heads of Government, I raised this frontally and said that the Commonwealth must be unequivocal about its seriousness in wanting to help the democratic process. I said we must be realistic in recognizing that there were limits to what we could do, but within those limits we must act. I actually suggested one way in which we might make a beginning – having a standing facility for observing elections. It is the kind of pragmatic thing the Commonwealth could attempt, and I was sure it would grow. I knew Governments would have to ask for its services, but the fact the facility existed would enlarge the pressure to ask for it in situations where there were problems about ensuring the integrity of elections.

I also felt that in the world of the 1990s and beyond, a Commonwealth of rich and poor, besides working for democracy within countries, should also be looking for a more democratic world. It could not just be a world of democratic states within an authoritarian, if not a feudal, world community, in which power and decision making are in the hands of a few. So there needed to be a consciousness that as we did more and more about democracy at the national level, we must also push for a more democratic world.

The other issue I mentioned is human rights which is quite closely related to the issue of democracy. […] There is not a country in the Commonwealth or elsewhere in which allegations of one kind or another are not sometimes levelled about human rights violations. But that is not what I am talking about. To get involved in such situations is really to be meddling, and that cannot serve anyone's purpose. But what about major violations such as those the Commonwealth had to face with Amin in Uganda in 1977? I did not think there was any point in blinking the issue or encouraging leaders to sweep it under the carpet. Commonwealth leaders would be meeting while horrible things were happening in Uganda – things which outraged African countries, which outraged the world community. Were we to pretend that they were not happening within the family? I urged the Commonwealth to take up the issue, to say that we are not in the business of meddling but, equally, there are some situations that cross the line – when it becomes everybody's business, especially our business within the family. I said that we might not know how to draw that line precisely but we would know when it had been crossed; and that wherever that line was, it had been crossed in Uganda. So let us speak out, I urged and urged publicly.

And Commonwealth leaders collectively did speak out. Within three weeks the UN Human Rights Commission found the courage to speak out as well. We had broken the mould of constraint. I think the Commonwealth is stronger today because it spoke out against Amin then. The Commonwealth must retain the capacity to speak out against such abuses; it is consistent after all with what the Commonwealth said and did over Southern Africa. We must not be accused of double standards or going soft on fundamental wrong doing. And, of course, far from acting in hostility to Commonwealth Governments, we would be showing solidarity with Commonwealth people. […]

It is that solidarity with Commonwealth people that will most assure the Commonwealth of a distinctive and enlarging role. The great conflicts of the present are not conflicts between countries but within them. The Commonwealth has to give a lead to the world in responding to them in solidarity with people. […]

Monarchy revisited

The relationship between the monarchy and the Commonwealth has of course always been a close one, with first the Crown and then (from 1949) the Headship providing the most visible symbol of Commonwealth unity. Few observers have faulted Queen Elizabeth II's performance of her role as Head of the Commonwealth, but by the 1990s there was increasing disquiet at what was thought by many to be the anachronistic linkage between monarchy and Commonwealth. In this article, the Queen's biographer reminded readers that the

> *link was not an automatic one, and that her successor as monarch would not necessarily succeed her as Head of the Commonwealth.*
>
> Ben Pimlott, 'Some Thoughts on the Queen and Commonwealth', *RT* 87/347 (July 1998), pp. 303–05

In its long history, the British Monarchy has played many parts – often parallel or overlapping. Since the 17th century, and especially since the late 19th, when Disraeli made Victoria 'Empress of India', a key role has been in relation to Empire and Commonwealth. In my recent book about the Monarchy[7] I discussed what I see as the present Queen's constitutional-cum-political achievements, as well as a few notable political mistakes. It seemed interesting to me that while the latter relate entirely to the British domestic context, the former relate to the Commonwealth. Certainly, on several occasions the significance of the Monarch has been more than merely symbolic.

For example, a number of observers who were present at the time have pointed to the emollient role played by the Queen at the Commonwealth Heads of Government Meeting at Lusaka in 1979, which helped to bring together Margaret Thatcher and the leaders of the frontline states, and contributed to the Lancaster Accord on Rhodesia/Zimbabwe. Another significant area of royal involvement – whether you call it an achievement is of course a matter of opinion – occurred at the time of the famous row involving Mrs Thatcher, Buckingham Palace and *The Sunday Times* in July 1986, over the issue of sanctions against South Africa. The newspaper was briefed – or believed it had been briefed – by a Palace official on the Queen's private attitude on a variety of policy issues, including the British Government's hostility to tightening sanctions against the apartheid regime, about which she was allegedly unhappy. The Palace denied the story, and sought to play it down. However, the embarrassment that was caused to the Government had the (arguably beneficial) side-effect of giving encouragement to the Commonwealth states that supported sanctions – and, thereby, of strengthening the association at a time of fragility and uncertainty.

South Africa provides an example of the way in which a continuing Royal Family interest has had an influence that extends beyond that of normal intergovernmental relations. The Queen's interest, as Head of the Commonwealth, in the affairs of southern Africa throughout the apartheid era seems to have stemmed partly from the celebrated visit of George VI, together with his wife and daughters, in 1947, shortly before the racist legislation that led to South Africa's international isolation. The Queen's known sympathy, and the sense that it was more than formal, for the plight of black Africans not only helped to bring about the Lancaster Accord, it also encouraged the idea that the Head of the Commonwealth stood apart from mere British Governments on such matters, and contributed to the decision of Nelson Mandela to take the new South Africa back into the Commonwealth as one of his first acts as President. Thus, when the Queen visited the Republic in 1995, she received an especially warm reception in the townships – not an inevitable response from poor blacks to a white, foreign Monarch. Significantly, she was greeted with placards saying 'welcome back' – a reference to the 1947 visit. [...]

If it is hard to see many royal mistakes in relation to the new Commonwealth, a case has been made for blaming royalty for failing to keep up links with the old. To some extent, this is unfair. A gradual diminution of the Monarch's role in those countries of which she remains head of state was inevitable, as Britain's world importance declined, and Commonwealth trade also diminished. Arguably, the remarkable thing is how long the connection has survived. That it has done so can be partly attributed to royal diplomacy – it helped, for example, the 'patriation' of the Canadian constitution, without the loss of the Monarch as titular Head of State, that the Queen spoke good French, and so was able to take a close and friendly interest in the negotiations. However, the Australian case is somewhat different: here, if the goal had been to maintain the monarchical link in perpetuity, then the Queen could be criticized for the infrequency of royal visits, and for failing to appear more of an Australian monarch. Certainly, the sense of the irrelevance of the monarchy to Australian national identity has increased over recent years, following an earlier period of intense – even wild – royal popularity. The marriage and other problems of the Royal Family in Britain have also undoubtedly contributed to a growing alienation, although a combination of the shifting demographic balance towards non-Anglo-Saxons, and a re-orientation of trade towards the Far East, must be counted as bigger factors.

What of the future? In relation to Britain, the position is fluid. Though the proportion of people in the United Kingdom favouring a retention of the Monarchy remains high, republicanism has increased, to the point at which it is a respectable and no longer marginal political position, on both sides of the political divide. Although the Labour Party is careful not to advocate it officially, the abolition of the institution would undoubtedly be on the private agendas of many backbench Labour MPs, as well as those of quite a few Liberal Democrat and even some Tory ones.

Nobody, however, regards a change in fundamental aspects of the status quo as likely in Britain for the foreseeable future. As far as the Commonwealth is concerned, the prospects for the institution are more uncertain: to say that the Head is widely respected, does not guarantee an indefinite lease. The Queen has actively helped to see the association through the period in which its survival seemed most in danger, to the point where a new generation has grown up that lacks the early post-imperial resentment and sees no particular reason to discard the set of relationships it provides. Yet, the days of the multi-state Monarchy are evidently numbered: and a reversion to a Britain-only institution – bar the odd distant island – is surely just a matter of time. In Canada the constitutional status of the Monarchy is now so reduced that it causes little controversy, and New Zealand may not choose to follow Australia's example and become a republic. But, the expected Australian decision will set a precedent, and a dwindling of the Monarch's remaining realms must be the virtually certain outcome.[8]

If a future Monarch ceases to be head of any significant state apart from Britain, what about the Headship of the Commonwealth? Although the two are connected in the minds of many people, they are in fact quite separate. On the basis of the Nehru formula, established at the end of the last reign, the position of Head of the Commonwealth is by appointment, not heredity. In 1952, the succession to the post by the present Queen seemed automatic, but in a very different climate: not only was the Commonwealth a smaller and tighter association, republics remained the exception among self-governing states, not the rule. Furthermore, Prince Charles has so far taken less interest than his mother in the Commonwealth. Hence it is more than possible that when she dies the new Monarch will not be asked to take over the same role. Much depends on the timing: but it may well be that the opportunity provided by the end of the present reign will be seized to devise a new basis for a headship or presidency, perhaps a rotating one, aimed at establishing a Commonwealth that no longer looks to Britain as the symbolically leading member state.

The Commonwealth and multilateralism

The third Secretary-General of the Commonwealth, Chief Emeka Anyaoku, was, like his predecessor, not lacking in any vision for the Commonwealth as a force in international relations, but he perhaps had to contend with a more unfavourable international environment. This environment deteriorated even more sharply after he had left office, with the policies of President George W. Bush of America undermining most multilateral approaches to the solution of international problems. In this article, Anyaoku reaffirmed the value of multilateralism, and of the Commonwealth in particular, in dealing with the complex international situation of the early twenty-first century.

Emeka Anyaoku, 'The End of Multilateralism: Whither Global Governance?', *RT* 93/374 (April 2004), pp. 193–97

[…] With the end of the Cold War at the beginning of the last decade of the past century, a new momentum was given to multilateralism. There was universal optimism that the nations of the world could now cooperate to promote international peace, democracy, human rights and sustainable development. There was hope that the paradigm shift away from the Cold War would lead to a revitalized multilateralism under the UN. Indeed, during the decade, the UN seemed to have acquired its Charter functions in the security field.

There was also a welcome expansion of the areas where multilateralism held out the promise of effective systems for regulating and managing issues of universal interest. From the Rio Earth Summit of 1992 to the Kyoto Conference of 1997, and even to the Johannesburg World Summit on Sustainable Development of 2002, there was hope that all countries had recognized the need for global arrangements for regulating and managing the environment if our planet was to survive.

In the area of trade and commerce the successful completion of the Uruguay Round of trade negotiations had led to the establishment of the World Trade Organization which, after the fiasco of the Ministerial Conference in Seattle in 1999, appeared to have achieved some significant success at the subsequent Doha Ministerial Conference. At Doha ministers had agreed, among other things, that the agenda for future global deliberations on trade liberalization and related matters would focus attention on development issues, including especially such issues as agricultural subsidies in the developed countries, which have serious adverse effects on the economies of most developing countries.

Underlying these trends towards new multilateralism were three principles that seemed to have gained universal acceptance. First, the principle of collective security based on the pre-eminent rôle of the UN Security Council. This was aptly illustrated by the fact that, even in cases where regional arrangements were made for dealing with conflicts, such as in Kosovo, East Timor and Liberia, the blessing of the Security Council was deemed to be necessary and pursued by all the parties concerned.

Second, by voluntarily agreeing to subscribe to global arrangements for managing matters of common concern, all countries were indicating their willingness to be bound by decisions reached at the multilateral [level] for all concerned.

The third underlying principle was the increasing acceptance by the international community of the reality of the interdependence of peoples and nations, leading to what had come to be commonly described as the 'global village'.

The first blow against this emerging new multilateralism was struck when the new administration of President Bush decided to reject the Kyoto Protocol to which its predecessor government of President Clinton had agreed.

The second and perhaps the decisive blow against multilateralism was delivered by the perpetrators of the inhuman and dastardly act in New York on 11 September 2001. It is, I believe, now without any doubt that 11 September 2001 has become a watershed in the evolution of multilateralism in the post-cold war period. On the one hand, the events of 11 September showed that even the most militarily powerful state human history has ever known cannot be invulnerable to such monstrous acts of terrorism. And on the other hand, that experience produced an unparalleled level of determination on the part of the US government and people to deploy their superpower resources in pursuing their national security. […]

The climactic development in this retrogression of multilateralism has undoubtedly been the Iraq war. The declaration and prosecution of the war against Iraq after a failed attempt to obtain UN Security Council support for it was a clear negation of the principle of the multilateralism which the UN was established to promote. The war and its aftermath have strengthened the forces of unilateralism, as well as challenged the UN either to act in accordance with its universal responsibility, or to face redundancy. They have also raised the question: whither global governance? […]

There is [*sic*] a number of areas where the need for arrangements for global governance has been widely accepted as necessary. They include:

1 sustaining the environment and the survival of the planet;
2 maintaining the security, not just of nations but also of peoples;
3 expanding national and international economic activity;
4 regulating international transportation and telecommunications;
5 controlling pandemic diseases;
6 deterring terrorism, especially after the events of 11 September 2001;
7 controlling illicit drug traders.

In some of these areas, such as controlling pandemic diseases and regulating international transportation and telecommunication, appreciable progress has been made through the concerned multilateral agencies within the UN. But, in others, progress has been slow thanks mainly to the ineffectiveness of the multilateral institutions concerned with managing the perceived interests of the diverse component parts of the international community. The areas where progress has been slow include sustaining the environment, meeting the Millennium Development Goals and deterring terrorism. […]

In seeking to achieve more effective global governance, there are aspects of the Commonwealth experience which offer useful lessons to the wider international community. First, the Commonwealth's core belief in one common humanity is a powerful antidote to the easy, and some would say, natural inclination towards an 'us and them' syndrome. The acceptance of common affinity has been shown to be capable of oiling the path to effective cooperation between peoples and nations, as was the case when the USA was willing to invest such colossal resources in the reconstruction of war-damaged western Europe.

Second, the Commonwealth's historical emphasis on a consensus approach to its consultations and decision making has often facilitated the implementation of its decisions. It is true that the decisions of the key organs and agencies of the UN are increasingly being made on a consensual basis, but it is also true that voting remains the norm within the UN family.

Third, empowering its collective machinery, its Secretariat, to act as the organization's executive agency rather than as just the 'facilitator' of its meetings and consultations, has enabled the Commonwealth to maintain a good record in the implementation of its collective decisions.

Fourth, the accepted role of the Commonwealth Secretary General as the apostle of the organization's fundamental principles, and its bridge-builder on occasions of divisive controversies within the organization, is an example which, if followed by the UN and its institutions, would strengthen their roles in promoting global governance.

Finally, civil society, through myriad NGOs, has always played an important role not only in keeping member governments alive to their commitments, but also in promoting practical co-operation and understanding between the countries and peoples of the Commonwealth. It is true that global networks of civil societies have exerted significant influence on such issues as the external debt of developing countries, and world trade negotiations in Seattle. But there is room for the UN and its agencies to pay greater attention to how world civil society might be mobilized in furtherance of multilateralism. […]

Multilateralism, which is the only way whereby our increasingly unequal yet interdependent world can progress in serving the common interests of humanity, has suffered a serious blow in recent months. And yet as globalization continues its inexorable forward movement, beginning with the economy and expanding to the environment and other areas of human activity, how to reconcile the interests of the world's diverse peoples and nations will remain the key challenge. It is a challenge that can only be satisfactorily met by co-operation between all regions of the world. With its fundamental doctrine of unity in diversity, the Commonwealth, working through the various regional organizations across the globe to which its members belong, can contribute effectively to the evolution of mechanisms for enabling global governance to tackle this challenge.

The Commonwealth in 2010

> *The centenary of the* Round Table *provided the chairman of its editorial board with an opportunity to reflect on the state of the Commonwealth in 2010. Weighing up the assets and defects of the organization with an empathetic but unsentimental eye, he concluded that the Commonwealth urgently needed to address its weaknesses if it was to rise to the challenges of the early twenty-first century – a conclusion which undoubtedly reflected the views of others on the editorial board, and indeed of informed observers of the Commonwealth more generally.*
>
> Richard Bourne, 'The *Round Table* at 100, in a Changing Commonwealth Context', *RT* 99/406 (February 2010), pp. 1–5

[…] What can one say about the Commonwealth in 2010, except that it is here, and not widely known or fashionable? This is a family of networks, going beyond the Commonwealth Secretariat set up in 1965, and the biennial meetings of heads of government whose ancestry goes back to imperial meetings of prime ministers.

It is swimming in the complex tides of globalization, frequently out-competed by newer or more pushy institutions in the 24-hour newsflow, ahistorical world of media, with its unreliable blogs, public relations stunts and short-lived summits. No formal element in the Commonwealth, intergovernmental or non-governmental, has significant resources. Those who take an interest in the Commonwealth, as a worldwide body with over fifty states in membership, amount to a small sect. Identifying oneself as a Commonwealth citizen is an eccentricity. It is common for international relations academics to focus on single countries, continents or regions, or the UN or total world community;

few invest intellectual effort in a diverse grouping that is anomalous except in its origin, its voluntary membership, and the fact that it is still around. For Foreign Ministry officials its meetings are another set in the long international list.

It is worth examining the assets, deficiencies, challenges and possibilities facing the Commonwealth, as *The Round Table* embarks on its second century. Starting with the assets, one can mention two to begin with – that the Commonwealth is a non-treaty organization, in its intergovernmental form, and that it uses the English language. De Gaulle once cynically remarked that treaties, like floral and feminine beauty, last while they last. The absence of any governing treaty for the Commonwealth, possibly a nod to the lack of a written constitution in the United Kingdom, has in reality made possible a series of evolutionary adjustments. The Commonwealth has traditions and precedents, but it is not hog-tied to any charter.

The English language, which became *the* international language in the second half of the twentieth century, is of course a second or third language for most of the 2000 million citizens of the Commonwealth. But the lack of interpreters makes for a free flow of discussion in any Commonwealth meeting which is the envy of other international gatherings. It does not mean that participants are more likely to agree, but they can engage more effectively.

A third asset lies in the voluntarist and 'clubby' spirit that attaches to Commonwealth activities. Countries do not have to join the Commonwealth. Individuals do not have to join Commonwealth associations. Since 1995, and the Millbrook programme to enforce the Harare Principles enunciated in 1991, those governments that fall short of the rules of the official Commonwealth risk suspension or expulsion. Volunteers often do more, more willingly, than conscripts.

A fourth asset, ironically, derives from things that the Commonwealth does not do. It is not a military alliance. It is not a significant development aid organization, although a majority of member states are developing countries and arguably a half of its citizens are poor. What this has meant is that the Commonwealth has worked hard to achieve what a recent committee chaired by Amartya Sen has called 'civil paths to peace' – peaceful and soft power solutions to intractable problems, such as apartheid in South Africa. It has led to a series of campaigns, at the World Bank, IMF and elsewhere, to write off debt, make trade fairer for poorer countries, and promote sustainable development. The Commonwealth has used its muscle, and its members' membership of other world or regional bodies, to promote coherent goals of value to its own. A particular benefit has been to small states, which comprise some three-fifths of its membership, living overlooked and unrepresented on the margins of international decision making. Many small Commonwealth states cannot afford to attend international gatherings themselves, yet are required to obey diktats which stretch their human and financial capacity.

Where it cannot produce troops or money, the Commonwealth can produce ideas and, sometimes, can build a global consensus for delivery. But there are serious deficiencies in today's Commonwealth also. The first is that few governments think first of the Commonwealth when they face a problem. People in London High Commissions, often not very senior, are their governments' interlocutors with the Secretariat between meetings of Heads. This places a burden of high-level consultation on a Secretary-General to be the political engine for the Commonwealth; it explains why all recent Secretaries-General have spent most of each year flying round it. Shridath Ramphal, the wily and imaginative Secretary-General who served for an unequalled 15 years, said later that no government would automatically use the Commonwealth; all have to be persuaded of its value for a particular task.

A second and related defect is that it is difficult, even for Foreign Ministries and international relations experts, to define what the Commonwealth is outstandingly good at, or for. In the 1990s, following Ramphal's developmental push which came up against the free market resistance of Margaret Thatcher and Ronald Reagan, Chief Emeka Anyaoku led the Commonwealth into a more defined commitment to democracy and human rights. This chimed with the end of the Cold War. But in the wake of the Iraq invasion and Zimbabwe's walkout after the Abuja summit in 2003, this thrust lost potency. For most of Don McKinnon's term as Secretary-General (2000–2008), the Commonwealth Ministerial Action Group on observance of rules of membership, of which he had been deputy chairman as New Zealand Foreign Minister, was largely inert. […]

A third defect is that there is a major divergence between propaganda for the Commonwealth, and performance. Conciliation and peacemaking form part of the advertising for the association, yet there are many conflicts within its members – from northern Uganda to Sri Lanka – where the official Commonwealth has never been seriously involved. Strategies by both official and unofficial Commonwealth bodies – the numerous regional workshops, or promotion of best practice – are sometimes cosmetic, lack follow-up, and result in benefits only to a handful and in unread reports. Relations between governments and civil society are not always as close and productive as claimed.

The fourth defect is that publicity for the Commonwealth is weak, and has little impact. Some enthusiasts argue that this is the obverse of a strength: that its servants work behind the scenes, and do not seek recognition. But there is something scandalous about publicly funded institutions which are so ineffective in explaining themselves to their owners – to over fifty governments and their taxpayers. There are static websites. Genuine achievements, like the remarkable turnaround in the Maldives in 2008 when a formerly imprisoned human rights activist was elected President, are not seen as they should have been, as the result of patient, successful Commonwealth advice.

The challenges the Commonwealth now faces are partly global – issues of climate change, wealth and poverty, migration and identity. […] The Commonwealth has its own take on issues of world trade, low-carbon energy and poverty reduction, even where the interests of member states differ. It has special, world-beating expertise in marine and maritime affairs. Its common educational traditions have led in recent decades to such innovations as the Commonwealth of Learning, the distance teaching service based in Vancouver, and the Virtual University of Small States. Its collaborative traditions have since 1990 led to such new institutions as the non-governmental Commonwealth Human Rights Initiative, the private sector-oriented Commonwealth Business Council, and the Commonwealth Local Government Forum.

The elephant in the room, of course, remains the role of the United Kingdom, the ex-colonial power which for so long has supplied 30 per cent of official Commonwealth budgets, and generous support for non-governmental initiatives. Arnold Smith once described the Commonwealth as the product of national liberation leaders, but without the ballast of UK funding it could have shrivelled. More recently, Krishnan Srinivasan, formerly Deputy Secretary-General, has described it as a political orphan because real UK political interest was so modest – but he could not envisage other governments taking more. […]

The Round Table, as a critical friend, has watched an extraordinary political evolution over the past century. An autocratic empire has become a voluntary association, of countries which aspire to be democracies. It is in the journal's interest, as well as that of millions of citizens, that the Commonwealth continues to be a framework for inspiration, cooperation, and practical utility.

Notes

1 [B. Howard,] 'Mr. Smith's Rhodesia: Damaged but Determined', *RT* 56/222, pp. 114–22; [H. M. Robertson,] 'The Rhodesian Tragedy: Britain's Betrayal of Partnership', *RT* 56/222, pp. 123–31.
2 [Robertson,] ibid.
3 1956 (Suez), 1965 (UDI in Rhodesia), 1970 (arms sales to South Africa), 1979 (Rhodesia again), 1986 (sanctions against South Africa).
4 In 1991, giving rise to the Harare Declaration.
5 In fact Cyprus joined in 1961 (two days before South Africa left).
6 *Our Global Neighbourhood: Report of the Commission on Global Governance* (Oxford: Oxford University Press, 1995).
7 *The Queen: A Biography of Elizabeth II* (London: John Wiley, 1997)
8 In fact, the Australian referendum, held in November 1999, resulted in a vote, by 55 per cent to 45 per cent, to retain the monarchy.

Index of articles

Notes on authors

Anyaoku, Chief Emeka (b. 1933): diplomat; Assistant Director (1966–71), Director (1971–75), International Affairs Division, Commonwealth Secretariat; Assistant Secretary-General (1975–77), Deputy Secretary-General (1977–83, 1984–90), Commonwealth Secretariat; Foreign Minister, Nigeria (1983); Secretary-General of the Commonwealth (1990–2000); hon. kt 20000.

Bailey, Sir Kenneth Hamilton (1898–1972): barrister; Professor of Jurisprudence (1928–30) and Public Law (1931–46), University of Melbourne; Solicitor-General, Australia (1946–64); Australian High Commissioner in Canada (1964–69); kt 1958.

Beaton, Leonard (1929–71): journalist (Montreal *Gazette*, Reuters, *The Times*, *Guardian*); Director of Studies, Institute for Strategic Studies (1963–65); Editor, *The Round Table* (1965–70); Strategic Affairs Correspondent, *The Times* (1971).

Bourne, Richard (b. 1940): journalist (*Guardian*, *New Society*, *Evening Standard*); Deputy Director, Commonwealth Institute (1983–89); Director, Commonwealth Human Rights Initiative (1990–92); Head, Commonwealth Policy Studies Unit (1999–2005); Chairman, *The Round Table* (2005–).

Brookes, Edgar (1897–1979): Professor of Public Administration, Transvaal University College (1924–33); Principal, Adams College, Natal (1933–45); Senator for Native Interests (1937–53); Professor of Political Science, University of Natal (1959–62).

Coupland, Sir Reginald (1884–1952): Fellow, Trinity College, Oxford (1907–13); Beit Lecturer, Oxford (1913–18); Beit Professor, Oxford (1920–48); Member, Royal Commission on Palestine (1936–37), Cripps Mission to India (1942); Editor, *The Round Table* (1917–19, 1939–41); kt 1944.

Curtis, Lionel (1872–1955): Town Clerk, Johannesburg (1902–04); Assistant Colonial Secretary, Transvaal (1904–06); Organizing Secretary, Closer Union Societies (1906–09); Organizing Secretary, Round Table (1910–21);

Beit Lecturer, Oxford (1912–13); Secretary, Chatham House (1920–30); Adviser, Colonial Office (1921–24); Fellow, All Souls College, Oxford (1923–55); refused knighthood, 1924.

Eggleston, Sir Frederic William (1875–1954): barrister; Australian delegation, Versailles Peace Conference (1919); Chairman, Commonwealth Grants Commission (1933–41); Australian Minister to China (1941–44) and United States (1944–46); kt 1941.

Hailey, William Malcolm, Baron Hailey (1872–1969): Indian Civil Service (1895–34); Governor of Punjab (1924–28); Governor of United Provinces (1928–30, 1931–34); Director, *African Survey* (1935–38); Head, Economic Mission to Belgian Congo (1940–41); Chairman, SOAS (1941–45); kt 1922, Baron 1936.

Hodson, Henry Vincent (1906–99): economist and journalist; Fellow, All Souls College, Oxford (1928–35); Editor, *The Round Table* (1934–39); Ministry of Information (1939–41); Reforms Commissioner, Government of India (1941–42); Ministry of Production (1942–45); Editor, *Sunday Times* (1950–61); Provost of Ditchley (1961–71); Editor, *Annual Register* (1973–88).

Howard, Sir Michael (b. 1922): Professor of War Studies, Kings College, London (1963–68); Fellow, All Souls College, Oxford (1968–80); Joint Editor, *The Round Table* (1970–71); Chichele Professor of History of War, Oxford (1977–80); Regius Professor of Modern History, Oxford (1980–89); Robert A. Lovett Professor of Military History, Yale (1989–93); kt 1986.

Howe, Geoffrey, Baron Howe of Aberavon (b. 1926): barrister; Conservative MP for Bebington (1964–66), Reigate (1970–74), Surrey East (1974–92); Solicitor-General (1970–72); Minister of State, Department of Trade and Industry (1972–74); Chancellor of the Exchequer (1979–83); Secretary of State for Foreign and Commonwealth Affairs (1983–89); Deputy Prime Minister (1989–90); kt 1970, Baron 1992.

Huggins, Molly, Lady Huggins (1907–84): 1929 married Sir John Huggins (kt 1943; Governor of Jamaica, 1943–51); marriage dissolved 1958; Director, United Newspapers (1965).

Huxley, Elspeth (1907–97): staff, Empire Marketing Board (1929–32); author (including *The Flame Trees of Thika*, 1959).

Jackson, Robert (b. 1946): Fellow, All Souls College, Oxford (1968–86); Joint Editor, *The Round Table* (1970–71); Editor, *The Round Table* (1972–75); Conservative MEP for Upper Thames (1979–84); Conservative MP for Wantage (1983–2005); Labour MP for Wantage (2005); Parliamentary Under-Secretary, Department of Education and Science (1987–90), Department of Employment (1990–92).

Jawara, Alhaji Sir Dawda Kairaba (b. 1924): veterinary officer; Leader, People's Progressive Party, the Gambia (1960–94); Premier (1962–63), Prime Minister (1963–70), President (1970–94) of the Gambia; kt 1966.

Kerr, Philip Henry, 11th Marquess of Lothian (1882–1940): Editor, *The State* (1908–09), *The Round Table* (1910–16); Secretary to Lloyd George (1916–21); Secretary, Rhodes Trust (1925–39); Chancellor of Duchy of Lancaster (1931); Parliamentary Under-Secretary, India Office (1931–32); Ambassador to Washington (1939–40); succeeded cousin as Marquess, 1930.

Lawrence, Thomas Edward ('Lawrence of Arabia') (1888–1935): archaeologist; army officer (1914–19); Adviser to Colonial Office (1921–22); Research Fellow, All Souls College, Oxford (1919–35); RAF (1922–23, 1925–34).

Lothian: see Kerr.

Lyon, Peter (b. 1934): Reader in International Relations, Institute of Commonwealth Studies, London (1975–95); Editor, *The Round Table* (1983–2004).

Marris, Sir William (1873–1945): Indian Civil Service (1895–1929); Reforms Commissioner (1919–20); Governor of Assam (1921–22); Governor of United Provinces (1922–28); Council of India (1928–29); Principal, Armstrong College, Newcastle (1929–37); kt 1919.

May, Alex (b. 1963): Hon Secretary/Treasurer, *The Round Table* (1997–); Research Editor, *Oxford Dictionary of National Biography* (1998–).

Milner, Alfred, Viscount Milner (1854–1925): Under-Secretary for Finance, Egypt (1889–92); Chairman, Board of Inland Revenue (1892–97); High Commissioner in South Africa (1897–1905); War Cabinet (1916–18); Secretary of State for War (1918); Secretary of State for Colonies (1918–21); kt 1895, Baron 1901, Viscount 1902.

Morrah, Dermot (1896–1974): Fellow, All Souls College, Oxford (1921–28); Mines Department (1922–28); Leader Writer, *Daily Mail* (1928–31), *The Times* (1932–61), *Daily Telegraph* (1961–67); Editor, *The Round Table* (1944–65).

Pimlott, Ben (1945–2004): Professor of Politics and Contemporary History, Birkbeck College, London (1987–98); Editor, *Samizdat* (1988–90); Chairman, Fabian Society (1993–94); Warden, Goldsmiths College, London (1998–2004).

Raison, Sir Timothy (b. 1929): journalist (*Picture Post*, *New Scientist*, *Crossbow*, *New Society*); Conservative MP for Aylesbury (1970–92); Minister of State, Home Office (1979–83), Foreign and Commonwealth Office (1983–86); Chairman, Advertising Standards Authority (1991–94); kt 1991.

Ramphal, Sir Shridath (Sonny) (b. 1928): barrister; Solicitor-General, British Guiana (1959–61); Attorney-General, Guyana (1965–73); Foreign Minister,

Guyana (1972–75); Secretary-General of the Commonwealth (1975–90); Chancellor, University of Guyana (1988–92), University of Warwick (1989–2002), University of the West Indies (1989–); kt 1976.

Sanders, Sir Ronald (b. 1948): Manager, Guyana Broadcasting Service (1973–76); Adviser, Government of Antigua and Barbuda (1977–82); Antigua and Barbuda Deputy Permanent Representative to UN (1982–83); Ambassador to UNESCO and EEC (1983–87); High Commissioner in London (1984–87, 1995–2004); Ambassador to World Trade Organization (WTO) (2002–04); kt 2002.

Seton, Sir Malcolm Cotter (1872–1940): India Office (1898–1933); Assistant Under-Secretary (1919–24); Deputy Under-Secretary (1924–33); kt 1919.

Smith, Arnold (1915–94): diplomat; Canadian Ambassador to United Arab Republic (1958–61), USSR (1961–63); Assistant Under-Secretary of State for External Affairs (1963–65); Secretary-General of the Commonwealth (1965–75); Professor of International Affairs, Carleton University (1975–81).

Todd, Sir Garfield (1908–2002): missionary (ordained 1931); Superintendent, Dadaya Mission (1934–53); MP for Shabani (1946–58); Prime Minister of Southern Rhodesia (1953–58); Senator, Zimbabwe (1980–85); kt 1986.

Whyte, Sir Frederick (1883–1970): Liberal MP for Perth (1910–18); President, Legislative Assembly of India (1920–25); Adviser to Government of China (1929–32); Ministry of Information (1939–40); kt 1922.

The *Round Table*: a selected bibliography

'Janitor' [J. G. Lockhart], *The Feet of the Young Men* (London: Duckworth, 1928).

J. Conway, '*The Round Table*: A Study in Liberal Imperialism', PhD thesis, Harvard, 1951.

E. Wrench, *Geoffrey Dawson and Our Times* (London: Hutchinson, 1955).

J. Eayrs, 'The Round Table Movement in Canada', *Canadian Historical Review*, 38 (1957), 1–20.

J. R. M. Butler, *Lord Lothian* (London: Macmillan, 1960).

D. C. Ellinwood, 'Milner's Kindergarten, the British Round Table Group and the Movement for Imperial Reform', PhD thesis, Washington, 1962.

W. Nimocks, 'The Kindergarten and the Origins of the Round Table Movement', *South Atlantic Quarterly*, 58 (1964), 507–20.

G. R. Allison, 'Imperialism and Appeasement: A Study in the Ideas of the Round Table Group', PhD thesis, Harvard, 1964.

W. Nimocks, *Milner's Young Men: The Kindergarten in Edwardian Imperial Affairs* (Durham, NC: Duke University Press, 1968).

P. A. Smith, 'Lord Lothian and British Foreign Policy, 1918–39', MA thesis, Carleton, 1968.

J. E. Kendle, 'The Round Table Movement and Home Rule All Round', *Historical Journal*, 11/2 (1968), 332–53.

M. Howard and R. Jackson (eds), *The Round Table*, jubilee issue, 240 (1970).

D. C. Ellinwood, 'The Round Table Movement and India', *Journal of Commonwealth Political Studies*, 9/3 (1971), 183–209.

J. E. Kendle, *The Round Table Movement and Imperial Union* (Toronto: Toronto University Press, 1975).

C. Quigley, *The Anglo-American Establishment from Rhodes to Cliveden* (New York: Books in Focus, 1981).

H. V. Hodson, 'The *Round Table*, 1910–81', *The Round Table*, 284 (October 1981), 308–33.

D. Lavin, 'History, Morals and the Politics of the Empire: Lionel Curtis and the *Round Table*', in F. Madden and D. K. Fieldhouse (eds), *Oxford and the Idea of Commonwealth* (London: Croom Helm, 1982).

D. Reynolds, *Lord Lothian and Anglo-American Relations, 1939–40* (Philadelphia, PA: American Philosophical Society, 1983).

L. Foster, *High Hopes: The Men and Motives of the Australian Round Table* (Carlton, Victoria: Melbourne University Press, 1986).

J. Turner (ed.), *The Larger Idea: Lord Lothian and the Problems of National Sovereignty* (London: Historians' Press, 1988).

H. V. Hodson, 'Looking Back: The Founders', *The Round Table*, 315 (July 1990), 254–56.

D. A. Low, 'Whatever Happened to Milner's Young Men: What of Their Successors?', *The Round Table*, 315 (July 1990), 257–67.

R. Symonds, 'The Round Table and Their Friends', in *Oxford and Empire* (London: Macmillan, 1986).

B. M. Magubane, 'The Round Table Movement: Its Influence on the Historiography of Imperialism', *SAPES Seminar Paper Series* No. 9 (1994).

G. Martel, 'From *Round Table* to *New Europe*: Some Intellectual Origins of the Institute of International Affairs', in A. Bosco and C. Navari (eds), *Chatham House and British Foreign Policy* (London: Lothian Foundation Press, 1994).

A. May, 'The Round Table, 1910–66', DPhil. thesis, Oxford, 1995.

C. R. J. Rickerd, 'Canada and the Elliptical Round Table, 1908–17', BA (Hons) thesis, Harvard, 1995.

D. Lavin, *From Empire to International Commonwealth: A Biography of Lionel Curtis* (Oxford: Clarendon Press, 1995).

G. Studdert-Kennedy, 'Political Science and Political Theology: Lionel Curtis, Federalism and India', *Journal of Imperial and Commonwealth History*, 24 (1996), 197–217.

A. Bosco and A. May (eds), *The Round Table, the Empire/Commonwealth and British Foreign Policy* (London: Lothian Foundation Press, 1997).

N. Rose, *The Cliveden Set: Portrait of an Exclusive Fraternity* (London: Jonathan Cape, 2000).

A. May, 'Empire Loyalists and "Commonwealth Men": The *Round Table* and the End of Empire', in S. Ward (ed.), *British Culture and the End of Empire* (Manchester: Manchester University Press, 2001).

D. Gorman, 'Lionel Curtis, Imperial Citizenship and the Quest for Unity', *The Historian*, 66/1 (2004), 67–96.

P. Roberts, 'Lord Lothian and the Atlantic World', *The Historian*, 66/1 (2004), 97–127.

——, 'World War I and Anglo-American Relations: The Role of Philip Kerr and the *Round Table*', *The Round Table*, 383 (2006), 113–39.

D. P. Billington, *Lothian: Philip Kerr and the Quest for World Order* (Westport, CT: Praeger Security International, 2006).

S. J. Potter, 'Richard Jebb, John S. Ewart and the *Round Table*, 1898–1926', *English Historical Review*, 122/495 (2007), 105–32.

Index

ROUTLEDGE PAPERBACKS DIRECT

Mail

Made in the USA
Las Vegas, NV
31 October 2024

10722866R00109